Captain William Ricketts, Wife, and Infant Daughter.

Two Centuries of
Costume in America

1620-1820

ALICE MORSE EARLE

In two volumes

VOL.

II

Dover Publications, Inc.

New York

Published in Canada by General Publishing Company, Ltd., 30 Lesmill Road, Don Mills, Toronto, Ontario.

Published in the United Kingdom by Constable and Company, Ltd., 10 Orange Street, London WC 2.

This Dover edition, first published in 1970, is an unabridged republication, with minor corrections, of the work originally published by The Macmillan Company, New York, in 1903.

International Standard Book Number: 0-486-22552-6
Library of Congress Catalog Card Number: 70-118167

Manufactured in the United States of America
Dover Publications, Inc.
180 Varick Street
New York, N.Y. 10014

Contents

VOL. II

v

Contents

List of Illustrations

In Volume II

vii

CHAPTER XV

THE PROVINCIAL GOVERNORS

" *Our Tailors know
How best to set apparel out to show.
It either shall be gathered, stitcht, or laced,
Else plaited, printed, jag'd, or cut and raced,
Or any way according to your taste.*"

— "Satires," GEORGE WITHER, 1613.

" *My mind very busy thinking of my great layings out lately
and what they must still be for clothes ; but I hope it is in order
of my getting of something the more by it ; for I perceive how I
have hitherto suffered for lack of going as becomes my place. I
being resolved to go handsomer than I have hitherto. I hope
I shall get better success than when for want of clothes I was
forced to sneak like a beggar. Thus I end. For Clothes I
perceive more and more every day is a great matter.*"

—"Diary," SAMUEL PEPYS, December 28, 1664.

Two Centuries of Costume

CHAPTER XV

THE PROVINCIAL GOVERNORS

IT has ever seemed to me that England and America under the three Georges, especially in the middle of the eighteenth century, fell on very dull days; it was all dull indeed till the Revolution came to enliven things. Everything was dull — history, literature, art, architecture, and almost dress, " our greatest recreation." I am confirmed in this notion by the difficulty I find in gathering anything new to tell about dress at that time.

The whole mid-century in whatever point you search seems stationary. Nothing was active but politics, hence men in political life were more important than many better men. The governors of the American provinces held much-sought-after positions. Religious interest was dormant if not declining in England, though Burton and Berkeley lived; in America a revival of religious feeling was sorely needed and prayed for — so states Jonathan Edwards. Art had no triumphs; there were portrait-painters in enough numbers to tell us of costume, but not to paint great pictures. Hogarth wrote that Art ever reflected the times; it was not great when the events of the day were small. Trade and agriculture did not advance; both were hampered by forestalling and regrating, by lotteries, by disastrous land speculations. Science offered no successors to Newton. There was little poetry, but there was a charming prose literature — and to that prose we owe all we have of interest in the period.

Governor William Burnet.

We see city life at this time in Hogarth's crowded perspectives; but it was not always gay and rollicking and cheerful in every London street and at all times, any more than all English country life was that of Sir Roger de Coverley. Hogarth has revealed to us also the dark corners and yawning holes, the want and cruelty, the heartlessness, misery, and vice. Life in London was not always cheery, as in Horace Walpole's letters — "a brilliant jigging, smirking Vanity Fair, with fiddles singing, where all is sparkle and glitter;

wax lights, fine dresses, fine jokes, fine plate, fine
equipages." There was formality enough and wickedness enough, and there was rich dress enough in
America as in London, yet life here was positively
dull. Occasionally the smooth little placid pond of
provincial society was agitated cheerfully by the
breeze of some welcome and not too wicked scandal, such as the life of Sir Harry Frankland and
Agnes Surriage, this being a scandal full of color
and picturesque of detail. Sometimes there was
the diversion of a little campaign against the
Indians, or even a single theatrical battle such as
that of Louisburg, an episode ever so unreal to
me, so like a stage battle, that I turn from the
officer actors and the regiment chorus to the one
real figure, that of the pious, praying gentleman, a
New England magistrate, who was sworn to solemn
secrecy for a term of days until certain difficult pre-
liminaries for the war were accomplished and supplies
bought, a magistrate who kept his word and the
secret in solemn and silent importance, save that,
when moved to prayer on a hot summer's night, he
prayed so loud and so long and in so detailed a
manner for guidance that he, in our expressive
modern slang, "gave the whole thing away." And
there are certain adventurers who give a bright and
unwonted color to the calm expanse of provincial
days. Here is the Princess Carolina Matilda,
Duchess of Brownstonburges, transported for steal-
ing from the queen, but masquerading, nevertheless,
from colony to colony richly dressed, bearing jewelled miniatures of the royal family, and then being

caught by the sheriff and whipped at the post. Here is the romantic Russian Princess Christine buried for dead and coming to life in America with a new husband.

Here is Elizabeth Canning, the most famous woman swindler the world has ever known. All London was wild over her case. Thousands of bets were made upon her; thousands of pounds changed hands. She was transported in 1753, but the truth was never definitely decided to the satisfaction of the public. Her story is printed in scores of books; her simple, dull face was painted and engraved scores of times. Here she is demurely spinning in a Wethersfield doorway, and here in the Connecticut Valley she died; and her secret is buried with her. Here is Bamfylde Moore Carew, the King of the Mumpers; and little Lord Annesley, the trepanned nobleman; and the delightful swindler, Reverend Henry Tufts; and several cozening rogues — many of them parsons; and here is Moll Flanders herself, and a score of other famous thieves and vagabonds, and "considerables," as Cotton Mather called such-like.

They file across our history and give life to it, yet are not a real part of everyday life. And we have the earliest of great preachers, fantastics like Gorton, some of them, and some fanatics. Others, like Roger Williams, are true men of God. The eighteenth century brought Bishop Berkeley with the portrait-painter Smybert in his train; and here are Whitefield and Wesley. Here is also that fascinating, amusing man, John Rogers, who founded the Rogerenes; and later Jemima Wilkinson, who founded the Wilkinsonians; and Mother Ann Lee, who founded the Shakers; and Father Rapp, who founded the community at Harmony.   Here are a

William Byrd of Westover.

band of Rosicrucian mystics practising their strange, weird rites in quiet Germantown.   They are in a garb of utmost simplicity.   And here are others wearing no wool, no skins, no part of anything that ever had sentient life, and eating no animal food.

One important London amusement was missing,

the theatre. A few players came here and recited moral adaptations of Shakespere to small audiences gathered in tavern parlors or tap-rooms, without scenery and with shabby costumes. Even in this they were hampered and hindered.

Theatres held no permanent place in American life till after the Revolution. Panoramas, perspectives, collections of paintings, took the place of the plays. Masked balls and fancy-dress parties, which were the chief and most constant of London pleasures, were not an American resource; they were frowned upon. This function of fancy-dress parties accounts for the strange costume-dresses worn in some portraits of this day. We did have "Gardens" in New York, with music and supper, following, though afar off, the Ranelagh and Vauxhall gardens beloved of Horace Walpole. Card-playing, too, and lotteries flourished in the American provinces. It was a wonderful zest to shopping to do it through lottery tickets. You might get a gold watch, or a scarlet roquelaure, or you might get an enamelled patch-box or a silver snuff-box — all for a shilling ticket. And you might — oh, dear me! — get a package of vegetable seeds or a wooden shovel. Raffling-shops were in every city. Even books — sensible, pious books — were sold by raffle.

This period of dulness of fashions for America and England came naturally enough through the different controlling conditions. England had no flippant gallant Court Abbé, as in France, whispering new fashions and new extravagances in women's ears; no intriguing priests, no overbearing milliners, no wonderful artist hair-dressers riding in state from house to house, taking pupils at high prices.

England had no French courtesans, dominating the king, securing royal funds and public moneys for their rich and fascinating costumes. England had — and they were America's rulers also — cold gloomy William; then, first, a dull German George; then, second, a very dull German George; and, third, a very narrow, virtuous, respectable, dull George, who came "with few of the graces and none of the liveliness of youth," and had ever a dull virtuous court. He had a queen as rigid, as decent and dull as himself, tasteless like her royal predecessor, who was not at all dull, however, the wife of George II. The wife of George I never came to England. There were two countesses who came with the dull old king; they might have set the fashions had they been French, but they were Dutch — one so thin that the street boys jeered at her. The other, who weighed three hundred, was stayless — and really you cannot be a fashion leader without stays. Four very dull courts; and a century of dull society.

We had constant balls and assemblies, simple affairs many of them. But read of London routs and ridottos; some of them were pretty dull things too. We had horse-races, foot-races, cocking-mains, and a few dull ventures at bull-baiting.

As a rule, however, American amusements were simple indeed. They were spinning-matches, and singing-schools, and various gatherings of women alone in country towns — and of men alone; and

in the capitals, the royal birth-night balls and
assemblies, a regatta, a horse-race, formal dinners
and high teas, and a "consort."

The mid-century of English dress from 1740 to
1764, as well as English daily life, is depicted for us
in every form and detail and in every rank in life in
the works of William Hogarth. To him we turn
rather than to description for a decision of any dis-
puted point. The plates in *Hudibras*, 1726, were
his first work ; but later the various series, such as
*Industry and Idleness, The Rake's Progress, Mar-
riage à la Mode*, and others, form an illustrated
panorama of the modes.

In the year 1768 a Boston painter named Christian
Remick made a water-color drawing which he called
a *Prospective View of Boston*. It is owned now
by the Concord Antiquarian Society, and a very good
reproduction of it has been engraved recently ; and
a few plates printed for sale. In the foreground the
Common is depicted with various promenaders in
the dress of the times. The children are dressed
precisely like the grown persons. Women and little
girls wear close caps surmounted by hats, as are the
women in Hogarth's works ; but the hats of *The
Boston Fair* are turned up in the back in a flap.
All the fine-lady promenaders wear very long aprons,
so long that the hems thereof touch the ground.
The servants in the picture are all negroes ; the
male servants wear knee-breeches and cocked hats,
but over the coats and breeches hang long heavy
aprons. The butcher wears a smock, and carries a
great cleaver. The simple dress of a negro servant

is shown in this old print of the poet Phillis Wheatley, on this page.

Around the governors of the various provinces gathered in each capital a little circle of card-playing, horse-racing, fox-hunting court attendants, who naturally wore the best dress in the provinces; English younger sons, sent to America to sober down, where they proceeded to liven America up. The constant correspondence of the governor and his officials with England kept this circle fully informed upon all the changes in dress; and many of these letters, both private

Published according to Act of Parliament; Sept. 1.1773 by Arch. Bell, Bookseller N° 8 near the Saracens Head Aldgate.

and official, have been preserved. From them we gain an excellent notion of the importance of good dress, and the prevalence of good dress in the colonies, and of good living in every respect — furniture, carriages, wine, food. There were proportionately more carriages in Boston than in London. Many had coaches. I have seen portions of the furniture of the short-lived Governor Osborne; and that of Governor Burnet; and of Governor Belcher. It was all exceedingly rich. Their clothing was also costly. The story is told of Lady Cornbury, wife of the extravagant and impecunious Governor Hyde, Lord Cornbury, that her means of replenishing her wardrobe was to admire a certain article of clothing worn by her Dutch or English neighbors in New York, to send for it the following day " for a pattern," and — to forget to return it. She owned the only coach in town, and the rumble of its wheels differed from that of all other New York vehicles; when the sound was heard approaching a house — all was animation. " Here! take this away!" " Run! hide that!" " Put this in the closet!" " Carry this to the garret!" else the new garment was lost forever.

A series of the portraits of the provincial governors found to-day in our state-houses shows them to be a fine, courtier-like, richly dressed group of men. Many are in full court-dress; others in armor; some wear turban and banyan.

In Boston the influence of the royal governor and his staff established a miniature court which closely aped English dress and manners, and rivalled English luxury. An English traveller, Bennett, wrote of Boston in 1740, " Both the ladies and gentlemen dress and appear as gay in common as courtiers in England on a coronation or birthday." Whitefield complained bitterly of the " foolish virgins of New England covered all over with the pride of life"; of the jewels, patches, and gay apparel commonly worn.

Hawthorne — keenest of observers and investigators — wrote thus of them : —

"There are tokens everywhere of a style of luxury and magnificence we had not associated with our notions of the times.   The gaudiest dress permissible by modern taste fades into a Quaker-like sobriety compared with the rich deep glaring splendor of our ancestors.   Such figures were too fine to go about town on foot; accordingly carriages were so numerous as to require a tax."

Let us read the letter-book of one governor, to learn of them all.

Jonathan Belcher was governor of Massachusetts from the year 1730 to 1741; many of his letters have been published in recent years by the Massachusetts Historical Society.   A man of method, he kept copies of all his letters, even those of minute importance.   But his thoughts moved in ruts; he had little choice of expression, and he owned a set of stock phrases and quotations which frequently reappeared.   In all things a conventional man, he naturally thought much of clothes.   He is, in fact, a strange product, a union of New Englander and English courtier; full of servility, corruption, and duplicity, and yet he was also ostentatious in piety. His pious references to the Bible and assertions of his religious faith, and moral advice to his twenty-year-old son, balance in every letter his solicitous querying as to the son's wig-wearing; the latter was "not to his goust" (or gust), he said.

" 1732. I find you are still desirous to cut off your hair.
For my own part I can't think a wigg will ever become you
so well.   After your having the small-pox you wore a wigg
and I thought it rather disfigured you.   I shall govern myself with what your uncle may say on this. . . .   The
Present Prince of Wales wore his own hair till he was
twenty-five.   Mr. Spencer Cooper wore his at the barr
after forty years of age. . . .   I will by no means have
you think of cutting off your hair without my special leave
altho' it shou'd cost you as much the yearly dressing as to
furnish yourself with wiggs."

We can see by the portrait of young Manigault
(facing page 424) and young Bowdoin (facing this
page), and others, that for many mid-years of the
century *young* men wore their own curling, flowing
hair, though their fathers all wore wigs.

Governor Belcher's own abundant means, acquired
by inheritance and in mercantile life, enabled him to
make much formal display in equipage, dress, and
lavish hospitality.   He writes to his son in 1733 :
" I am in great want of a footman that can shave,
dress a wigg, and do all things about a gentleman.
Let him be a Dissenter, sober and honest if you
can ; but one I must have, the best you can get.
For my servants are all free and set up for themselves."   He sent the following letter to his tailor.
It is dated January, 1733.

" To Mr. Tullit :

" I have desired my brother, Mr. Partridge, to get me
some cloaths made, and that you should make them, and
have sent him the yellow grogram [a fabric of silk and
mohair] suit you made me at London ; but those you make

Governor Bowdoin, in Youth.

now must be two or three inches longer and as much bigger. Let 'em be workt strong, as well as neat and curious. I believe Mr. Harris in Spittlefields (of whom I had the last) will let you have the grogram as good and cheap as any body. The other suit to be of a very good silk. I have sometimes thought a rich damask would do well, or some good thick silk, such as may be the Queen's birthday fashion, but I don't like padisway. It must be a substantial silk, because you'll see I have ordered it to be trimm'd rich, and I think a very good white shagrine will be the best lining. I say, let it be a handsome compleat suit, and two pair of breeches to each suit. I hope Mr. Belcher of the Temple is your customer, and that he don't dishonour his father. I am, Sir,

"Your ready friend, J. B."

With this yellow grogram suit was also ordered " a very handsome sword-knot, cane-string and cockade all of orange ribbon richly flowered with silver and crimson." These were to be woven for him specially, and this cockade and sword-knot of orange and crimson ribbon worn with the yellow grogram coat and the orange trooping-scarf must have made his ruddy face in its flowing peruke look

Dress Coat and Waistcoat. Worn in British Navy by American and British Officers. 1750.

like one inflamed pumpkin with his body for another.
His portrait by Liopoldt hangs in the Boston State-
house — a goodly personable figure in velvet with
flowered waistcoat.   The buttonholes on the coat
and deep cuff are works of art; they are embroidered
in the shape of a curled ostrich plume, the end of
the plume being formed by a little tassel of fringed
silk detached from the coat save at one end.   Steinkirk and sleeve-ruffles of richest lace complete an
elegant costume.   Other beautiful buttonholes of
this date are shown on page 403, on the formal
dress-suit of an English admiral.

The following year he orders a fine three-pile
velvet suit, "the best that can be had for money,"
the lining deep gold color either of "shagrine" or
other good lining silk; also a "night-gown of best
Geneva damask that is made for men's wear." The
color of this was to be a deep crimson. He pru-
dently requests several extra yards of both velvet and
damask. In 1739 he orders from London a roquelo
(or roquelaure). Then he sends across seas a leathern
waistcoat and breeches to be laced with gold in the
handsomest manner, "not open nor bone lace, but
close lace something open near the head of the lace."
The buttons were to be of metal with eyes of the
same, "not wooden buttons with cat gut loops which
are good for nothing." These buttons were to be
"gilt with gold" wrought in imitation of cloth buttons. To wear with these riding-breeches he ordered
"a fine cloth jocky coat" of leather color lined with
same color. Hat, buckles, shoes, stockings, all are
ordered to match, silver buckles and pinchbeck also,

General Samuel Waldo.

and everything the very best.   Another glimpse of
modes is seen in the score of fine otter skins sent to
Europe from which to make a muff for the Duke
of Argyle, though "I am sensible muffs are out of
high fashion in London."

No one was better fitted to give tone and flavor
to society than Hutchinson, who, as governor of
the province under the king, was destined to be rejected by the people when they seized a choice.
There were gay doings then at his home at Milton,
as well as in the fine mansions of Boston town.   The
memoranda relative to the Governor's "cloaths" are
enough to paint a picture of the stately scene wherein
he figured, bravely arrayed.   Like all the proper
men of his day, he was distinctly exacting over his
wardrobe.   October 5, 1769, found him in a delib-
erating mood; this was after his elevation to the chief
magistracy.   He then sends to London for appropriate furbishing for his person : —

" To Mr. Peter Leitch :

"I desire to have you send me a blue cloth waistcoat
trimmed with the same color, lined, the skirts and facings,
with effigeen, and the body linnen to match the last blue
cloath I had from you : — two under waistcoats or camisols
of warm swansdown, without sleeves, faced with some cheap
silk or shagg.   A suit of cloaths full-trimmed, he cloath
some thing like the enclosed, only more of a gray mixture,
gold button and hole, but little wadding lined with effigeen.
I like a wrought, or flowered, or embroidered hole, something though not exactly like the hole upon the cloaths of
which the pattern is enclosed ; or if frogs are worn, I think
they look well on the coat ; but if it be quite irregular, I

would have neither one or the other, but such a hole and button as are worn. I know a laced coat is more the mode, but this is too gay for me. A pair of worsted breeches to match the color, and a pair of black velvet breeches, the breeches with leather linings. Let them come by the first ship.

"P.S. If there be no opportunity before February, omit the camisols, and send a green waistcoat, the forebodies a strong corded silk — not the *cor du soie*, but looks something like it — the sleeves and bodies sagathee or other thin stuff, body lined with linen, skirts silk. My last cloaths were rather small in the arm-holes, but the alterations must be very little, next to nothing."

Again, in 1773, his wardrobe needs a further replenishing : —

"I desire you to send me by the first opportunity a suit of scarlet broad-cloth, full trimmed but with few folds, and shalloon lining in the body of the coat and facing, the body of the waistcoat linen, and the breeches lining leather, plain mohair button hole ; also, a cloth frock with waistcoat and breeches, not a pure white but next to it, upon the yellow rather than blue, — I mean a color which has been much worn of late, button-holes and lining the same, the coat to have a small rolling cape or collar. — Also, a surtout of light shag or beaver, such color as is most in fashion : a velvet cape gives a little life to it. . . . Write me whether any sort of garment of the fashion of velvet coats, to wear over all, which were common some years ago, are now worn, and whether of cloth, and what color and trimmings. I should not chuse velvet."

We can trace in portraits the alteration in shape of coats ; William Browne's coat-skirts reach well down to the knee, indeed are almost below it. There is still no coat-collar. In 1745 laces disappeared from the coat, though they still edged the long waistcoats. The coat-skirts were stiffly lined. The stockings were drawn over the knee, and met the kneeband of the breeches which was neatly buttoned or buckled. A writer of 1753 gave a hint of the mode in his complaining letter : —

"What gentleman now rolls his Stockings? or lets his Breeches cover the cap of his Knees? Who suffers his coat-skirts to hang low enough to hide his thighs?"

This word "coat" means a waistcoat.

In 1757 a "coatee" was in fashion; no definite description of it can be given, save that it was very short.

"Horseman's coats," "Watch-coats," "Grego Watch-coats," "Thunder and Lightning Coat"—this last is explained to be a coat of German serge.

In the *Boston News Letter* in the first year, 1704, was advertised a runaway servant who eloped in a "sad colour'd old Coat or a new light Drugget Coat with Buttonholes and Trimmings of black." Another deserter wore a "White Cape-cloth Watch-coat."

The skirts of men's coats were at first stiffened with wire to make them stand out well; but this fashion was given up in the second half of the century. A certain tilt of the coat-skirts marked the dandy, just as the swing of the hoop told the belle. The set and swing of the coat-skirts was ever a

matter of much pride and concern.   Great care was
taken not to wrinkle and crease and crush these
skirts; yet it was not till the nineteenth century, till
1802, that the inventive genius of the great cabinet-
maker and designer, Sheraton, shaped and made a
chair which he called a "conversation chair," and
which was intended solely for masculine use, and to
protect the masculine coat-skirts.   This chair was
very narrow, the coat-wearer sat astride it, and leaned
his arms upon the back, which was cushioned on the
top like the side arms of a chair; and at the precisely convenient height for elegant leisurely lolling.
Of course the coat-skirts stuck out or hung down
unwrinkled and uncrushed, to the admiration of all
beholders and the confident satisfaction of the coat
wearer.   We can imagine the fine velvet court-suit
of Governor James Bowdoin thus safely displayed.

All the portraits of the provincial governors show
tight, plain breeches, varied only at the knee, where
one year may be a band or a button, another has a
paste knee-buckle, and for some of the early years a
rich garter.

In the list of household goods and clothing which
the governor of Acadia asserted that " Mr. Phips,"
the governor of Massachusetts, had stolen from him,
or deprived him of, were four pair of silken garters;
with which borrowed finery possibly Governor Phips
cut a fine figure.   Judge Sewall had a rare pair of
garters given to him in 1688 — "a pair of Jerusalem
Garters which cost above 2 pieces 8 (Spanish dollars)
in Algeria."   Snakeskin garters were constantly worn
to ward off cramp in the leg.

By the latter part of the eighteenth century breeches were worn skin tight. A gentleman ordering a pair is said to have told his tailor, " If I can get into 'em, I won't pay for 'em."

An ancient gentleman, telling of Alexandria in Washington's day, asserted that breeches were hung on hooks, and the wearer donned them by going up three steps and then letting the person down into

Wedding Waistcoat of Blue Uncut Velvet. 1704.

them from above. Such breeches-hooks remained till the present day in the Roberdean house, in Alexandria, and can there be seen.

Breeches-making in this century became a trade in itself, aside from tailoring, because the breeches were commonly made of leather, deerskin or sheep-skin, and required different workmen.

Some of these waistcoats were " exceeding mag-nifical," with their embroidered pocket-flaps and buttonholes and their beautiful paste buttons; these latter were rich in colored enamels and jewels, in odd natural stones, of lovely tints, such as agates, carnelians, bloodstones, spar, marcasite, onyx, chalcedony, lapis lazuli, malachite. The pink-tinted tops of fine shells were beautiful on black velvet garments. George Washington had several sets of shell buttons. A rose-pink waistcoat embroidered in silver with buttons of darker pink shell in silver settings was worn by a Boston groom with a silver-gray velvet coat, also with shell buttons, and white satin smallclothes. And there is a tradition in the family that his dress was so much more striking than the bride's that she had a hearty fit of crying over it. Here are a few of the names of buttons taken from tailors' lists. These are buttons for men's garments, not for women's: Thread, metal, and worsted buttons; death's head buttons; mohair buttons; gold and silver wire buttons; death's head black vest buttons; gilt buttons; shell buttons and tortoise shell buttons; carnelian and marcasite buttons; Lapps-azure buttons (which were doubtless lapis lazuli); knit buttons; steel buttons; coin buttons; French gilt and London plate buttons; basket buttons; horsehair buttons; pewter buttons. Fashionable button-makers covered buttons with the cloth of the coat or cloak, and then embroidered these with gilt bugle, steel beads, spangles, etc.

One very beautiful waistcoat is covered with a trellis design in brown over which run vines with tiny single roses. On the flaps of the pockets these vines form the initials of the wearer, "E. M." The border of this waistcoat is in silks the colors of the embroidery, and has also flat bits of green glass (a flat glass bead) sewed in a fine design. This was a wedding waistcoat. And it is a curious example of the indifference of the day to all save external effects, to find this waistcoat lined with a printed cotton stuff.

One detail of men's dress at this date I gather wholly from advertisements in the newspapers. I find no items in inventories of wardrobes, no mention in letters, but the newspapers of the middle of the century give in every shopkeeper's list, knit waistcoats and knit breeches. Sometimes the item is knit breeches - pieces ; or breeches patterns ; at other times the arti-

Embroidered Waistcoats of Governor James Bowdoin.

cles appear to be made up or knitted in shape. " Saxon green knit waistcoats," " black worsted knit breeches," " black silk-knit breeches," " silk-knit waistcoats," are named as for sale; one tailor had a " white silk knit waistcoat-piece." Women also advertised that they would repair knit waistcoats and

knit breeches, would "graft" where spots were worn
— which would indicate that these knitted pieces
were hand knit. At one time I thought they were
knit on the new knitting-machines. With the short
knee-breeches, stockings were an important detail of
dress. When every young woman was a diligent
knitter, stockings were plentiful. Five pairs of silk,
thirteen of cotton, and a like number of worsted
stockings were in Captain Parker's possession.

Stubbes tells of "cunningly knit hose, curiously
indented in every point with quirks, clocks, open
seams, and everything else accordingly."

The cost of these silk hose is often a surprise to
us. A man's silk stockings could cost more than
the coat on his back; a guinea for a coat perhaps,
but the clocked silk hose embroidered on the instep
cost two guineas. But when I look at them, I cannot wonder. Here is a pair of my great-grandfather's, the minute-man of the Revolution, of
purest, whitest silk closely spun, thickly woven;
they shine like silver. Were they worn on his head
instead of his heels, you would call them a fit crown
to his whole costume. See this portrait, painted by
Copley in his best manner, of old Jeremiah Lee in
his best manner. Head well up, peruke flowing,
hand proudly extended, he is "making a leg" as he
was taught in his Comenius's *Janua*, "Rise up, put
off thy Hatt, extend thy Hand, make a Leg." And
a goodly leg it is. There are compensations in all
conditions. If Jeremiah Lee mourned over the too
vast spread of his brown velvet waistcoat and the in-
creasing inches of his embroidered sword-belt, the

extra weight would permit him to set out this goodly white silk leg, and he could try to forget the paunch ; while Joseph Browne, with a slim waist like a young maid of honor's, wrapped his shrunk shanks in shame in an Indian banyan, and wore three pairs of thick stockings when he walked abroad. The artist Copley gratified the harmless pride of Jeremiah by painting his silken leg and the fine triangular clocks so deftly that you could never forget them. General Waldo has equally rich and beautiful hose, but he has not Jeremiah Lee's leg. (See facing page 404.)

Castor hats continued to be imported ; Pepperell ordered six dozen from England in one invoice. They appear on the heads of runaways in many an advertisement. But a change was coming from the centuries' wear of straight-brimmed beavers. Cocked hats came in vogue in New England when they did in England, and varied widely in shape from year to year as they did in looping, sometimes being turned up only in front with a button, at other times having three laps. In 1670 hat-brims had been about six inches wide. Dr. Holyoke said that in 1732 his father wore one seven inches wide. In 1742 it became

> " . . . a fashionable whim
> To wear it with a narrow brim."

A " Ramillies cock" was worn with a Ramillies wig.

> " When Anna ruled and Kevenhueller fought
> The hat its title from the hero caught."

This Kevenhueller was a large hat, and was much affected in the army. Hatters named Remington and Brown, in Hanover Square, advertised " Gentlemen's plain and laced Hats, dress'd and cock't by the most fashionable hatter in England."

A certain affectation of hat-wearing was seen. It consisted in letting the corners, which should stand out from the forehead, stick up perpendicularly. The wearers of these hats were called gaukies, an appropriate name.

The shape of the hat and the cock of the hat were matters of importance.

" My Mother . . . had rather follow me to the grave than see me tear my clothes, and hang down my head and sneak about with dirty shoes and blotted fingers, hair unpowdered and a hat uncocked,"

says *The Rambler*, No. 109.

During the Revolutionary War, the sentence of whipping with five lashes was imposed on any soldier whose hat was found carelessly unlooped, " uncockt," as it " gave him a hang-dog look."

Tied loosely around the neck of well-dressed gentlemen, there now appeared a ribbon of black silk. It was worn first at the court of Louis XV, and was known as a solitaire. Sometimes it was fastened to the bag of the wig. It was most becoming; the clear black ribbon formed a frame to the powdered hair, the pretty shirt-ruffle, the stock, and the jewelled stock-buckle; it was really a delightful addition to a man's dress. I can fully agree with the fribble in Anstey's *Bath Guide* (1766) : —

Front of Court Suit worn by Governor Bowdoin.

Back of Court Suit worn by Governor Bowdoin.

" But what with my Nivernois hat can compare
Bag-wig and laced ruffles, and black solitaire.
And what can a man of true fashion denote
Like an ell of good riband tied under the throat."

Often it was tied to the bag of the wig, and the ends were tucked loosely into the front of the coat or shirt, as shown in the portrait of Dr. John Morgan. Solitaire ribbons were advertised widely in American newspapers. The accompanying feminine fashion was a ribbon of black velvet tied round the throat, given in several portraits in this book. The solitaire lingered until the great pouf of ribbon and lawn, adopted by the macaroni, entirely changed neck-dressing.

One great dress contrast seen everywhere in England was never found in the New World; this was the sombre formal garb of the English clergy. Neither surplice or cassock in the pulpit nor the decorous shovel-hatted dress of English clerical street wear was seen; even in Virginia, where the parson wore his gown in the pulpit, he was not carefully arrayed in conventional garments when out of the pulpit. In New England the minister wore a respectable black suit — often, alas ! sadly rusty — alike on week-days and the Sabbath.

An entry in the diary of Anna Green Winslow, a Boston schoolgirl in 1771, shows the hatred of New England Puritans of anything savoring of Episcopacy.

" Dr Pemberton & Dr Cooper had on gowns; In the form of the Episcopal cassock; the Doct^s deign to distinguish themselves from the inferior clergy by these strange habits (at a time too when the good people of N. E. are threatn'd with & dreading the coming of an episcopal bishop). N. B. I dont know whether one sleeve would make a full trimm'd negligee as the fashion is at present, tho' I cant say but it would make one of the frugal sort with but scant trimming. Unkle says they all have popes in their bellys. Contrary to 1 Peter v. 23. Aunt says when she saw Dr. P. roll up the pulpit stairs, the figure of parson Trolliber recorded by Mr. Fielding occur'd to her mind & she was really sorry a congregational divine should by any instance whatever give her so unpleasing an idea."

A few years ago, at an anniversary in the Congregational church at Northampton, Massachusetts, a beautiful bas-relief of the figure of Jonathan Edwards was erected as a memorial. When the design was being made, a great questioning arose whether Parson Edwards wore a gown in the pulpit. If so, the draping folds made a far more graceful dress for the artist's use than the plain black coat and knee-breeches of the layman. The portrait known to the artist displayed a small clerical band, but the dress might be coat or gown. The original portrait, however, owned by Mrs. Johnson-Hudson, of Stratford, Connecticut, a descendant of Jonathan Edwards, plainly shows a Geneva gown; and the bas-relief displays a figure thus attired. Many sermons exist in which the wearing of a gown in the pulpit is deplored; and one parson, in derision, donned the black cambric pulpit-cover and thrust his arms through the holes make for the pulpit lamps, and thus attired delivered his sermon. We have a few early portraits which prove the wearing

of clerical robes by some, such as the portrait of
John Cotton (page 42), and later of Cotton Mather
(facing page 42).   But it is also true that they were
abhorred by many Puri-
tan believers.   There
had been much contro-
versy in the fold of
the Church of England
about clerical gowns.

After the Reforma-
tion the graduates of
English universities
wore the comely aca-
demical apparel assigned
to their wear ; this was
the wide-sleeved gown.
The Puritan preachers
adopted in England a
dress of Genevan devis-
ing ; though some wore
" Turkey gowns, gaber-
dines, frocks, or night-
gowns of most lay
fashion for avoiding of
superstition." Hogarth
shows us many of his
clergymen wearing a
full-sleeved gown, some-

Everyday Suit of Clothes of Dr.
Edmund Holyoke, of Salem, Mass.

times closed with a button at the top, and sometimes
open to display a cassock and cincture beneath.

A description of dress was written for the Old
Colony Memorial in 1820, giving the costume and

appearance of everyday plain folk in the years previous to the Revolution. I have always deemed this account of value, being the words of people then living, writing without exaggeration, and without being contradicted, as they would certainly have been if the record were untrue. It does not give the dress of Copley's sitters, the garb of fine folk who had their portraits painted, but tells what was worn by the men who lived upon the farms, who worked in shops; the dress of tradespeople, artisans, craftsmen — in short, the people. It runs thus : —

"In general, men old and young, who had got their growth, had a decent coat, vest, and small clothes, and some kind of fur hat. These were for holiday use and would last half a lifetime. Old men had a great coat and a pair of boots. The boots generally lasted for life.

"For common use they had a long jacket, or what was called a fly coat, reaching down about halfway to the knee. They had a striped jacket to wear under a pair of small clothes like the coat. These were made of flannel cloth.

"They had flannel shirts and stockings and thick leather shoes. A silk handkerchief for holidays would last ten years. In summer-time they had a pair of wide trousers reaching halfway from the knee to the ankle.

"Shoes and stockings were not worn by the young men. Few men in farming business wore them either. As for boys, as soon as they were taken out of petticoats, they were put into small clothes summer and winter. This lasted till they put on long trousers, which they called tongs. They were but little different from the pantaloons of to-day. These were made of linen or cotton, and soon were used by old men and young through the warm season.

"Later they were made of flannel cloth, and were in

general use for the winter. Young men never thought of greatcoats; and overcoats were then unknown."

It will be proved plainly by the illustrations shown in these pages that the only unquestionable record of the dress of the past is presented in the portraits of the wearers. Sometimes a group of those of certain dates may be studied together, as at the Copley exhibitions in Boston, in the portrait group by Gilbert Stuart, now in the Pennsylvania Museum of the Fine Arts, or in the Trumbull collection owned by Yale University. Even more compact as well as extended in presentation are the collections in such works as Miss Anne Hollingsworth Wharton's *Heirlooms in Miniature.* In this book the little gems of art which the author has gathered can be shown in the size of the originals, and form a pleasant study, not only from the dress, but the skilful and concise sketch offered with each miniature as a presentation of the character of the wearer of the dress.

I have collected from which to choose the illustrations in this book, over five hundred portraits of Americans. They form a beautiful collection — a gallery of American history. All of these pictured faces have not names great in our public history, but all are, nevertheless, a part of our national life and progress. All are not beautiful; but some of the most commonplace faces and figures display costumes that make them serve wonderfully well in this book, while some of the fairest faces are valueless. Some are very crude art, yet are of use; while others, masterpieces, are thrown aside. For example, I have the beautiful engraving of Sir Joshua Reynolds's portrait of Joanna Leigh, Mrs. Richard Bennet Lloyd, whose husband, a Maryland gentleman, brought his beautiful bride to Annapolis. Standing in a park carving her name upon the bark of a tree, this fair Joanna is beautiful to look upon. But she wears simply a graceful drapery of long, soft folds held in place by a knotted sash and displaying bare sandalled feet. It is scarce a gown, though it is looped and folded into sleeves; and certainly no mantua-maker or tailor had any part in its making, hence it is in no sense representative of the dress of her day.

It will be seen that many of the portraits are the work of unknown painters — ones who could not in truth be termed artists. But these have been chosen because they reproduce faithfully the articles of dress; they could be painted, and well done, too, by painters of no talent. It was easier to copy elaborate lace ruffles than to paint flesh tints. But even these crudities have their own standard of value. Horace Greeley was shown one of the unspeakable statues of Abraham Lincoln which, in respect to a nation's outcry of grief and affection, were turned out to us in bronze and marble and stone in such numbers in so short a time, some by artists, more by stone-cutters who were scarcely craftsmen and certainly not sculptors. The wily old journalist walked critically around this statue at the first un-veiling of its appalling awkwardness and ill form, and when asked what he thought of it, responded cheerfully, " Certainly the buttons are natural."

Court Suit of General Thomas Pinckney.

So have I, not finding a good portrait with such buttons as I wish to illustrate, chosen a daub where "the buttons are natural," not fearing in the least that any will be deceived, or deem me deceived, in fancying them high art.

That there was a resident portrait-painter in Charleston, South Carolina, as early as 1705 is certain, for there is still existing an admirable picture of Sir Nathaniel Johnson, knight in armor, which was painted then and there. This picture bears, written on the background by the artist's hand, the words, "Aetatis 61, April, 7, 1705." It was the work of Henrietta Johnson, who was a pastel artist, and marked her pictures with date and the legend, "Henrietta Johnson Fecit." She was buried in St. Philip's graveyard, March 9, 1728–29.

Governor Broughton, South Carolina.

Fifteen of her portraits have been identified — the earliest dated 1708. Most of these are in the original black wooden frames.

It is most interesting to me to find that few as were women artists in Europe, the New World developed several who made art their means of livelihood, and became successful portrait-painters. There was this Miss Johnson of Charleston, who has the distinction of being the first American artist as well as the first woman artist, since Smybert and Blackburn were not painting in Boston till 1725, and John Watson in Philadelphia till 1728; and the single

allusion to Tom Child in Boston scarcely gives him
shape and form.

Another woman painter was Miss Mary Wrench,
of Philadelphia; this young lady was so retiring and
so proper, that she was unwilling to paint gentlemen's
portraits, but was constrained to do so since she
needed the money for her support.   The unprinted
Recollections of the artist Charles Willson Peale gives
a sentimental story of his call upon her, his exam-
ination of her work, and his disclosure of his name
with an offer to teach her.   Whereupon, as became
so modest a young woman, and according to the
fashion of the day, she was overcome with confusion
and blushes, and was speechless.   She married a Mr.
Rush, a carver of ship's heads; and in matrimony
ceased to paint miniatures.

There was an artist named John Watson, who
came to America from Scotland at the age of
thirty, in the year 1715, and set up his easel as a
portrait-painter at Perth Amboy, New Jersey; but
little is known of him or his work.

The erstwhile coach-painter, Smybert, came to
America through the urgent requests of Bishop
Berkeley.   He landed in old Narragansett, and naturally painted the friends of Dr. Berkeley in that
plantation, Dr. Honeyman of Newport, Dr. Mac-
Sparran and his wife of Kingston.   When he came
to Boston in 1725, he painted there in the best
families: the Lyndes, Quincys, Sewalls, Faneuils,
Bromfields, Phillipses, Greens, and other Boston
solid men — hard-featured they are, as are all of
Smybert's men; and their wives (when they had

wives) were painted too — they are not all hard-featured, but certainly are monotonous in style. But he was faithful in his representations; and his dry, bloodless faces and stiff figures serve well enough for our study as figures to display the dress of his day, which was a little meagre, too, in comparison to what preceded and what followed. Smybert died in 1751.

Robert Feke is said to have been a Rhode Island Quaker. He was in Newport in the year 1746, for he then painted portraits of the Rev. John Callender, of Newport, and the beautiful wife of Governor Wanton. He may have visited Philadelphia, as a remarkably fine portrait by him of Mrs. Charles Willing, wife of the mayor of Philadelphia, and one of Tench Francis, signed " R. Feke, 1746," are in the possession of their descendants. The following story is told of his life: Feke, although of Dutch descent, was a Quaker; but he joined the Baptist church in Rhode Island. He then turned to a seafaring life, was taken prisoner by the Spaniards and carried off to a Spanish prison. While a captive he relieved the tediousness of imprisonment by rude attempts at painting. The sale of these pictures after his release procured him the means of returning to America. He is believed to have had a home on Long Island; and there is a tradition that some of his portraits are there, but inquiry among the leading Long Island families has failed to reveal where they are. He died in Bermuda, aged forty-four years.

I am inclined to give to Robert Feke the palm for

the painting of fabrics over Smybert and Theus;
and he is not excelled by Copley. His paintings
extend over a short time only, and are of persons
who were often close kin, and thus of like station.
There is little variety in their dress except in the
case of the rich brocade of Mrs. Willing, which has
what Mrs. Delany called "great ramping flowers."
His presentation of this brocade is wonderful; nor
have the light and lustre faded from his satins, nor
the richness and depth from his velvets, though it is
two centuries since they were painted.

Feke's capacity for delineating fabrics is discovered amply in the portrait of Governor Bowdoin
(facing page 402); though that is not the only power
displayed. His drawing is good, the flesh tints are
still excellent. Altogether this is a fine portrait,
holding its own in worth by the side of Stuart and
Copley in a way to make us regret the few of Feke's
portraits known to be in existence. The number
twelve has been said to me; I know but eight.

In Virginia all the earlier portraits are the work
of Lely, Kneller, Van Dyck, and other foreign artists. There is no positive record of native attempts
at face-limning until John Hesselius, who lived in
Annapolis, painted some portraits in Maryland and
Virginia. Some of his work was done previous to
1759; but his father, Gustavus, who called himself
"a face painter" in his will proved in 1754, probably painted some of the earlier portraits attributed
to John.

Gustavus Hesselius was born in 1682, and was,
therefore, several years older than Watson and two

Hon. Peter Manigault.

years the senior of Smybert. He arrived at Wilmington, Delaware, in May, 1711, and soon " flyted " on account of his calling to Philadelphia.

When he died in 1755 he left a comfortable property to his children. His portrait, now at the Pennsylvania Historical Society, displays a well-ruffled shirt, and a head of hair which might be either a wig, or artificially curled natural hair.

The lovely Charlotte Hesselius, daughter of John, became the first wife of Thomas Jennings Johnson; a winning, vivacious creature. Her pretty face is shown on a later page in a hat which might have been made in New York this year, so modern is its shape as well as its trimming. But the bare neck with shepherdess bodice shows that the wearer is of another century.

Jeremiah Theus, or Thews, was one of three brothers who came to South Carolina from Switzerland about 1739.

During a residence in Charleston of nearly forty years, Jeremiah impressed the community with the influence of his talent and high personal character, and he was the undoubted pioneer of legitimate art in South Carolina as well as the founder of a family honorably connected with Revolutionary history.

He died on May 18, 1774, leaving a handsome fortune and a homestead. His drawing was accurate and coloring excellent, and his execution of fabrics fully equal to that of Copley. This last-named characteristic has led to some of his work being called that of Copley.

The portrait of Mrs. Peter Manigault is by

Thews, but the portrait of Mr. Peter Manigault, see facing page 424, is a fine example of the work of Allan Ramsay, the last court-painter of the English court.   Mr. Manigault was born in Charleston in 1731, and when eighteen years old went to London where this portrait was painted in 1751. He went to school and university, and studied law in England, and became a barrister of the Inner Temple; later he was Speaker of the House of Commons of South Carolina. He was always splendidly dressed, and his first act when landing in England, when a little lad, was to buy a costly watch with his indigo money. Perhaps he had a love of time-pieces, since his portrait is painted with one — an unusual accessory. The satin and velvet suit was of the richest sea-green of a singular tint. The hair is unusually simple for the times.

The portraits by Sir Godfrey Kneller found in America are nearly all of the size a little less than half length, but including the hands, called kit-cat — a name immortalized by being that of the club of forty-eight members whose portraits were painted by Kneller and presented to the secretary and founder of the club.

> "Whence deathless Kit-Cat took its name
> Few critics can unriddle,
> Some say from pastry cook it came
> And some from cat and fiddle."

This club was instituted about the year 1700, and is believed to have lasted but twenty years. Kneller was one of the members.

CHAPTER XVI

NIGHTGOWNS AND NIGHTRAILS; BANYANS AND TURBANS

" *Get on your nightgown, lest occasion call us*
And show us to be watchers."

—"Macbeth," II, 2, 70, WILLIAM SHAKESPERE.

" *Others came in their night-gowns, to saunter away their time.*"

—"The Spectator," No. 49, RICHARD STEELE.

" *Eight miles beyond any Ordinary I arriv'd at Col⁰ Martin's who rec'd me with Gravity and saluted me with a glass of Good Canary. I found him⁻ in his Night Cap and Banian, which is his ordinary dress.*"

— " A Progress to the Mines," WILLIAM BYRD, 1723.

CHAPTER XVI

NIGHTGOWNS AND NIGHTRAILS; BANYANS AND TURBANS

BY the middle of the seventeenth century many new and pleasing things came to English and American folk from far Cathay, and were eagerly welcomed. We find one colonist, Higginson, writing from Salem to England, in the first years of that little Massachusetts town, for a reshipment of India goods, such as leather-ware, spices, a few toys, and some silks. A very delectable product, agreeable for both food and drink, then written "chockellata," was imported and quickly loved; a second ambrosial drink, called coffee, was a rival, but was received with some suspicion; "thea," a China drink, had some votaries and many enemies. Besides the lacquered ware came pieces of India china — cups for the costly tea, and splendid punch-bowls to hold the new and welcome India drink, punch. Rich spices delighted colonial gourmands; they valued them like precious stones. Gay, silken stuffs pleased milliners and tailors. Among the fine gauze and crape and thin silk fabrics came one Oriental garment which was quickly adopted by the race who already loved a nightgown; and it was called by various names, besides nightgown, such

429

names as Indian gown, Indian robe, banian, banjan, banyan, and dressing-gown.

The nightgown of colonial days was not a sleeping-garment. In truth it was a loose gown worn in conditions and under circumstances such as a dressing-gown was worn by our fathers forty years ago ; and also worn at more formal meetings where a dressing-gown would have been deemed inadmissible.

The opening of Oriental trade and the importation and use of Oriental articles came first to the Dutch. And attempts have been made to show that early Oriental influences can be traced readily in Dutch Delft ware, in Dutch embroideries, in the Dutch language, and still more far-fetched in Dutch costume.

The nightgown might be, for both men and women, a very handsome article of dress, either " ruffled with great Care," as we are told of one in *The Spectator*, No. 45, or made of rich silk, brocade, or even velvet. American gentlemen wore nightgowns in their counting-houses, both words having given way, the one to a Norfolk jacket or occasionally a smoking-jacket, and the other to the word " office."

Men not only wore these nightgowns in their own homes, but " sauntered abroad " in them, says *The Spectator*. They were, ere Addison's time, I believe, somewhat more undress, for literally " a scandal about Queen Elizabeth," when she was a reckless and hoydenish princess, is told that Admiral Seymour used to come every morning to see her " at hir boke," he garbed " in his nightgown, bare-legged in his slippers." However, he but " looked in the gallery-dore, bade hir good morrow and so went his way."

In an order given by Queen Elizabeth she specifies "twelve yardes of purple vellat frized on the
backsyde with white and russet silke to make us a
night-gowne; also 14 yardes of Murray Damaske
to be employed for making a Night Gowne for the
Erle of Leycester," which certainly formed a garment formal enough to silence any scandal.

These nightgowns had been worn in the time of
Henry VIII. Lady Lisle had one then of black
satin, and her friendly gossiping steward writes : —

"Your night-gowns are made in every point as my Lady
Beauchamp's and it is the very fashion that the Queen doth
wear, and so were the caps. Divers of the ladies have their
night-gowns embroidered, some with gold, some with silk.
I have given to Mr. Skeet (the tailor) twelve yards of satin
according to order, who shall make it (a night-gown) after
the best and most used fashion which is large and long, with
double placards as you wished : And when the fur cometh,
see it trimmed after the best manner."

What we now term a nightgown was then a night-
rail; though all rails were not for night wear. An
old play, by Middleton, speaks of the impropriety
of men wearing stomachers or nightrails. The
fashion of wearing "immoderate great rayles" was
prohibited by law in Massachusetts in 1634. The
garment at that date must have been a woman's
loose gown or sacque worn in the daytime, for even
a meddling Massachusetts magistrate would scarce
dare to say what kind of a nightrobe a woman
should wear. Some men certainly had nightshirts,
as we learn from the formal rules for servants in

dressing their masters, and for court attendants in waiting on the king.

But when we have accounts of the rich nightgowns of royal bridegrooms, the gowns are not for wear while sleeping. At the marriage of the father of George IV, the groom came to the bridal chamber, where the royal family were all assembled, in " a night-gown of silver stuff and cap of finest lace." Lord Hervey described a similar scene at the wedding of the Prince of Orange to the eldest daughter of George II. The poor groom was somewhat misshapen, and when he entered the bridal apartment in brocaded nightgown and nightcap, a vast number of staring people were present. Said the chronicler, " From the shape of his brocaded gown and the make of his back, he looked behind as if he had no head, and before as if he had no neck or legs. His appearance was as indescribable as the astonished countenances around him."

I may state here that I think it very doubtful whether night-clothes were generally popular even in the early years of the eighteenth century. In Fielding's *Joseph Andrews* (1736) several references are made which indicate that night clothing was not worn by his characters. However, the famous Mrs. Glasse advertised in 1751 that she made " bed gowns, night-gowns and robe de chambers." We must not infer from the use of the word naked that absolute lack of clothing is indicated. Thus, in *Joseph Andrews*, Parson Adams is referred to as naked while standing in his shirt. In the oft-quoted *Mundus Muliebris*, 1696, we read of " twelve day smocks of

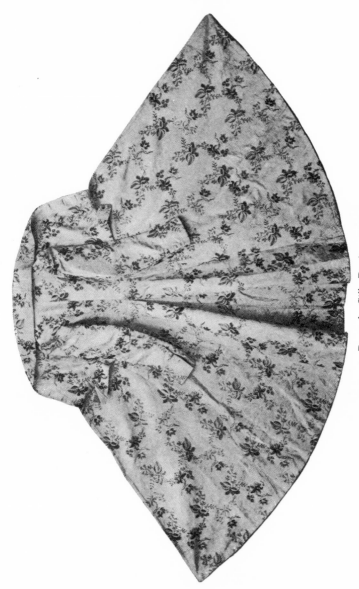

Brocade Silk Banian.

Holland fine with cambric sleeves, and twelve more for night all Flanders laced." The author adds, " The same her night-gown must adorn, with two point waist-coats for the morn."

There were nightrails; but they seem to have been for special wear, when visitors were shown to the bedroom as they were in certain functions, as, for instance, the christening of a child, and throughout the week of caudle drinking, when men and women thronged the mother's bedroom and drank caudle by her bedside. This custom was kept up in America until well into the nineteenth century. To return to the nightrails, Massinger writes in *The City Madam* : —

> " Sickness feigned
> That your night-rails of forty pounds apiece
> Might be the envy of the visitants."

Pepys makes reference to night clothing, but in other entries plainly shows that he slept at times in his day shirt.

Every one — men, women, and children — wore nightcaps apparently as part of sleeping attire, until modern times; at first they were made of silk, gold laced and embroidered.

When the governor of Acadia sent to the government of Massachusetts the list of goods stolen from him by " Mr. Phips " he named "four nightcaps with lace edge; eight nightcaps without lace."

We may well exclaim with Taylor, the " Water Poet," " A nightcap is a garment of high state; " for Queen Elizabeth had among her New Year's gifts night-coifs of " cut-work flourished with silver and set with spangles," and of "camerk [cambric] cut-work and spangells, with a forehead-cloth and a night-border of cut-work with bone lace." But did she really wear these while sleeping, or were they an undress cap? Did not young Gilbert Talbot, son of the Earl of Shrewsbury, catch her walking in the tilt-yard in one of these caps? And did not the queen that evening give him "a good flap" on the forehead and tell her chamberlain that the youth had caught her "unready and in her night-stuff," and how much ashamed she was thereat, and so on, with more of the comedy play she so loved to divert herself and her courtiers with.

When the nineteenth century was reached, the silk nightcap lingered for men, and seems to have been regarded as a gift of much sentiment; but women's nightcaps were always of some washable stuff. Two of the nightcaps of a bridal outfit a hundred years ago are given facing page 434. It will be noted that one is closely covered with a close seeding of French knots, a manner of trimming we have revived within the past two years.

Samuel Pepys was ever punctilious to painful particularity in securing the very ultimatum not so much of fashion as of what he termed gentility; the extreme of wear of those persons whose esteem and approval he and his whole London world and English court valued. In 1665 this "glass of fashion" had his portrait painted in what he termed an Indian gown, which he hired; soon he bought one of his own. So established and modish a dress were these gowns that the making of them became a

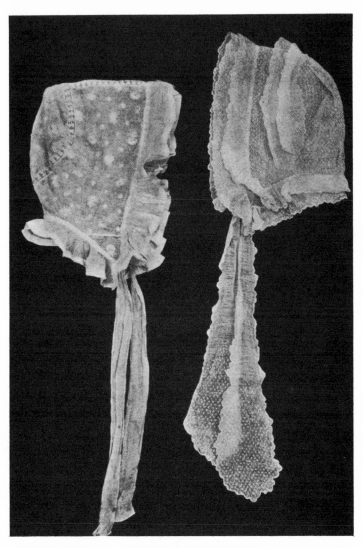

Bridal Nightcaps.

special calling. In Chamberlain's *Present State of England*, 1684, Robert Croft is named as Indian-gown maker to the king, and Mrs. Mary Mandove Indian-gown maker to the queen.

The fashion of painting portraits in these night-gowns was favored by Kneller, who painted them often with great wigs. As Horace Walpole said : —

" In the Kit Cat Club, Kneller poured full-bottomed wigs over night-gowns ; if these streams of hair were incommode in armour, in a battle, I know nothing they were adapted to that can be done in a night-gown."

The collar of these nightgowns was the plain turnover straight or rolling collar, without revers or corners, familiar to us to-day on Chinese robes and on Japanese kimonos. The broad sleeves also had a straight rolled-over cuff like a kimono cuff. Collar and cuffs show Oriental influences. The lining of the gown was generally of a different color, and thus afforded a contrast in the collar and cuffs. Excellent examples of these gowns may be seen in many of Copley's portraits. He delighted in them ; for they gave him ample opportunity for the gay colors and contrasts he rejoiced in. Often these gowns were of the richest brocade, or silk, or even velvet; and were heavily lined, and were reversible. For summer wear an unlined gown of soft Chinese silk, like lutestring, was a welcome relief from the formal, stiff, buckram-lined coat. By the year 1730 certainly, and possibly earlier, these Indian gowns had become known generally by the name banyan, banjan, or banian.

When I first read of banians, I had a notion that the term applied only to loose cotton gowns, and I fancied these gowns had been brought ready-shaped from India, in the cotton stuffs made so widely and variedly in India, and desired so much in America. But on turning to the never-failing assistant and friend of the historical writer — the press, then not even the daily press — I found in the advertisements of old weekly news-letters ample evidence that wool stuffs were used for banians just as much as cotton stuffs. In the *Boston Weekly Gazette*, for several months in the year 1738, appeared a notice of a Boston shopkeeper who had banians made of worsted, damask, and brocaded stuffs; also Scotch plaids and callimancos. A Scotch-plaid banian does seem a bit queer. Then came starrets, and scarlet cloth and masqueraded stuffs all specified for banians. Then I read of a banian with a silver clasp. The definition of banian, given by the new Historical English Dictionary, is very misleading and limited, and conveys no manner of notion of the use of the word in America. This word was the title of a dignitary in India, who usually wore such gowns; the name was transferred from the wearer to the garment. I am sure at first they retained the Indian shape in collar and cuff. Old and young alike revelled in banians; even little infants are described as "wrapped up in a banyan." For a time the word was applied to women's "night-gowns," but had there no long or extended use.

A lutestring silk banian which, for many years, was the summer comfort of an estimable Salem worthy, Dr. Edward Holyoke, is shown on this page. He was a thrifty old gentleman and one of very quiet tastes ; but this banian is of a bright orange, with pink and brown stripes.   The very striking Copley portrait of Nathaniel Hurd, now in the Boston Museum of the Fine Arts, affords us a distinct example of a banian.   This banian is a rich golden-brown tint with bright pink lining rolled over in kimono cuffs and collar.   It has elaborate pink loops and frogs. It is worn over a waistcoat which is partly unbuttoned, and the collarless white shirt is unfastened and opened back at the full throat. The sensual face, blue black, with a strong-growing though close-shaven beard, the tur-

Banian worn by Dr. Edward Holyoke.

baned head, and unfastened shirt, with no collar or neck-ruffles, give an extraordinary effect of indolent comfort-loving carelessness, extraordinary to find in a Boston physician and much more to be perpetuated.

A splendid example of banyan and turban, unexcelled by any English portrait, may be seen in a copy facing page 438 and at Harvard Memorial

Hall. It is the likeness of Dr. Nicholas Boylston, a benefactor of the college; and this portrait
was an order to Copley as a memorial of the generous giver. Remembering this, it is to me an extraordinary portrait, and in extraordinary taste; that
any sober Boston gentleman of that day should be
limned for perpetuity in the negligée dress of a banian of bright blue brocade, scarlet morocco slippers,
and scarlet turban cocked well on one side, is a bit
startling. , The canvas is very large; and this gay
little figure sits with "shrunk shanks" carelessly
crossed, as blithe and debonair as a comic-opera figure. And he has such a "pittivanted look," as says
the old play, such a self-satisfied air, that we feel
sure he chose them because he cut a fine dash in
them, and believed he really did look "the top of
the jant" in his toggery, else he would have chosen
to wear his sober everyday dress or his rich court
costume.

John Lovell, the Boston Latin master, was painted
by Smybert. His portrait is also in Memorial Hall,
and is in turban and a plain banian. Thomas Hub-
bard, another man of note, hangs by his side in similar dress. Here is Edward Bromfield, by Smybert.
He died in 1746 when but twenty-three years old;
but he had already made a name for himself by his
generous gifts and his scientific attainments. He
made the first microscope ever set up in America.
His portrait has a great velvet turban and a furred
banian, with cuffs turned back from white undersleeves. Here is that "princely knight and courtly
gentleman," Jonathan Jackson, the son of "Doro-

Dr. Nicholas Boylston.

thy Q.," who lost his fortune in the War of the Revolution. There are five Copley portraits of him. He is in a wonderful green-figured banian with crimson collar.

The reader of this book will weary of the constant noting of the correspondence of men's and women's fashions. If they did not conform in shape, they did in spirit; this is most plainly shown in these years. For the masculine undress of banian and turban found its counterpart in the negligée, the sacque, and the mob-cap and nightgown.

We have a very good description of a feminine nightgown from the pen of the old Duchess of Marlborough, who ordered such a garment from Paris; you will note that she specifies it is not worn in bed : —

" A Night-gown easy and warm, with a light silk wadd in it, such as are used to come out of bed and gird around, without any train at all, but very full. Tis no matter what color, except pink or yellow — no gold or silver in it; but some pretty striped satin or damask, lined with a taffety of the same color."

The Duchess of Devonshire wrote in 1765 : —

" My sister and I were very smart for Carlton House. Our gowns were night-gowns of my invention. The body and sleeves black velvet bound with pink, and the skirt, apron and handkerchie crape bound with light pink, and large chip hats with feathers and pinks. My sister looked vastly pretty."

One of the handsomest garments I have ever known is depicted facing page 438. It is so long

that it must have touched the floor even when worn
by a tall man.   It is of superb cream-colored damask silk, brocaded with high-colored flowers and
with a self-colored figure in the background of a
pattern known as à la Dauphine.   This banian is
lined with heavily ribbed cream-colored silk quilted
in a pattern of infinite
intricacy.   It would not
be called a banian but
for a half-belt which
defines the waist-line.
Dress-coats had no belts.
A waistcoat of the same
material accompanies it ;
and it was worn with
cream-colored or black
satin knee-breeches, with
diamond knee and shoe
buckles and rich lace
frills at neck and wrist.

Old " Redcap."

All these are also preserved in perfect condition.
This was worn by Admiral Jackson, and must have
graced some important and familiar conclave with
royalty.   I have never seen in any court collection
or elsewhere a garment of equal elegance of shape
and material.

We find many American portraits of men with
turbans, especially when banians are worn.   Copley
was given to painting turbans ; and not only did
artists love to depict a turban, but they loved to
wear one.   The portraits of Hogarth and his contemporary artists in England all wear turbans or velvet

caps: Zincke, Rysbrach, Roubiliac, Delvaux, Kent, John Pine, Arthur Pond, John Smith, Winstanley — I take the names as they run in Walpole's *Anecdotes* and as their jaunty turbans peer out of his pages. I suspect they dreaded the test of time on the periwig, dreaded lest it make their faces heavy or ridiculous. They preferred to trust the more natural outlines of the twisted turban or simple cap. It afforded also what they never forgot, a point of bright color.

It may be noted that under all these turbans the head is close shaven. They were worn at a time when large wigs were in fashion, and evidently alternated with the wigs; the latter being worn on dress occasions, the turban in more informal circles, or at home. It is plain that they were very welcome to the colonists, were a relief from the heavy cumbersome wig and the trying powder.

Naturally the head, accustomed to the hot wig, would soon become distressingly neuralgic if left uncovered, therefore, these turbans and nightcaps took turns in protection.

Horace Walpole.

A curious head-covering is this of Horace Walpole. A cocked hat is on top of a half-cap, and singular bags confine the two sides or "wings" of the wig. This must have been the very top of the mode, else Walpole would not have been painted in it. A frilled nightcap was chosen by the poet Cowper (see page 442).

It is not wholly a notion of mine, I believe, since others with a keen sense of the humorous have also noted it, that I see distinctly on the faces of our American turban-wearers an expression of satisfied, albeit innocent vanity. Each wearer fancied the gay-colored jaunty turban becoming, and bridled with that fatuous pride which to-day makes all men so gratified with themselves when once they don, though apparently unwillingly, a rich, gayly colored fancy-dress costume. Those good staid citizens of many years ago rejoiced in their rich, high-colored velvet and satin finery.

William Cowper.

All banians were not of the stately richness and riot of color that are displayed in these portraits of Smybert and Copley; some were of heavy cotton stuffs lined with other cotton. A large figured patch or copperplate cheney like bed-hangings for the outside, and a striped cotton of green and black, red and brown, blue and yellow, for the lining, made a less costly and less elegant garment. I have seen a long and full banian of heavy cotton fabric figured with a palm-leaf design of many hues and lined with a soft sarcenet silk of bright orange hue spotted with white and green. On one cuff was sewed a bit of white linen inscribed in ink with these words : —

" This Banyan was made in Canton in 1792 for Archelaus Brown by Chinese taylors. It was made by order of his son, Rufus Brown; Supercargo of the bark The Lively Nancy. He cleared $100,000 of Chinese gold Cash for a venture of $100 of Ginseng; and 1 Barrel of dried Sage of his Mother's Venture cleared a Chiney tea set, 2 Crape Shawls and $100. All lost by Shipwrack but one small Chest of mostly Books. He was mourned 1 year as Dead & He came in on horse-back waring this Banyan for the last of his clothes was wore out and Rotten with Salt Water and Sun. A very live dress he sayd for a Dead Man. Which is Kept for Thankfulness."

CHAPTER XVII

TWO MASCULINE VANITIES — MUFFS AND EAR-RINGS

"*Any Man that took up a Man's Muff dropt on the Lord's Day between the Old Meeting House and the South Meeting House are desired to Bring it to the Printer's Office and Shall be Rewarded.*
— "Boston News Letter," March 5, 1715.

Superbus swaggers with a ring in his ear;
And likewise as the custome is doth wear
About his neck a riband and a ring;
Which makes me think he's proud of a string.

— "Epigrams," HUTTON, 1619.

CHAPTER XVII

HE advertisement given on page 445 brings naturally to our mind through the suggestion of its grammarless words some young Boston dandy, or perhaps an English officer, mincing along the snowy Boston streets, setting an extreme of star-tling fashion by carrying a mon-strous muff, not at all to the liking of sober, decorous Boston folk. Yet such need not have been the case; for in 1725 Dr. Prince lost his " black bearskin muff," and ad-vertised for it in a Boston news-paper. Now Dr. Prince was

Man's Muff. From Hogarth.

the honored minister at the Old South Church, a Puritan, severe and solemn of countenance, if we

447

can trust his portrait, and anything but a foolish dandy; yet he, too, carried a muff, as did other sober Boston gentlemen; another one lost a " sable skin man's muff," another a " black bear-skin muff," which they duly advertised. In this fashion they simply followed, as in all other articles of dress, the English modes which were sent to them across seas.

From very early days Englishmen wore muffs as well as Englishwomen. The earliest English drawing extant in which a muff is depicted is dated 1598. It is by Gaspar Rutz, and shows an English lady with a cloth muff hanging from her girdle. The wardrobe accounts of Prince Henry of England (that beloved son of James I who died in youth) are still in existence. Two entries under date 1608 read thus : —

" Two muffes ; one of cloth of silver embroidered with purles plates and Venice twists of silver and gold ; the other of black satten embroidered with black silk and bugles ; viz. the one for £7, the other 6os."

The muffs of that day, both for men and women, while yet a French fashion, seem seldom to have been of fur ; but rather of some rich material embroidered, and trimmed with rosettes of ribbon or lace ; and they were often worn hung around the neck with varicolored ribbons. When they became naturalized in England, they were more commonly made entirely of feathers, and then of fur.

> " Where's my dear delightful muff ?
> Muff, my faithful Romeo's present !
> Tippet, too, from tail of pheasant !
> Muff from downy breast of swan ! "

One of the first mentions, in the poems and plays of that day, of muff-wearing by men is in a poem by Samuel Rowlands, written about the year 1600. It reads : —

" Behold a most accomplished cavalier
That the world's ape of fashion doth appear
Walking the streets his humour to disclose
In the French doublet and the German hose.
The muffes, cloak, Spanish hat, Toledo blade,
Italian ruff, a shoe right Spanish made."

From that never failing well of artless information, Pepys's *Diary*, we gain proof of the continued prevalence of muff-wearing. Pepys, torn

A Spark of the Bar, with his Wig and his Muff.

between equal desires to be fashionable and economical, and economical and generous, records that he took his wife's last year's muff for his own wearing, and made a gift to his mother of his wife's old muff.

Muffs were not worn only by beaux — " A spark of the Bar, with his wig and his muff " — but by dignified professional gentlemen. With gold-headed cane in one hand, a truly fashionable doctor ever held a muff in the other. In *The Mother-in-law* one of the characters is discussing the advisability of becoming a doctor. One friend says to him : —

" 'Tis but putting on the doctor's cap and gown, and you'll have more knowledge in an instant than you'll know what to do withal. Besides, if you had no other qualification than that muff of yours, 'twould go a great way. A muff is more than half in the making of a doctor."

Alexander Weddesburn, telling of his youth in the middle of the eighteenth century, speaks of his wearing a muff and trying to look thoughtful and steady, and thus inspire confidence.

From the pages of *The Tatler* and *The Spectator* we learn of muffs and masculine muff-wearers, still assuming the muff as a distinct mark of dignity. It is told of a somewhat eccentric head of a college at Oxford University at about this date, that, like a certain college president to-day, he had a vast aversion to the undergraduates wearing long hair. And he *carried in his muff* a pair of scissors with which he slyly clipped off offending locks.

Muffs were so commonly used by men that Dr. Josiah Tucker, Dean of Gloucester, wore his muff in the cathedral.

Among constant wearers of muffs among Englishmen were Francis, second Earl of Guildford, who died in 1790, Charles James Fox, and Dr. Samuel Parr. The Earl of March wrote to George

Selwyn in 1766, "The muff you sent me by the Duke of Richmond I like prodigiously; vastly better than if it had been tigre or any glaring color."

In 1757 took place in England that cruel tragedy in public life, — the official murder of Admiral Byng. Sent by an incompetent war ministry with an ineffectual fleet on an impossible errand, — the relief of Minorca, — the brave officer, with undoubted good judgment, declared success impossible, and abandoned the ruinous attempt. He was found guilty of neglect of duty, was sentenced to death, and was shot on board his ship in Portsmouth harbor. A famous satirical print of the affair was published at the time. In it Admiral Byng carries a large muff, not to mark

Adam Winthrop.

him as a dandy, but as a true man of dignity. At a much later day, even after the war of the Revolution, Judge Dana of Boston carried always a large muff in winter; and in various inventories of masculine wardrobes in New York and Boston men's muffs appear at that time.

Horace Walpole carried a muff, and gave them to his friends. He wrote on Christmas Eve, 1764,

to George Montagu : " I send you a decent small-
ish muff, that you may put in your pocket, and
it costs but fourteen shillings." It is easy to fancy
him with a muff, and Samuel Pepys also, but it
does not seem suited to the garb of a New England
Puritan, albeit warmly meet for the temperature of a

New England win-
ter, either for man's
or woman's wear.

From 1790 till
1820 great muffs
never went out of
fashion for women,
and part of the
time for men. They
were biggest in
1810. Two kinds
of fur often were in
one muff, a square
or single skin of
black fur alternat-
ing, checker-board
fashion, with sable
or squirrel. Some-

Chandos Portrait of William Shakespere.

times a strip of ermine was edged with a darker fur,
that of the weasel called gris. Gathered cloth and
velvet were used with the fur. A pretty knot or
rosette of ribbon, a tiny sprig of artificial flowers,
or even a paste buckle with ribbon ornamented the
middle of the outside of the muff. It was ever
small, often but a cockade knot and seemed almost
lost in the dark, fluffy fur of those muffs, some of

which were two feet long, so that when in use the arms were covered entirely to the elbow. Some of these barrel-muffs are illustrated in later pages of this book.

One curious muff-knot was of two colors of narrow ribbon woven in checks into a little bag known in my youth as a May basket. This was fastened to the muff, and may have served as a purse or an equipage to carry folderols.

It is always a surprise to me to find a sedate old English gentleman wearing an ear-ring. Adam Winthrop, grandfather of the first governor, John Winthrop, was painted by Holbein. With his furred robe and flat citizen's cap, this dignified Master of the Guild of Cloth-workers wears an ear-ring (page 451). Philip Stubbes, in his indignant outbursts at excess of fashion, says: —

"Worse than all, they are so far bewitched as they are not ashamed to make holes in their ears; whereat they hang rings, and other jewels of gold and precious stones, but this is not so much frequented among women as among men."

Holinshed in his *Chronicle* confirms this statement: —

"Some lusty courtiers also and gentlemen of courage do wear either rings of gold, stones or pearls in their ears."

Courtiers, it is not strange to know, wore them. That effeminate creature, Henry III of France, and his followers delighted in them, and that courtier of courtiers, the man who seems the very personification of the life of luxury, amusement, cleverness, and extravagance of the English Court under James I, that courtier of courtiers, the Duke of Buckingham, wore diamond ear-rings.

In the reign of Charles I ear-rings continued in fashion; for the king hung a beautiful pearl in his ear; he even wore it on his way to the scaffold. There he took it from his ear and gave it to a faithful follower, and ever since it has been carefully preserved as a sacred relic, and is now owned by the Duke of Portland. This pearl was given to the Earl of Portland by King William, with an attestation in the handwriting of the Princess of Orange. It is pear-shaped, about five-eighths of an inch long, mounted with a gold top, with a wire to pass through the ear, and a tiny knob to place behind the ear to hold it in place. It is shown in a portrait of the King when he was but fourteen years old.

Robert Carr, Earl of Somerset.

Many of the portraits of men of the sixteenth and

seventeenth century show ear-rings, usually pearls. A great pearl is in the left ear of Thomas Dutton (nat. 1507, ob.1582), the founder of one branch of the Cheshire family of his name; his right ear is not shown; generally but one ear was pierced. I have a fine old print of the infamous Earl of Somerset which has a double pearl in the right ear. This portrait of him is in the National Portrait Gallery. In it he wears a ruby ear-ring.

It must not be held that the wearing of ear-rings was only by men of "dandaical body," as Carlyle would say; they hung at the ears of men of action, of men of parts—of Sir Walter Raleigh, of Shakespere, of the Earl of Southampton. Two great pear-shaped pearls, one an inch and a quarter certainly in length, dangle in Raleigh's left ear in a well-authenticated portrait, while the portrait of the Earl of Southampton (facing page 190) shows a goodly ear-ring. His friend Shakespere, in the so-called Chandos portrait (see page 452), is shown with mustache and beard, and an ear-ring like a sailor's. He wrote:—

> "Her beauty hangs upon the cheek of night
> Like a rich jewel in an Ethiop's ear."

This passage in *Romeo and Juliet* refers to the custom of "Ethiops"—African negroes—wearing ear-rings.

Sailors and fishermen, as did the Ishmaelites of the Bible, commonly wear ear-rings. They have a belief that piercing the ears will both cure and prevent sore eyes. I find that a hundred years ago American

men who "followed the sea" often had their ears
pierced and wore ear-rings.   On page 457 is a copy
of a miniature portrait of Captain George Taylor, a
Salem ship-owner, a man of wealth, who wore ear-
rings.   This was painted in Lisbon in the year 1800.
It was a safe inference, until recent times, that an
American man who wore ear-rings had seen the world
and been round the Horn; and I am told that it was
as common for sea-
farers (whether ship
captains or super-
cargoes, or men be-
fore the mast) to
have their ears
pierced as to be tat-
tooed.

I have seen a
splendid portrait by
Gilbert Stuart of a
New England gen-
tleman who wore
ear-rings and was
painted in ear-rings.

M. St. Quily.   By Saint Memin.

The presence of the ear-rings in the portrait so
annoyed a granddaughter, that she has had them
painted out.

Many portraits of French gentlemen have ear-
rings.

In the play *Cupid's Revenge*, when the old
duke tries to play the gallant, he has his ears
pierced.   In the Saint Memin portraits, which were
painted in America in 1797 to 1810, are several

with ear-rings bearing French surnames, dated 1798
to 1805. A copy of one of these is given on page
456. As Saint Memin was a gentleman, a nobleman, I cannot doubt that his friends were also men
of note, but some of them look like Brussels sailors.

Lady Morgan, as late as 1816, noted the gold
ear-rings worn by men in France. These were not
only on the custom-
house officials, but
she remarked spe-
cially upon the Duc
de Biron Gontaut,
whose resemblance
to the portrait of his
ancestor, the Duc de
Biron, who was de-
capitated by Henry
IV, was much in-
creased by the fact
that both wore
"very long gold ear-
rings."

More singular
still to me, even than
ear-rings, are the

Captain George Taylor.

black silken strings tied in holes made in the edge
of the ear. There is a portrait at Hampton Court
with these ear-strings, which is said to be of Shakespere, but with no authority.

Planché gives, from *Desiderata Curiosa*, an account of a fray in Gray's Inn, in 1612, when one
quarrelsome gentleman seized another "by a black

string which he wore in his ear, a fashion then much
in use." Planché also gives a portrait of Henry,
Prince of Wales, at that date, with this black string
in his ear; and he conjectures the peculiar fashion
may have travelled to England from Denmark with
Anne, mother of this Prince Henry, for a portrait at
Hampton Court shows Christian, King of Denmark,
wearing this ear-string.

Frequent reference to these ear-strings are found
in old plays by Jonson, and Beaumont and Fletcher
In one of Marlowe's we read : —

> " Yet for thy sake I will not bore mine eare
> To hang thy durtie silken shoo-tires there."

Another allusion is to drawing ribbons through the
ear. Women also wore these ear-strings. A portrait of Anne of Denmark by Vansomer and one
of Elizabeth, Queen of Bohemia, by Honthorst
have them.

To wear a rose in the ear was a prettier fashion.
A portrait of Thomas Lee (about 1590) shows him
with a red rose over his ear. The red rose suited
love-lock and pearl ear-rings then just as a red rose
suits a black lace mantilla to-day.

CHAPTER XVIII

MID-CENTURY MODES

" *In teacup time of hood and hoop*
And when the patch was worn."

— AUSTIN DOBSON.

" *Flowing loosely down her back*
Draw with art the graceful sack
Ornament it well with gimping,
Flowers, furbelows, and crimping
Let of ruffles many a row
Guard her elbows white as snow ;
Knots below and knots above,
Emblems of the tyes of love.
Let her hoop extending wide,
Show what petticoats should hide ;
  Garters of the softest silk
  Stockings whiter than the milk."

—" London Magazine," in July, 1755.

CHAPTER XVIII

MID-CENTURY MODES

HERE was much monotony in woman's dress in the eighteenth century, but since the dress was good, that should not be a great hardship to look back upon; it might be harder to endure. The mid-century gave us the Watteau dress with its swelling skirts, clouds of lace, and gay ribbons, a costume deemed by many the most charming of all of women's dresses. We can see the very best of this mode in the great pastel of Latour, his portrait of Madame de Pompadour, which is a mantua-maker's dream of artificiality and prettiness in dress, " a poem in satins, ribbons, and laces." Even this fashion lasted too long a time. You can see gowns by the score like those of Madame de Pompadour's in Saint-Aubin's *Le Bal Paré*. They are loose gowns or sacques open over stomachers and under-petticoats; caught in perhaps at the waist by ribbons; raised high sometimes on the side by swelling paniers; fluttering ribbons at certain points, bands of fur at others, satin folds, pleated robings, lace, flowers, gauze and ruches. This dress seems suited to sedan-chairs; and though Governor Winthrop had a sedan-chair in Boston in 1640, when few Europeans had seen them, and fewer owned them, and though sedan-chairs, both private and for hire, were in ample number in the eighteenth century in all our larger American cities, still American women were not of a nature for sedan-chairs.   It was a time, too, of very flat coquetry and inane idleness, a time when musk was constantly used, a rococo time — and American women are not rococo nor idle.   The first distinct change came in 1770, in hair-dressing ; the very tight-drawn small heads, accented in their small-ness by the spreading hoops, were to be replaced in Marie Antoinette's time by some of the greatest monstrosities in head-gear that a civilized world (or indeed an uncivilized) has ever known.

There was a simple dress, which was worn fifty years before the Watteau dress was known, was not vanquished while the coquettish French robe was the rage, and continued to be worn after the sacque disappeared and until the short-waisted empire robes were the mode.   I do not mean, of course, that it never varied, but it varied little.   It was a rather plain, gathered, full skirt, a pointed waist low in the neck, with a ruffled elbow-sleeve.

We have in America many portraits of women with a dress such as was much painted by Sir Peter Lely in his later work.   The hair and shape of the bodice differ from the beautiful portraits of the time of Charles II.   The hair is more graceful, being raised unpowdered in a light roll, sometimes with a suggestion of a parting, and with a loose curl on the left shoulder.   The modest low neck has a ruffle of white, either of close lace or of mull or lawn, which is fulled scantly into a little tucker or ruffle at the middle of the bosom. The sleeves vary, often opening over a loose, plain undersleeve of white. Often a rich *ouche* or ornament, a pendent pearl perhaps, catches the slash of the sleeve. With it were worn elbow-ruffles. It is a good dress, simple rather than graceful. You can see it with slight variations on many of the mid-pages of this book. The first woman of any prominence to wear it, I find from the full notes I have made of hundreds of English portraits, was Queen Anne, as shown in her portrait of 1695.

Fair Evelyn Byrd.

She was painted then by Dahl with her poor little son William. The Duchess of Marlborough is a still more familiar example of the dress. This dress was before commode-time, and all through commode-time. The waist was small, and tightly stayed, and seemed smaller from the spread of the hooped skirt; but the general figure of women at that time

demanded a small waist.   The shoulders were not
broad, the arms were slender — a great waist would
have been incongruous indeed.

The lovely portrait of fair Evelyn Byrd may be
taken as an example of the simple dignity of the
dress of that date.   The beautiful girl was painted
in England by Sir Godfrey Kneller, when she was
presented at court.   The fragile fan she carried at
her presentation is still preserved among the precious
relics at Brandon.   The romance of the short life of
this fair Evelyn was her love for Charles Mordaunt,
the grandson of Lord Peterborough.   But the
Peterboroughs were leading Roman Catholics, and
William Byrd, her father, was a staunch churchman.
She was deported from England to Westover-on-
the-James, her father's Virginian home, and, "refusing
all offers from other gentlemen, died of a broken
heart."   On her tombstone we read that "God was
pleased to call this Lady on the 13th Day of November, 1737, in the 29th year of her Age."   The
portrait was painted probably in 1727, or within a
year of that time.   She wears a rose in her hair, and
a scarlet bird (an allusion to her name) is perched
in the shrubbery at the right hand.   Her lovely
hands bind flowers around a simple straw hat.

Facing this page is a portrait of Mary Burnet
Browne of Salem, Massachusetts.   She was the
daughter of Governor Burnet, and granddaughter
of Bishop Burnet, the chronicler of the reign of
King Charles I.   She was reared in one of the finest
homes in the colonies; her father lived in great luxury.   As an example of his house-furnishing, let

William Browne.

Mary Burnet Browne.

me state that in the inventory of his estate at his
death the pewter had what would be a value to-day
of over a thousand dollars, and the china and glass
over two thousand.   He had eleven hundred and
seventy-two ounces of large silverware, and an infinite number of small pieces.   He had a collection
of prints, and one hundred and fifty pictures, four
pieces of rich tapestry, and "a fine piece of needlework representing a rustick," which may have been
the tapestry given to Bishop Burnet by William of
Orange.   His furniture was superb ; part of it is in
the library of Yale University.   In his cellar were
twelve hundred bottles of wine, many flasks of
Canary, a pipe of Madeira, a quarter cask of
Fayal.

Governor Montgomery, his successor, also had
rich belongings, and the finest wines in the country.
Indeed, a wine cellar of a value of $50,000 would
be a goodly belonging to-day.

Madam Browne died in her twenty-third year,
though I think her portrait looks twice that age.
In Mr. Lynde's diary, 1737, we read, "Coz. W.
Browne set out for N. York where in November
he married Mrs. Mary Burnet, ye late Gov.r. Bur-
net's only daughter then $14\frac{1}{2}$ years old and brot her
home in May."   She left two children.   Her husband, though he married a second wife, never ceased
to mourn her ; and at his death was buried by her
side.   In his will made late in life he termed her "my
dear, my beloved, my affectionate, and my constant
wife, friend, and companion" ; and he added that
she was "the best wife and best earthly friend any

mortal could boast of." The portraits of the twain went to Virginia with the fine Holbein portrait of Sir Anthony Browne, an ancestor who by royal favor and grant " need not unbonnet before the King." The great hatchment, used at funerals in the family until Revolutionary times, remained in Massachusetts, and is now in my cousin's home.

In the background of her portrait is seen Folly Hall, the Salem home of this happy married pair. It was built in 1740, and was a copy of the old Browne manor-house in Lancashire. It was a noble house, with many rooms, and a great hall with a gallery for musicians. It was sawed apart; some portions were pulled down, and others carted away. The fields and gardens where it stood are now untilled; and when I visited last summer this home of my ancestors, every inch of ground was a blaze of glory with the golden bloom of broom, the sole relic of all the luxuries and necessities of life which came so lavishly from England to that remote New England home.

To show how little the fashions changed as the years went on, look at the mid-century portrait of Martha Washington (when she was the Widow Custis). See also the portrait of a Virginia dame, Elizabeth Carter, who married the third William Byrd, and died when twenty-eight years old, in 1760. Her plump, complacent face displays the apple-cheeks and double chin of good health, and a smile also of much self-satisfaction. Her buxom figure is well revealed in a pale blue gown, with rich lace at the elbow-sleeves. She wears a simple but prettily shaped hat on her

dark head. She had rather a hard time in life in
spite of her careless eyes and satisfied air, for she
grieved bitterly for the little sons who were sent
away from her to school in England ; and she had a
mother-in-law ; — a mother-in-law who wrote sharply
of Betty's frivolity and extravagance, and said the
silly creature would
think herself ruined
" if she could not have
two new lutestring
gowns every year."
With due respect to
the economical head
of the house, two new
rich gowns would not
seem over many for the
wife of so prominent a
citizen, nor for the
daughter of Secretary
Carter. It is the tra-
dition that the prudent
elder Madam Byrd
hid Betty's finery up-
on the top of a great

Mrs. Betty Carter Byrd.

wardrobe ; at any rate, this hearty young woman, so
full of life and strength, was killed by the pulling
over and falling over upon her of a heavy wardrobe
which she was searching.

The shocking news was brought to Colonel Byrd
as he sat at cards at a neighbor's house, playing, it is
told, with the very Molly Willing who became Willing Molly, and married him speedily — within a year.

It is curious to note, in the oldest gowns I have seen, that the method of cutting and shaping the waist or body is precisely the same as at the present day. The outlines of the shoulder and back seams, of the bust forms, are alike, though not so gracefully curved, and the number of pieces is usually the same. Very good examples to study are the gorgeous brocaded gowns exhibited in the Boston Art Museum. Two are presented in this book.

Nor have we to-day any richer or more beautiful stuffs for gowns than had our far-away grandmothers. The silks, satins, velvets, and brocades which wealthy colonists imported for the adornment of their wives and daughters, and for themselves, cannot be excelled by the work of modern looms ; and the few laces were equally beautiful.

Whitefield complained justly and more than once of the " foolish virgins of New England covered all over with the Pride of Life " ; especially of their gaudy dress in church, which the Abbé Robin also remarked, saying it was the only theatre New England women had for the display of their finery. Other clergymen, as Manasseh Cutler, noted with satisfaction that " the congregation was dressed in a very tasty manner."

Though the shops were full of rich stuffs, there was no ready-made clothing for women for sale either in outside garments or in under-linen. Occasionally, by the latter part of the eighteenth century, we read the advertisement of a " vandoo " of " full-made gowns, petticoats and sacs of a genteel lady of highest fashion," — a notice which reads un-

Green Brocaded Satin Gown.

commonly like the "forced sales" of the present day of mock outfits of various kinds.

A very interesting link of kinship in my own family has ever been to me the marriage of the daughter of Lady Alice Lisle, the martyr to English law, to Dr. Leonard Hoar, President of Harvard College. After the doctor's death, she married a Boston merchant named Usher; and at her own death in 1725 her clothing was sent back to England to her daughter. In the list of her "apparell" made by Judge Samuel Sewall, the executor, is the only reference I have ever found to woollen underclothing; with the holland linen shifts he names one flannel shift. Other items of interest are nine aprons, "five of them short," nine hoods "of various sorts," four head-dresses, three pairs of pockets, one stomacher, eighteen handkerchiefs, "one red silk Purse filled with Knots and Girdles." All the garments seem to have had rich linings. "One New Suit of blew Damask Lined with blew Lutestring; one Satin Night-gown and Coat Lined with Red Lutestring; One full Suit of Striped Satin lined with Cloth-colour'd Lutestring." There were several silk nightgowns, quilted coats, three bonnets, three pairs of stays, stockings, scarfs, screens. It may be noted in this and in other inventories of the garments of elderly ladies that there was no sobering or darkening of colors on account of the age of the women. Old ladies wore light blue and saffron and "pinck-colour" just as did young girls. In fact the richest and brightest tinted brocades were worn by elderly women.

We have excellent descriptions of English dress through the agreeable pages of Mrs. Delany, a delightful old lady who was attached to the court for many years, and wrote many sprightly letters of the court doings.

She knew great folk intimately, observed their dress minutely, recorded it carefully. The sacques and gowns of the Duchess of Portland and her interesting family were more hung with "coloured jewels and diamonds" than those of American ladies of wealth — but the gowns themselves, on both sides of the ocean, were of the same fashion. In 1733 Mrs. Delany herself wore at a wedding of "Cousin Spencer" (Georgiana Carteret and John Spencer, brother of Duke of Marlborough) a brocaded lutestring, white ground with "great ramping flowers of purples, reds, and greens." She adds, "I shall wear dark purple and gold ribbon and a black hood for decency's sake." In 1738 she wore at a royal birthday "pink damask, white and gold handkerchief, plain green ribbon, and Lady Sunderland's buckles for my stays." There was much borrowing of finery constantly going on. The queen even borrowed rich jewels for her coronation. In these she made "a good showish figure." Mrs. Delany's description of the caps, which she calls "frippery whims," is very striking. One was "a French cap of blond which stood in the form of a butterfly with wings not quite extended, frilled lappets crossed under the chin and tied with pink and green ribbons — "a feast she was." Some of these "chapsey" gowns she described at length.

Light Blue Brocaded Satin Gown.

Embroidery prevailed. Her own needlework was exquisite, but she deemed her designs too restricted, too simple. Silver ostrich feathers and purple violets embroidered on a dove-colored gown produced a modest effect, but was lost beside other court robes, as we can believe from her descriptions : —

"The Duchess of Bedford's petticoat was green paduasoy, embroidered very richly with gold and silver and a few colours; the pattern was festoons of shells, coral, corn, corn-flowers, and sea-weeds; everything in different works of gold and silver except the flowers and coral, the body of the gown white satin, with a mosaic pattern of gold facings, robings and train the same of the petticoat; there was abundance of embroidery, and many people in gowns and petticoats of different colours. My Lord Baltimore was in light brown and silver, his coat lined *quite through* with ermine. His lady looked like a *frightened owl*, her locks strutted out and most furiously greased, or rather gummed and powdered; Lady Percival very fine in white satin, embroidered with gold and silver; Lady Carteret in a feuille mort uncut velvet, trimmed with silver flounces — grave and handsome; Miss Carteret a flowered silk with coloured flowers, and glittering with all her mama's jewels; she danced with a very good air, her person is really fine; but my Lady Carteret's agreeable countenance and easy air pleased me more than younger beauties. Miss Fortescue looked like Cleopatra in her bloom; I thought her *the handsomest woman* at the ball; she was in pink and silver, and very well drest."

Mrs. Delany was held to be a woman of unerring taste; but she has placed her taste on record in these words which she wrote in 1740, describing a reception at the residence of the Prince of Wales : —

"The Duchess of Queensberry's clothes pleased me best. They were white satin embroidered, the bottom of the petticoat *brown hills* covered with all sorts of weeds, and every breadth had *an old stump of a tree* that run up almost to the top of the petticoat, broken and ragged, or worked

Mrs. Curwen.

with brown chenille, round which twined nasturtiums, ivy, honeysuckles, periwinkles, convolvuluses, and all sorts of twining flowers, which spread and covered the petticoat. Vines with the leaves variegated, as you have seen them by the sun, all rather smaller than nature which makes them look very light; the robings and facings were little green banks with all sorts of weeds, and the sleeves and the rest of the gown loose twining branches of the same sort as those on the petticoats : many of the leaves were finished with gold, and part of the stumps of the trees looked like the gilding of the sun."

In another letter she describes a similar monstrosity, and deplores her labor spent on a simpler sprig embroidery when she might have accomplished a robe so much more striking.

" A petticoat embroidered with chenille, the pattern a *large stone vase* filled with *ramping flowers* that spread almost over a breadth of the petticoat from the bottom to the top : between each vase of flowers was a pattern of gold shells and foliage, embossed, and most heavily rich ; the gown was white satin, embroidered also with chenille mixt with gold ornaments, no vases on the *sleeve*, but *two or three on the tail.*"

There was a certain type of woman's dress which was worn in this century in many shapes and in rich and varied materials : sacques, " polonezes," levites, trollopees, negligées, slammerkins — all forms of the same loose dress. Women wore hoops and paniers, and stays and stomachers. Capuchins, cardinals, riding-hoods — all were forms of the same hooded cloak.

We are constantly reading references in old letters and descriptions to sacques — French sacques. We now use the word " sack " or sacque for a loose outer garment, but a hundred and fifty years ago it referred to a gown. A careful drawing of a sacque exists in a New England family with full descriptions and rules for the making. It is precisely the dress shown facing this page; it opens in front over a handsome petticoat. It is familiar to us in Watteau's pictures; indeed it is often called a Watteau sacque.

Among the many silly communications to the newspapers of the day, occasionally a few lines of description will be found which are worth reading. Part of the *Receipt for Modern Dress*, 1753, ran:--

> " Let your gown be a sacque, blue, yellow or green,
> And frizzle your elbows with ruffles sixteen ;
> Furl off your lawn apron with flounces in rows,
> Puff and pucker up lace on your arms and your toes ;
> Make your petticoats short that a hoop eight yards wide
> May daintily show how your garters are tied.''

These sacques varied in material. In 1751 there were advertised in the *Boston Evening Post*, " white calico with work'd sprigs for sacks," and " Rich Tobine & tissues for men & women's wear, chiefly Gowns and Sacks."

The sacques worn everywhere were made, in 1781, " with scarcely any figure in the back ; train with a Sash tyed the Right side : in Winter of white Dimity ; in Summer Muslin, with chintz borders."

The negligée, or sacque, was a costly dress. It took many yards of silk to make one. We learn this from such letters as this of William Mollison's, of the 8th of November, 1766, to Captain C. Ridgely, of Baltimore : —

" You wrote for a piece of Lutestring, which Mrs. Mollison thinks you must only have meant a sufficient quantity for a Negligee & therefore by her advice I have only sent a proper quantity for that, a *piece* would have made *four*

Sacque worn by Mrs. Carroll.

gowns. I hope I have done right . . . all the things for
her have been chosen by Mrs. Mollison. I could not get
in London a piece of India chintz that I liked & therefore
have omitted it for the present. . . . Mrs. Mollison
desires her compliments & that you will tell Mrs. Ridgely

Martha Custis.

the fashionable trimmings for a Black Satten is a narrow
black Lace which is sent & that the Lutestring must be
trimmed with its own silk edge with a narrow white Blond
Lace, which is sent for that purpose.

Another form of polonaise was called a Levite.
Lady Cathcart, an American by birth, writing to her
aunt in 1781, gave thus the London Fashions : —

" They wear for morning a white poloneze or a dress they call a Levete, which is a kind of gown and Peticote, with long sleeves made with scarcely any pique in the back, and worn with a sash tyed on the left side. They make these in winter of white dimity, and in Summer of Muslin with Chints borders."

This explains the advertisements, in the *Boston Evening Post* of 1783, of " callicoes for Levites."

The Levite was originally a long, straight frock-coat somewhat like that worn by a priest. Horace Walpole satirized it as resembling " a man's night-gown tied round with a belt." The robe Levite imitated it with a train added. A " monkey-tailed Levite" had a curiously twisted train, and was a French fashion. In the translation, by Mrs. Cashel Hoey, of Robida's *Ten Centuries of Toilette*, there is shown on page 177 a Levite robe — and a very mod-ish-looking garment it is. The word " Levite," like the robe, is now obsolete.

The Watteau-back sacques were worn very low in the bust. Sometimes a large ruff was fastened around the bare neck; a smaller ruche or ribbon was still more common, as is shown in the beautiful portrait facing this page, that of Madam Scott of Boston. She has a small, closely dressed head, and the pretty, ornamental throat-band. For many years this band lingered, dying out in the narrow black velvet such as is shown in the portrait of Madam Dorothy Lynde Dix.

The open gown which was looped at the sides and trailing behind was sometimes called a polonese. The Century Dictionary says these were worn

Mrs. Scott.

" toward the close of the eighteenth century," and
Fairholt gives the date of introduction as 1770; but
both are entirely wrong, for even in America " polo-
nees " were advertised in 1755, in the *Boston Evening
Post*. The next year, in the same newspaper, they
were spelt polonese; and the following year, pulla-
nees; and in 1758, pullonees. They must have
been known in England at a much earlier date.

A description given of an " Irish polonese " in
1774 in the *Lady's Magazine* conveys a good notion
of the shape of the garment. " It buttons half
down the arm, no ruffles, quite straight in the back,
and buttons down before and flies off behind till
there is nothing but a kind of role behind except
the petticoat, a large hood behind the neck." I
have never seen a polonaise with a hood; that may
have been the Irish portion of it.

Another name for these loose, ruffled gowns was
slamkin or slammerkin, which later became an
opprobrious term applied to a slattern. These two
words and shambling are evidently allied; slam also
is a word applied to an ill-shaped, shambling fellow.
All are derived from the German *schlampe*, a slattern.
It is an ugly name, but it was used for some years.

Of course, when the open sacques, negligées, and
polonaises were so much worn, and the petticoat was
consequently so exposed to view, it became a still
more important and costly article of attire than in
early colonial days.

In the year 1688 was introduced to Fashion one
of the most charming accessories which women's
dress has ever known, namely, lace elbow-ruffles.

They may be termed the typical feminine sleeve of the eighteenth century, as the virago-sleeve was of the preceding century.

We may say that engageants appeared with the cravat and the commode, — they were sister frivolities, — but the commode was meaningless, and naturally found its time and season very short, while the others were what might be termed natural and reasonable fashions; one was a suitable and sensible, as well as charming, finish to a sleeve, the cravat a graceful finish at the throat. Engageants remained in fashion till the time of the French Revolution; indeed, with very short temporary disappearances they have been popular ever since. In the *Mercure Galant*, 1683, we read that two elbow-ruffles of fine and wide "fil de point" are the fashion, and that such sleeves are called "Engageantes." A year or two later we read of "Engageantes of Malines lace." The word was adopted at once by English women. Evelyn says in his *Mundus Muliebris*, 1690, "About her sleeves are engageants." And the *Ladies' Dictionary* of the same date calls them engageants, and describes them fully. In the lace bills of Queen Mary in 1694, are "broad engageants of Point lace," and "double engageants." I will not call attention to the portraits in this book which show these elbow-ruffles — they are too numerous; nor need I multiply references such as this entry of Mrs. Delany's in 1756: —

"Mrs. Spencer's negligee sleeves are *treble;* the ruffles are much the same as at Bath, long at the elbow and pretty narrow at top.

Silk Gown and Petticoat.

These engageants have been varied in shape, in depth, in width, in ornamentation, but custom cannot stale their infinite variety ; they are ever pleasing, ever satisfying, ever becoming. We can say of them in the expressive phrase of praise used by old Pepys, they are " the best flowers blooming in the garden."

Accompanying the sleeve-ruffle were several new

gown trimmings. Furbelows were invented — falba-
las — by one Langlée, son of a waiting-maid of the
French queen. These were quilled pleatings, or
narrow flounces pinked, hemmed, lace-edged, disposed often in curving lines, such as we now term
festoon-shape. They were used lavishly on the
petticoat and sparingly on the trained overdress or
sacque, provided that sacque were not looped up at
the sides.

Another novelty were *prétintailles*, appliqués of
colored figures, cut from brocaded materials and
sewed upon other backgrounds, sometimes very
thin ones, with unusual embroidery stitches. Two
breadths of a sacque I have before me, which were
formerly the plait at the back of a Watteau sacque
of the year 1740. The material is a salmon-pink
thin silk, stronger than a sarcenet and thinner, yet
not exactly a silk gauze. It is something like a
Liberty silk. It is faded nearly white, save under
the figures. These are dark green velvet leaves and
single great pink flowers like magnolias or tulip-tree
blossoms. The coral tint of the outer petals, the
light pink and the dark green of the velvet, give it
all the coloring of an open watermelon. The petticoat was of coral pink with furbelows of pinked-
out silk of the different melon tints. It must have
been a smart and handsome thing in its day. Another
sacque of bright pink satin had *prétintailles* of scarlet velvet, a lattice-work of inch-wide white Swiss
lace insertion forming part of the pattern. This
is a distinct novelty which might be revived and
adopted to-day, the lattice of insertion with appliqué

Gold-covered Brocade Gown of Mrs. Eliza Lucas Pinckney.

vines. A pair of high-heeled, purple kid shoes has always been kept with this gown, and is believed to have been worn with it, for the lining of the flaps is scarlet. A design of gold beads is sewn on these shoe-flaps. They seem dull and ugly in color with the vivid-hued green.

Besides the furbelows and *prétintailles*, or "whatnots," were hurly-burlies and *fanfreluches* — little puffs of silk or gauze.

Ruffles gathered or pleated in the middle, or on either or both edges, and disposed in various waving, circling, or even regular parallel forms on the gown or polonaise, were called robings. Many and ingenious were the ways in which these were plaited and twisted into ruches, rolls, folds, and bands. They were often made of strips of

Fly-fringe.

the dress material, and I have seen them of gauze ribbons and of pinked silk. Pinking was very fashionable in those mid-century years, even on the heaviest silk and velvet. Robings and cuffings were constantly advertised for sale in the middle years of the eighteenth century. I have no doubt that the handsome trimmings of fine silk cord, knotted with gold-colored silk and fly-fringe and woven to match the gold brocade gown (shown facing the previous page), were called robings.

Fly-fringe was a universal trimming of the eighteenth century. It is composed, as you may see, of simple tufts of silk, alternating two and four tufts.

This gold-colored silk robe was made of silk raised and spun by Eliza Lucas Pinckney, who was, perhaps, the most remarkable of all South Carolina women. She introduced indigo-culture to the state, bringing thereby vast wealth and prosperity.

The plaited ruffles disposed in semicircles and waves on Mrs. Rudd's gown were known as robings, as were similar undulatory ruffles on Mrs. Mercy Warren's polonaise.

The portrait of Mrs. Daniel Horry had some exceedingly delicate robings made for the gown in the shades of light blue, pale green, and raisin tints of the figures of the brocade of the gown. The dress, fan, and exact attitude of the original portrait of Mrs. Horry, of Hampton, South Carolina, are here displayed upon Mrs. Horry's great-granddaughter. Mrs. Horry was the daughter of Eliza Lucas Pinckney.

Some of these gowns with their fal-lals and robings show to me plainly the source of Aubrey Beardsley's whimsies. He never wholly escaped the influence of *The Rape of the Lock*, his earliest important work, but carried the modes of that day into all his illustrations, even of the ancient classics.

In addition to the artists named in the previous chapter, to depict in perfection for us the Levite, sacque, and cardinal, we have Copley.

In the spring of the year 1774, Copley was thirty-seven years of age, and he sailed for Europe. His son, Lord Lyndhurst, declared late in life that Copley had then never seen a decent painting, though I think that there is ample proof in the pages of this book that there were more than decent portraits to be seen. However, he had had no instruction, as Pelham and Smybert had died when he was fourteen —if they could have taught him anything. After a few weeks he started for Italy, where he had, as congenial travelling companions, Mr. and Mrs. Ralph Izard. Izard was a rich South Carolinian indigo-planter, who had been edu-

Mrs. Ralph Izard.

cated in England. His wife was Alice de Lancey of New York. Copley painted their portraits in Rome on a single canvas. This was his first group and the only portraits he painted while in Italy. He was to receive £200 for it; but the war of the American Revolution made it impossible for Mr. Izard to pay for it or even take it. After Copley's death in 1815, his widow retained it for ten years, when Izard's grandson, Charles Manigault, found it, bought it, and brought it to Charleston, and the Manigault family have owned it till this year. Mr. Izard is in grayish buff broadcloth, a beautiful tint — the one described by Governor Hutchinson in a preceding chapter of this book. Mrs. Izard is in Copley's favorite blue-green, but a much better color than his wife's gown because greener and less startling. It is the same nasturtium-leaf tint as the sacque of Mrs. Mercy Warren. They are seated on either side of a table with gilt frame and red porphyry top. The furniture-covering and draperies are old-rose damask. In the middle distance can be seen the marble group, *Orestes and Elektra*, which was in the Villa Lodovisi. Mrs. Izard has apparently drawn this group, and shows her drawing to her husband. The Colosseum is in the background.

Mrs. Izard was a graceful and beautiful creature, and her great refinement is shown in her dress. It was at a time when filigree trimmings and cheap paste ornaments were much worn, but her dress is noticeably simple. Her gown is a Watteau sacque of plain taffeta. Her gauze apron is absolutely plain, and her charming cap is of plaited fine mull or lawn, and has a pretty little close trimming of satin ribbon. These look like little overlapping squares, but it is really a ribbon ruche. I have a lace cap of that date with the precise trimming, and it is made of white satin ribbon plaited in a certain manner, with the plaits turned all the same way, and not sewed down on the face of the trimming, but left loose and pulled over flat into the little overlapping lozenges.

Brocade Gown of Mrs. Daniel Horry.

This same shaped cap, sometimes a bit longer, sometimes smaller, was very fashionable. I have grouped some of the illustrations from *Town and Country* on page 486, to show these "dormouse" caps. These are said to be portraits of London women who were much in the public eye, and their dresses serve as fashion-plates. Little white ribbon plaitings and ruchings and robings of various forms are on them all. Milliners tired their brains inventing new robings, and brought out one after the other until the fashion was worn out — and the inventors also.

Copley was fortunately a great lover of fine dress. His granddaughter says that " the beautiful costumes which we admire to-day on the stately portraits of our grandmothers' times were the results of his combined taste and study." He had theories about women's dress, which he carried out with scrupulous elaboration in his portraits. Not only the dress, the hair, the jewels, were much thought upon, but other adjuncts were studied, and their values weighed ; birds, a spaniel, or his favorite squirrel, seen in several portraits, were never painted by accident. His own dress was rich and full of color. Trumbull found him in rich claret color — a favorite either of his or of the day, for it is seen in many of his masculine portraits. He bought in Genoa, in 1774, lace ruffles, silk stockings, rich Genoese velvet for a coat, and crimson satin to line it. He writes to his wife, " I believe you will think I have become a beau to dress in so rich a suit of clothes ; and truly I am a little tinctured ; but you must remember you thought I was too careless about my dress. I wish to reform

Caps with Ribbon Ruches.

from all my errors, and particularly from those that
are most painful to you."

Aprons varied from year to year in form.   In
1744 they were worn so long that careless girls were

Mr. and Mrs. Ralph Izard. 1770. By Copley.

warned severely not to tread upon them when walking, but to lift them daintily. They covered the petticoat, which was displayed by the open-fronted robe. Even Queen Anne wore these aprons, and they often formed part of a wedding dress. In 1752 they were shortened. A year or two later efforts were made to make them unfashionable, but a lace apron was too pretty a thing and too costly to be lightly cast off. They appear still in every inventory. Sometimes they were attached to a stomacher and were then usually of brocade. In the portraits of Mrs. Izard and of Mrs. Cadwalader in this chapter both wear handsome lace aprons. Letters were written clamoring for patterns for drawn-work and other embroideries for aprons. As tidy adjuncts to preserve the dress, aprons lingered to our own day. The sculptor Nollekens relates that his wife wore on her wedding-day " a sacque and petticoat of the most expensive brocaded white silk, resembling network, enriched with small flowers, which displayed in the variation of the folds a most delicate shade of pink, the uncommon beauty of which was greatly admired. The deep and pointed stomacher was exquisitely guimped and pinked, and at the lower part was a large pin, consisting of several diamonds, confining an elegant point lace apron." This description, even the dress of pink, might serve as an attire of " Dorothy Q.," Mrs. Hancock (given in this chapter). The gimped and pinked stomacher, lace apron, and cap are the same.

This day of hoop and hood was one of curious contrasts and incongruities. We find these sacques

and Levites and negligées hanging loose from the
neck, flowing apparently in easy undress fashion.
Indeed, the name "flying-gown" was given to these

sacques. We find the
hood thrown negligently
on the head, or hanging
dangling on the arm,
and the apron, certainly
not a formal dress, was
also worn everywhere.
But the negligées and
the ease and the aban-
don were all artificial,
like the times.   Under-
neath the sacque, women
were laced up in the
fiercest of stays; and
under the furbelowed
petticoat was a rigid
hoop. So little of the
bodice was definitely
outlined that such heavy
stays seem wholly su-
perfluous. But some-
times the gown was
without a sacque back,
and then the corsets

Stomacher and Apron of Figured
Damask.

were worn outside the chemisette, and formed the
bodice. Sometimes a whaleboned stomacher or fore-
body was worn under the sacque. There was never
any total ease or relaxation for the body of the
wearer; for if the stays had yielded, the hoop still

Mrs. Livingstone.

dominated. Variations in dress during these years came chiefly through changes in the shape of hoops.

In 1713 there was printed in Boston a pamphlet entitled *A Satyr, in Verse, origin of the Whalebone Petticoat*. This was not the first straw to show which way the wind blew. As usual the first note of alarm came from the parsons; allusions in sermons show that hoops were trundling into Boston. In 1701 a correspondent of Judge Sewall's had written to him in puritanical alarm of hooped petticoats that they "trenched on morality." In 1722 a little book was offered for sale in Boston for a few pennies, "intituled" *Hoop Pettycoats Arraigned and Condemned by the Light of Nature and Laws of God*. Evidently Judge Sewall did not regard them as immoral or irreligious, for he permitted his granddaughter, Mary Hirst, to receive one from her bridegroom, William Pepperell, as a wedding gift.

Soon hoop coats, hooped coats, hooped petticoats, long-bone hoops, short-bone hoops, hooping holland, Quhaill bone, and reeds were offered for sale on all sides. Thrifty Merchant Amory in 1728 shipped back to England a consignment of petticoats because they were too scant in width to wear with hoops. Some of these hoops were five yards in circumference. Bell hoops were offered in 1731; fan hoops in 1758. Pocket hoops to spread out the paniers were worn on each hip in 1750. Mrs. Delany wrote thus in 1756: —

"Hoops are as flat as if made of pasteboard, and as stiff, the shape sloping from the hip and spreading at the bottom, enormous but *not* so ugly as the *square* hoops. There *are hopes* they will be reduced to a very small size, and two very fine fashionable ladies appeared at Court with *very small ones*. I expect soon to see the other extreme of thread-paper heads and no hoops, and from appearing like so many *blown bladders* we shall look like so many *bodkins stalking about*."

The word "pannier" applied to a hoop has one of the strangest and most distasteful, as well as silly derivations of any of our many strange dress names. It is such a "witless bravery"—to use Shakespere's words. A well-known official, a Master of Requests named Panier or Pannier, perished in a shipwreck on his voyage home to France from the Antilles, and his name was given to an article of dress which might well have had the same name in a less heedless and heartless way. For some time the large panniers went by the name *maître des requêtes*. I think none but French women could have done this.

The pretty sacque-gown of Mrs. Carroll was made to wear with a much larger hoop than is shown in the photograph ; a pannier hoop, too, which naturally could not be supplied in 1903.

But it is surprising that so few of our portraits display the hoop when we remember its dominance. Artists both in England and America seem to have been a bit shy about perpetuating such extremes as commode and hoop. Madam Flucker's portrait painted by Feke gives a faithful presentation of the Boston hoop of her day worn below a fiercely laced and lengthened waist; she looks like a maid of honor of the English court. She was a very

Mrs. Judith Bowdoin Flucker.   1740.

fashionable woman and she had the aristocratic bearing, the elegant carriage of her family. She was
Judith Bowdoin, sister of Governor Bowdoin, who
founded Bowdoin College. She was born March,
1719; and in 1744 was married to Thomas Flucker.
This portrait must have been painted at about this
time.

Several of her kinsfolk are shown in these pages;
for they seem, as a family, to have loved to have
their portraits painted. They had great wealth, and
they were handsome; two very good reasons for this
love of placing their faces on canvas. I should fancy
they were both proud and vain — they had reason to
be — of themselves and each other. I can see little
harm in having pride in handsome and good and
intelligent men, and in handsome and good and lov-
able women; nor can I see how any woman could
be so handsome and not be vain. It is an amiable
and harmless failing, one we would all doubtless
succumb to had we the faces of these Bowdoins and
their ilk. Lady Temple was a sister of Mrs.
Flucker. Her head by Copley is on a later page.

Dr. Manasseh Cutler visited Lady Temple in New
York in the first years of our national existence, and
she made a profound impression on him. " The
greatest beauty I ever saw," he writes, " notwithstanding her age. To a well-proportioned form, a
perfectly fair skin, and completely adjusted features,
is added a soft but majestic air; an easy and pleasing
sociability, a vein of fine sense which commands
admiration and infuses delight. Her dress is exceedingly neat and becoming, but not gay. She is

now a grandmother; her real age is forty-four, but I should not suppose her more than twenty-two."

Besides the portrait of Lady Temple in childhood and this fine head by Copley, I have a photograph of a head of her by Gilbert Stuart painted in 1806: and John Trumbull painted a family group, of Sir John and Lady Temple and two children, which I have not deemed interesting or pronounced enough as to costume to reproduce herein.

Lady Temple was, as may be seen in her portrait, what old Pepys called "a good-bodied woman, but not over-thick."

Many New England families were assiduous in having their portraits painted. The members of the Pepperell family, I am sure, were unfailing in this duty.

There were in the Pepperell homestead at Kittery, Maine, fifty family portraits, some in hoops and furbelows. The assigned dates of these began about the year 1730. This noble array has been disbanded; the whereabouts of about twenty of the fifty are known. Not only members of the family were painted, but friends gave portraits of themselves to each other. Sir Peter Warren and Sir William Pepperell thus exchanged. The splendid Copley portrait of Colonel Scott was painted for his friend, Joshua Winslow.

Smart-looking, high-colored embroidered stays were worn outside a chemisette. One continually meets with mention of stays in descriptions of full-dress costume, but I cannot recall seeing them in portraits. I have seen a few that were like a deep,

Lady Temple.

pointed, heavily boned waistband, with straps at the shoulders. In 1734 stays were worn extremely low, and again in 1795, when a paragraph in the *Times* declared, in a satirical comment on the fashions, that " corsettes about six inches long, and a slight buffon tucker of two inches high, are now the only defensive paraphernalia of our fashionable belles between the necklace and the apron strings." The

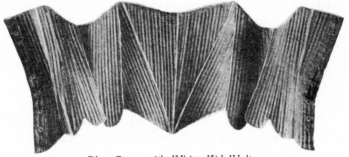

Blue Stays with White Kid Welts.

high stays worn at several periods were very ugly, and produced an unnatural-looking figure.

These were, to use the extreme expression of approval from the lips of the fribbles of the day, "in the high kick of fashion." Another expressive phrase from a jesting rhyme, —

> " Last Sunday at St. James's prayers
> I drest in all my whalebone airs,"

seems to display to us in the two words " whalebone airs " as clear a picture of the stiffly boned stays and hoop as could be given by the ordinary adjectives of an entire sentence.

We learn of these gay stays through the very prosaic record of articles stolen ; cherry color seems to have been a favorite tint for them. An advertisement of stolen goods runs thus : —

" A black silk petticoat with a red and white calico border, cherry-coloured stays trimmed with blue and silver, a red and dove-coloured damask gown flowered with large trees, a yellow satin apron trimmed with white Persian, and muslin head-cloths with crow-foot edging, double ruffles with fine edging, a black silk furbelowed scarf and a spotted hood."

Among the goods of Benjamin Franklin, printer, which were stolen from his Philadelphia house in 1750, was a pair of women's stays, covered with white tabby before and dove-colored tabby behind, with two large steel hooks. Another pair is described as cherry colored, with white kid welts and silver lace edging. A pair of stays is on the preceding page, which are light blue silk with " white kid welts." They were costly and deservedly so, as they were difficult to shape, and to make neatly ; often a pair would contain sixty or seventy pieces of material, all carefully cut from a rigid pattern. I have counted over eighty pieces in one pair. Whole fronted and laced in the back was the rule of the day in shape. Stern busks give added stiffness of form.

The eighteenth century witnessed many pretty adjuncts of dress besides the engageants, the furbelows, and hurley-burlies.

Every lady carried a fan. It was an indispensable

part of a costume. The eighteenth century witnessed the apotheosis of the fan. The fan was so distinctly French in "spirit" that I hardly think of

one as important in American dress, while no French costume was complete without one. The management of a fan seems to have been a study in elegance and grace, and the plebeian seldom learned to manage her fan well, even when by circumstance she acquired one.

Fans and Piece of Brocade Gown. Worn by Mrs. John Adams.

I will not attempt to give a history of the fan or its use. It has been ably done by a competent hand and by a Frenchman, Octave Uzanne. When even in the seventeenth century there were more than five hundred manufacturers of fans in Paris, we may know that many of the beautiful things came to America. We have seen how eagerly Madam Symonds sought them in 1685.

In the first news-letters appear these advertisements : —

" George Harding lately from London, now at Mr. John Potters, Confectioners, Mounteth all sorts of Fans as well as any Done in old England.   He likewise hath a large Sortment of Curious Mounts which he will dispose of very Reasonably, not purposing to stay long in These Parts."

Old Painted Kid Fan.

By 1732 other fan-mounters had come to town, and set up business on Beacon Street, near the Common.

" The Person that mounts Fans having a Parcel Just arriv'd.   All Gentlewomen that Desire to be Supply'd may have them.   She intending to Mount no more desires they would be speedy in Coming."

Soon several Boston women supported themselves by fan-making and mending.   All kinds of scenes and legends found their way on to the French fan, until, as a correspondent wrote to one of the fashion journals, a lady hardly knew whether to blush before or behind her fan. Under the term "classical," almost anything could be brought before the public; and drawings which would not have been tolerated otherwise were, with that single word for apology, passed from hand to hand to admire. I suspect that Mary, daughter of Deacon Vans, who painted fans in Boston, knew naught of these "classical" subjects.

Nearly all the dresses of this century had breast-knots; and every order sent to England contained breast-knots. Washington ordered them for wife and stepdaughter. You may see them in many of the portraits in this book. They were apparently simple enough. But I presume then, as now, there were some women who could not tie a graceful, pretty knot. They have been made with tasselled ends, or agletted, as in the seventeenth century. A writer in 1720 said : —

"As the breast-knot allows a good deal of ingenuity in the delicate choice of colors and disposition of figure, I think it may be indulged, but very sparingly, and rather with a carelessness than the least affectation. It seems there is a fashion even in the colors of ribbons, and I have observed a beautiful purple to be lately the general mode. It is not the beauty of the color that recommends it, so much as the symbol it is said to bear."

Without books on costume one might know that flowers were soon to appear in dress at this time. For English gardens were being most thought upon;

Addison, Pope, Thomson, Mason, Shenstone, had
written upon gardening and gardens. Linnæus
was laying out a system of botany. It was a day
of arbors, of summer-houses, of grottos. A love
of flowers was the rage. Ladies made wonderful her-
bariums and illustrated flower beds ; others painted

Carved Ivory Fan.

and embroidered flowers; and Mrs. Delany cut
wonderful flowers from paper. Waxen and silken
flowers were made, and flowers of shell. Whole
dresses were embroidered with flowers. Natural
flowers even appeared upon the breakfast table,
where I fancy no one had seen them since Sir
Francis Bacon had them.

With the interest in gardens and in botany came
an assumption of rural simplicity in dress, came the
wear of natural flowers. Fair Evelyn Byrd wreathes

her simple straw hat with a garland of country blossoms. Of course these flowers quickly faded, and a withered knot, dull of color and dead of leaf, is neither beautiful nor becoming; and soon a new means was found to keep these graceful breast-bouquets fresh. Horace Walpole writes in 1754: —

"A new fashion has my Lady Henry brought from France; it is a tin funnel covered with green ribbon and it holds water, which the ladies wear to keep their bouquets fresh."

This was a clumsy thing, and more delicate substances were soon sought, silver and glass. I was much puzzled by the advertisement in the *Boston Evening Post* of July 26, 1756, and in subsequent New England newspapers, of "Bosom Bottles." I now believe them to be small, flat glasses, covered with green ribbon perhaps, like Lady Henry's, which, filled with water, were worn in the stomacher of the dress, and in which the stems of "bosom flowers" were placed. I found two of these bottles, of a flattened pear shape, about four inches in extreme length, of ribbed glass, thrown in an old trunk which had held for nearly a century an honored great-great-aunt's maiden finery. This ownership was a bit puzzling when we considered the accompanying story of the purpose and being of the bottles. And it always seemed to amuse all who saw them and heard the family tradition, which was that these two curious, flat, opalescent glasses were infants' nursing-bottles. It was, one can see, a very natural perversion of their name and nature.

But when their true use was discovered to us we understood why Aunt Vryling Phillips cherished them throughout her long, unmarried life. They were mementoes of a happy girlhood; some lover's gift of rose or violet perfumed to her for half a century these curious bosom bottles.

We must not fall into the notion that every American or every English woman wore a brocade or satin gown or petticoats. There were working-women who had clothes simple of shape and stuff. You can see similar ones in Hogarth if you will, or in other works of his day.

This dress, consisting of a warm, wool gown with double-puffed sleeve, with linen kerchief and collar, white or woollen apron, and loose hood tied under the chin, was seen in scores of prints; such as, for instance, Tempest's *Cries of London*, 1702. If the scene be without-doors, a hat surmounts the hood. A young woman would have her bodice laced or strapped, and have ribbons on her shoes, and pockets on her aprons, and would wear mittens. Sometimes the overskirt was turned up to form what is known as a washer-woman's skirt or apron, and was used by ballad-mongers, and the sellers of the gazettes and news-letters — all tiny sheets — as a deep pocket to hold their wares. A street vendor could also and did carry a basket on her arm, in which she displayed her " Dutch biskets," laces, minikin pins, cotton reels or ribbons.

The skirt did not touch the ground, and the shoes had low heels; the neck was protected by the hood, and the eyes shaded by the hat brim; and I

Mrs. Benjamin Smith. Painted by Jeremiah Theus.

think it altogether a neat, trim, comfortable, warm, sensible dress; one which could be adopted for working-women with advantage to-day. The only improvement would be to have the hair show a bit under the hood; for a woman's face never seems rightly framed unless her hair shows.

I have quoted in the previous chapter a description written by an old gentleman for the Old Colony Memorial at the meeting at Plymouth in 1820 to celebrate the two hundredth year of the settlement of Plymouth. He thus described the dress of plain country women, in the years from 1750 to the Revolution: —

"As for the women, old and young, they wore flannel gowns in winter. The young women wore wrappers in the summer, and about their ordinary business they did not wear stockings and shoes. They were usually contented with one calico gown, and another of camel's hair goods; and some had them made of poplin. The sleeves were short and did not come below the elbow.

"On holidays they wore one, two, or three ruffles on each arm. They wore long gloves coming up to the elbow, fastened by what were called glove-tightens, made of black horsehair. They wore aprons made of checked linen or cotton, and, for holiday use, of white cotton, lawn or cambric.

"They seldom wore caps when about their ordinary affairs; but they had two kinds. One kind they wore when they meant to be much dressed up. One was called a strap-cap; it came under the chin; the other was called round-cord cap, and did not come over the ears.

"They wore thick leather, thin leather, and broadcloth shoes, all with heels an inch and a half high. These had peaked toes, turned up in a point at the toes.   They generally had small, very small muffs; and some wore masks."

In one thing the fifty years of stationary fashions were not idle, — in lace-making.   That prospered. More laces were made, and more kinds of laces were made, than ever before.   Beautiful new laces were invented.   Every one wore lace.   Men's neckwear vied with women's " heads."   There seemed scarcely lace enough for all demands.

Madame de Pompadour died in 1764 after more than twenty years of absolute control of French internal politics, foreign affairs, the French king, and fashions.   Du Barry reigned in her stead over the king and the modes.   Poor France! under her everything and everybody sunk very low; too low for Marie Antoinette, when she became queen in 1774, to succeed in pulling up again.

Rebecca Orne.

CHAPTER XIX

WOMAN'S HAIR

" *But if a woman have long hair, it is a glory to her, for her hair is given to her as a covering.*"
— 1 Corinthians xi. 15.

" *If they would keep under a power as they ought to do there should not any Tussocks nor Tufts be seen as there be; nor such laying out of the haire; nor braiding it to have it open. Of these Tussocks laid out now-a-days there is no mention made in the Scripture; because they were not yet come to be so far out of order as to lay out their hair in such tussocks and tufts.*"

— "Sermon to 'His Sisters the Women,'" BISHOP LATIMER, 1550.

" *Seabank Hog did say that she would pull off her head-clothes and come to them in her hair, like a parcel of pitiful beggarly black curs that they were.*"

— Testimony at Trial in New Hampshire, MARY RANN, 1686.

CHAPTER XIX

HE portraits of Englishwomen contemporary with our first colonists, and the earliest portraits we have of the wives of the emigrants, show little hair, and that little simply dressed. The Lady Armine has prim stiff curls at either side of the face, while a few stray curls may lie on the forehead. Rebecca Rawson has like ringlets. Penelope Winslow's are more luxuriant and beautiful. In general, however, the hair is severely covered with caps and veils and scarfs and the omnipresent hood, so that we really have little notion of their mode of hair-dressing.

Were you to judge, however, from the sermons of the Puritan preachers, you would fancy that the heads of New England women were dressed like the heads at the court of Marie Antoinette. Even the Massachusetts court complained of the " cutting and curling and laying out of the hair especially among the younger sort." One parson said severely, " The special sin of women is pride and haughtiness, and that because they are generally ignorant and worthless." I wish I knew what Madam, the parson's wife, said to him about that last clause, after the service was ended. A comet was seen in the sky in 1683, and our Puritan forbears were fearsome indeed of the wonder. Increase Mather, of course, hinted that the vanity and extravagance of his sober Boston neighbors were attracting the tail of the comet; and he called out: "Will not the haughty daughters of Zion refrain their pride in apparell? Will they lay out their hair, and wear their false locks, their borders, and towers like comets about their heads?" You would fancy the women wore court head-dresses, commodes, from what he said; but I presume they were all sitting there in a row with their demure black hoods over their little coifs, and not one curly hair showing.

Madame de Sévigné.

The curling and laying out of the hair objected to so bitterly by the Puritan magistrates was, I believe, a French fashion which had been quickly adopted in England. A parting was made horizontally across the forehead and this front hair cut short and curled loosely, "as our English women wear their hair." The hair was knotted at the back and a brush of curls or a great roll with a few dangling ringlets spread out at the sides. You may see this in scores of English and French portraits. These knots of curls were generally artificial and were often called "a pair of perukes." In a letter written by Knollys, in Chalmers's *Life of Mary Queen of Scots*, we read that Queen Mary wore them at one time.

"Mary Seaton, who is praised to be the finest busker, the finest dresser of a woman's head of hair whereof we have seen divers experiences since her coming hither, among other pretty devices yesterday, she did set such a curled hair upon the Queen that was said to be a Peruke that showed very delicately ; and every other day she hath a new device of head-dressing without any cost, and yet setteth forth woman gaylie well."

Poor Mary ! "pleased with a rattle—tickled with a straw ;" having her fast-whitening locks dressed diversely to help to pass her dragging days.

The "cutting of the hair of the younger sort" was, I think, a cutting of the hair across the forehead in a fashion known to us ten years ago by the word "bang." Many Puritan men and women wore their hair thus cut. Higginson, in writing of the Indians in 1692, said, "Their hair is generally black, and cut before like our gentlewomen's." The false hair (if any really was worn) must have been these same bunches of curls called also "heart-breakers." Mr. Felt gives an account of one bill in Salem in 1679 for wire, catgut, and hair for a woman's head-gear.

These heart-breakers are familiarized to us by many portraits, among them those of Madame de Sévigné, who seems to have worn them for many years. An old copperplate print of Madame de Sévigné, given many years ago to a systematically idle little girl, as "a reward for proficiency in her

French exercises," has always been carefully preserved as the sole prize she ever received for scholarship or anything; and it is reproduced in these pages.

Madame de Sévigné thus wrote to her daughter of this mode: —

"Knot the hair low at the back of the head so as not to conceal either its purity of outline or its harmonious proportions. The short 'undergrowth' of hair in light curls on the forehead gives piquancy to the physiognomy, while bunches of light ringlets at the temples add softness to the expression."

It is difficult to think of Madame de Sévigné as a contemporary of the first generation born to the American colonist. She was born in 1626, died in 1696. She seems so modern, so fully in the spirit of our own time when compared with our Yankee forefathers. These ringlets at the side were sometimes called in France mustaches. After a time they were not cut in short bunches, but hung in long ringlets over the bosom.

It would seem strange and doubtful to draw the early residents of Boston and New York with these bunches of curls, but we should certainly err if we did not do so. These heart-breakers were sometimes wired that they might flutter alluringly, and stand out at a distance from the head, like butterfly wings. The stern old Puritan Stubbes writes of them: —

"Then followeth the trimming and tricking of their heades, in laying out their haire to the shewe, whiche of force must be curled, fristed, and crisped, laid out (a world to see) on wreathes and borders, from one eare to another. And least it should fall down, it is vnder propped with forks, wiers, and I cannot tell what, like grim sterne monsters, rather than chaste Christian matrones."

An old Puritan preacher named Perkins, denouncing " curled and embroidered hair," called those knots of curls "winkles," and another called them " wink-a-peeps." The word winkle is a good one to choose for etymological research. It is allied to winkers, blinkers, or blinders, part of the harness of a horse's head, worn relatively as were these winkles on a woman's head. As for wink-a-peep, under the spelling win-co-pipe, we find that this is a folk-name for the scarlet pimpernel. I have noted that the history of dress is allied to the fine arts; it is also in close connection with the sciences, especially botany.

Another reference to perukes, this time by Pepys, on March 24, 1662, runs thus : —

"Comes La Bell Pierce to see my wife; and to bring her a pair of peruques of hair, as the fashion now is for ladies to wear; which are pretty and of my wife's own hair; or else I should not endure them."

Three years later he notes her beginning to wear " light locks, white almost," which made her look very pretty.

At this time women wore periwigs under their riding hats, and brought down the indignant verse of the Quaker Ellwood : —

" Some women (Oh the Shame,) like ramping Rigs
Ride flaunting in their powder'd Perriwigs."

" Female wigs," as they were advertised in the News Letter, had their times and seasons, but these

said times and seasons were short. Pepys tells with
repulsion that on a June day in 1666 he saw the
maids of honor walking on the galleries at White
Hall dressed in riding garb, " with coats and doublets with deep skirts just for all the world like mine,
and with periwigs and hats." He adds, " It was a
sight that did not
please me." *The
Spectator*, No. 435,
speaks of ladies in
riding dress and peri-
wigs. A hundred
years after Pepys, in
Nugent's Travels,
1766, some fair
dames are described
as wearing bagwigs.
I cannot think that
wigs were common
wear; certainly not
within doors.

"Peggy" Champlin.

The style of wear-
ing the hair for a
time became some-
what mean in ap-
pearance. It is a
safe rule for all times
and all faces that a woman's countenance should
have a certain framing of hair. It is better, even,
to have it brought down smoothly in front of and
over the ears, or to let it hang in shiny ringlets, or
to have it in a frowzle, than to have it drawn back

tightly from the face, strained back, so that it scarcely shows. I would rather see a creation like Marie Antoinette's (see it, not wear it) than to see the face bare, with no hair in view.

The portrait of Martha Washington when she was the Widow Custis is a good example of the period when women's hair was very little in evidence. This portrait was painted by John Woolaston, an artist who was painting in Philadelphia as early as 1758. He too, was influenced by Kneller; and his work is cold and meagre, though we are led to think otherwise from the enthusiastic tribute

Head from *Plocacosmos*.

of that clever, gifted man of many enthusiasms, Francis Hopkinson, "the Signer."

As soon as the roll known to us as the pompadour came into vogue, hair-dressing was much more elegant. It varied little for fifty years save in the size of the roll.

We see the various heights and forms of this roll in the portraits by Lely, such as that of fair Evelyn Byrd, and likenesses of other pretty Vir-

ginians; we see it in the Feke and Smybert and
Blackburn portraits reproduced in this book. The
date, in general, is given of each, and the slight
changes can be watched.

When we read in the *Boston News Letter* of
1768 that "Black and White and Yellow Poma-
tum is from Six Coppers to two Shillings a Roll,"
and in New York newspapers that "Orange Butter
for Ladies' Rolls" is for sale, we know a change has
come in the wearing of the hair. Soon powdering-
puffs, and powdering-bags, and powdering-machines
are advertised; and "Hair powder plain and scented,"
blue, brown, maréchal, and white. Great hair-rolls,
and puffs and cushions appear likewise. A tower was
rising, — a *talematongue*, which was soon to assume
vast heights. Like everything else worn by pretty
women, these high constructions were admired by
fond lovers. One of the latter wrote of his Hartford sweetheart, "Her hair covered her cushion as
a plate of most beautiful enamel frosted with silver."

The history of the use of hair-powder is somewhat obscure. We can gather it from scattered
references, such as this in an account-book of the
year 1634, noted in Whitaker's *History of Craven*.
"Paid for a Quayle pipe for poudring hair." A
quail pipe was a call for alluring quail; it was a
simple tube, and apparently the hair-powder was
blown through it.

A very striking picture exists by Vernet called *The
Toilette*. The hair-dresser stands with powder-bag
in one hand and broom-whisk in the other, his comb
thrust in his own hair, his head thrown back, while

he shakes powder over the head of his customer.
The latter covers his face with a paper cornucopia
or cone, in order not to inhale the powder. Powdering was certainly French in origin ; various manuals
and encyclopædias state that " Hair powder was introduced by Marie de
Medicis." She was
born in 1573, and mar-
ried the French king
in 1600. In 1593, long
before her days of in-
fluence, L'Etoile writes
that the nuns in Paris
were powdered and
curled. Rowlands, in
his book, *The Human
Hair*, says that in 1614
certain ballad singers at
St. Germain covered
their heads with flour,
in order to appear ri-
diculous ; just as the
clown in the circus now
paints his face.

Le Bandeau d'Amour.

In the year 1770, that delightful little child, Anna
Green Winslow, wrote in her diary a frank description
of the manufacture and assumption of fashionable
head-gear. This description is most vivacious and
witty ; in fact, it is far more clever than any similar
account that I have read by any other writer : —

" I had my HEDDUS roll on ; Aunt Storer said it
ought to be made less, Aunt Deming said it ought not to

be made at all.   It makes my head itch and ach and burn
like anything, Mama.   *This* famous roll is not made *wholly*
of a red *Cow Tail*, but is a mixture of that & horsehair
(very coarse) & a little human hair of a yellow hue that
I suppose was taken out of the back part of an old wig.
But D. (the barber) made it (our head) all carded together
and twisted up.   When it first came home, aunt put it on
& my new cap upon it, she took up her apron & measur'd
me & from the roots of my hair on my forehead to the top
of my notions I measur'd above an inch longer than I did
downward from the roots of my hair to the end of my chin.
Nothing renders a young person more amiable than virtue &
modesty without the help of fals hair, red Cow Tail, or D."

Anna had ere that seen D., a fashionable hair-
dresser, at work upon a lady's head, and the observ-
ing little creature wrote : —

" How long she was under his opperations I know not.
I saw him twist & tug & pick & cut off whole locks of
grey hair at a slice, (the lady telling him he would have no
hair to dress next time,) for the space of an hour & a half,
when I left them, he seeming not to be near done."

An entertaining and very popular book was published in 1782 entitled *Plocacosmos, or the Whole Art
of Hair Dressing*.   I have seen several old copies of
it in America, and feel sure it was widely read.   It contained ample rules for " the young artizan " (the word
" artizan " throughout the book being used in our
sense of artist), and for "ladieswomen," and valets ;
and even directions for unfortunate persons who had
to dress their own hair.   There were rules for cos-
metics, care of the hair, history of hair-dressing,

"interspersed with Moral Thoughts, necessary for all Families." The dedication is to the Prince of Wales, " All that is Graceful, All that is Amiable, Where the Graces all concentre, the Idol of every Heart, the pattern for All inborn and Outward Accomplishments, in whom blend the immortal heroism of the third Edward and the valour of his darling son, with the glorious ambition of the fifth Henry, and the caution of the wise and economical seventh Henry, and the endearing domestic virtues of the pious martyr Charles." Think of it! wise, economical, domestic, virtuous — oh, what a Prince of Princes was George IV!

Mrs. Alexander McComb. 1789.

The rules for hair-dressing, in this book, are couched in words worthy the highest intellectual performance, or deeds of great heroism; they are classic. High resolves, pious fervor, patriotic ambition, noble art, virtuous kindness, generous courtesy, all (as the author says in an ill-chosen phrase) "animate his dressing comb." His abhorrence of hair "in a state of nature" is deep even to pathos; it would move the most hardened heart. Every detail is made of fearful importance, even the quality of the curl-papers, their exact size and shape. The comb must be a "well-turned tortoise-shell tail-comb," smooth, slanting regularly to the point that the hair may readily slip off. Rules are given for the use of every finger in turn, and injunctions never to vary the sequence. Page after page is devoted to the placing of the hair in papers, so that —

"When all is done they look like regular rows of trees truly set with their heads bending to the crown as if blown

Mrs. Duthill.

thence by a gust of wind from the face, that in idea you could walk a file of men three deep not only from the front to the crown through one of these rows without meeting the least obstruction, but traverse from one ear to the other in the same regular line when properly done, they have in paper a very pretty effect besides the utility. Unless they are done so, they will not have the proper curl nor sit as they ought when dressed."

The rules for pinching these papers with hot irons are elaborate to a degree. The actual dressing-rules fill a hundred pages, and equally careful instructions are given to the lady's maid for the care of her mistress's head when sleeping. The frizzing

or craping of the front and top hair is his delight
— and could be made an exquisite bit of workmanship, as may be seen on the head of Miss Champlin
and Mrs. McComb. A lady's hair frizzed by an
" artizan " should " carry with it the idea of your
standing on the beach and viewing the sea as far as
your eye will carry you, till by a gentle swell it falls
from your sight."

Many startling inventions were announced for fix-
ing the hair in immovable position. Among other
advertisements, I find this in 1782 : —

> " A new method of stuccowing the hair in the most
> fashionable taste, to last with very little repair during the
> whole session of Parliament. Price only five guineas.
> N.B. He takes but one hour to build the head, and two
> for baking it."

The high heads of the ladies brought forth much
public abuse in print and even to the wearers. During the famous " Dark Day," May 19, 1780, when
candles were burnt at mid-day, and the cocks roosted
as at the coming of night, fear seized on all except the
sailors in port, who drank deeply and frolicked through
the streets, calling into houses as they passed and to
timid ladies on their hurried and terrified way to
the religious services, " Now you may take off your
rolls and high caps and be damned."

Little thought of what we now deem cleanliness,
or even decency, was present in the hair-dressing of
that day. Not only was the hair left untouched for
a most revoltingly long time, but materials were
used in the dressing of the hair and making up the

rolls (as Anna Green Winslow related), and other
adjuncts were used, which are most incredible.   The
Boston Gazette of May, 1771, tells of a young woman
driving in Boston streets who was thrown from a carriage, and her high tower partly torn off.   It proved
to be stuffed with yarn, tow, wool, curled hair, and
even hay; and the detached mass was kicked about

Macaroni Head.

the streets like a foot-ball.   A shrewd woman im-
postor, named Jemima Wilkinson, had a wonderful
career of successful fraud at about this time.   She
gathered followers, land, and wealth, and *kept them.*
In reading of her career, I am impressed with a belief
that her dress had much influence in her success.   While
women were all wearing much-betrimmed garments
and those monstrous, untidy head-towers, she ap-

peared in garments of richest material, but exceedingly plain. Her complexion was extraordinarily
fine, while her splendid hair was always kept in exquisite order and dressed very simply, part of it in
long curls; and hair and dress were ever noticeably
and radiantly clean, and were so noted by all chroni-
clers. I believe a large
part of her influence
was *personal;* the
power, though un-
consciously to the
subject, of absolute
cleanliness.

Lady Kennedy.

A New England
clergyman, Manasseh
Cutler, wrote thus
of the head-dress of
Mrs. General Knox
in 1787 : —

" Her hair in front is craped at least a foot high, much in
the form of a churn bottom upward and topped off with a
wire skeleton in the same form, covered with black gauze
which hangs in streamers down her back. Her hair behind
is in a large braid turned up and confined with a monstrous
large crooked comb. She reminded me of the monstrous
cap worn by the Marquis of La Fayettes valet, commonly
called on this account the Marquises devil."

This head-dress must have been like that worn
by Mrs. Robert Morris.

The Abbé Robin wrote of New England women
in 1781 : —

" The hair of the head is raised and supported upon cushions to an extravagant height somewhat resembling the manner in which the French ladies wore their hair some years ago. Instead of powdering they often wash the head, which answers the purpose well enough as their own hair is commonly of an agreeable light color, but the more fashionable among them begin to adopt the European fashion of setting off the head to the best advantage."

The fashion of the roll was of much importance, and various shaped rolls were advertised; we find one of " a modish new roll weighing but 8 ounces when others weigh fourteen ounces." We can well believe that such a heavy roll made poor Anna Winslow's head " ach and itch like anything." A Salem hair-dresser, who employed twelve barbers, advertised thus in 1773 : " Ladies shall be attended to in the polite constructions of rolls such as may tend to raise their heads to any pitch they desire."

In 1781 the towering heads were lowered. Lady Cathcart, keeping her American friends thoroughly posted as to all the modes, writes in June of women's head-gear : —

" They wear their Heads about 2 inches high and not very broad with two small Curles of a side. Their necks are a good deal covered."

In 1783 General Huntington wrote to his wife of Philadelphia fashions in hair-dressing: " The Roll is much less than formerly, and is Raised to a Peak above the Forehead ; Frowzled (or frizzed) and Powdered." This form of frizzed and pointed roll was known as the macaroni roll.

Frances Cadwalader (Lady Erskine).

It was similar to the head-gear of men at that date, whether the man's hair was a wig or his own frizzed locks. It was a French macaroni fashion, which I have noted in French pictures as early as 1772. It is very probable that it was communicated as the height of fashion by the many French officers who took part in the war of the Revolution and took an equally lively interest in American women.

It seems superfluous to call attention to any of the illustrations in this book as of special use in this chapter; for all the illustrations which show women's hair illustrate the subject. Two of the cuts from the book *Plocacosmos*

Mrs. Clinton.

are given in much-reduced sizes in this chapter; and the copies of the old copperplates of Mrs. Rudd show distinctly the most fashionable hair-dressing of the year 1775. Her portraits and others in these pages give the stiffly " buckled " or rolled curls which demanded so much time and attention of hair-dressers. One mode which was in high favor in America, and in France as well, had thirteen of these rolls; and was termed *à l'Indépendance* — a tribute of fashion, and a proof of American popularity in thus commemorating our thirteen brand-new states.

Even demure Quaker dames had barbers Fay
and Duchateau to dress ladies in fifty different
manners with their natural hair, while ladies with
scant hair could be " dressed satisfactorily with False
Curls not to be distinguished from Natural ones ";
they also set on the heads false flowers and brilliants,
" to the greatest advantage."

In 1797 there came into fashion a long, straight
or waved lock of hair, looped low in the back of the
neck, brought up to the crown of the head, and
there fastened, with the end left in another loop or
a free curl.   The picture of Mrs. De Witt Clinton
(1797), on the previous page, displays well this loop ;
also of Lady Kennedy and Lady Johnson.   Men's
hair followed the same fashion ; and often combs
were worn by both men and women to keep this
looped lock of hair in place.   The Saint Memin
portrait of Landon Carter, 1808, shows such a
comb ; and others by that artist.   I remember well
an ancient gentleman in New England who wore as
late as 1870 a loop of hair caught up with a comb.
He was then over eighty, and his hair was still
thick.   He boldly attributed baldness to the constant cutting of men's hair.

In the opening year of the nineteenth century a
French fashion of hair-dressing for both men and
women was invented and called the Titus.   La
Mésangère, the fashion-purveying priest, wrote that
the Titus mode consisted in having the hair cut
close to the roots, so as to restore the natural stiffness to the tube and make it grow in a perpendicu-
lar direction.   It was cut closely at the back, while

a few untidy, unattractive, two-inch-long curls hung into the eyes.

Frenchwomen who adopted the cut *à la Titus* felt compelled to wear a scarlet shawl and a red necklace to complete the harmony (?) of the costume. *À la victime* was another and most unpleasant name. I cannot comprehend how any grown woman of any dignity ever tolerated this fashion, but the ugly shock heads were everywhere. By 1804 the Titus style of haircutting had become provincial in Paris; and we were not one whit behind in America. Of course there was no recourse, after such shearing, save to wigs; and for several years wigs had full sway.

Lady Johnson.

The reign of wigs for women's wear must have come as a great relief. The years of twisting, frizzing, burning, had effectually worn out and worn off the hair from the heads of women of fashion; and to clip the hair closely and wear a wig must have been a great rest to the tortured scalp. During this period of capillary rest and recreation, wigs seem to have been universal, save where elderly caps served as a cover. From the sprightly pages

of Eliza Southgate in the year 1800, we will let her
introduce to us, as she did to her parents, the subject of wig-wearing.   She writes thus : —

"Now Mamma, what do you think I am going to ask
for ? — a wig.   Eleanor has got a new one just like my
hair and only 5 dollars, Mrs. Mayo one just like it.   I
must either cut my hair or have one, I cannot dress it at all
stylish.   Mrs. Coffin
bought Eleanor's and
says that she will write
to Mrs. Sumner to get
me one just like it ;
how much time it will
save — in one year we
could save it in pins
and paper, besides the
trouble.   At the assembly I was quite ashamed
of my head, for no-
body has long hair.   If
you will consent to my
having one do send me
over a 5 dollar bill by
the post immediately after you receive this, for I am in
hopes to have it for the next Assembly — do send me word
immediately if you can let me have one."

Mrs. Cox in Curled Wig.

Her miniature, reproduced in this book, shows,
doubtless, this wig.

The snowy hair of Mrs. Oliver Ormsby is obvi-
ously a wig ; as is that of her husband.   The twain
were married in Pittsburgh when eighteen and twenty
years old.

Children of Colonel Moultrie. 1805.

They rode on a wedding journey to Philadelphia across the mountains on horseback. There they both had their thick handsome hair cut close and bought powdered wigs. Finding Saint Memin's portraits and engravings the height of the mode, both had their profiles taken proudly in their new " bandoes."

Mrs. Oliver Ormsby.
By Saint Memin.

Mrs. Erskine, of Philadelphia, writing at this date, says she paid six guineas for a wig, which is so costly that she intends it shall last the rest of her life. I presume it lasted till out of fashion.

Another young woman, the wife of the first Secretary of the Navy, wrote very explicitly at the same time from Philadelphia about ladies' wigs : —

" Instead of a wig I have a bando which suits me much better. I had it in contemplation to get a wig, but I have got what I will like much better for myself. It is called a Bando. I think the former best for those who dress in a different style from myself, but the latter suits me best. I heard the ladies with whom I was in company last night say that the fashionable manner of dressing the hair was more like the Indians — the hair without powder — and looked sleek and hung down the forehead in strings. Mine will do that to a nicety. I observe powder is scarcely worn, only, I believe, by those who are gray, too much so to go without powder I mean. How these ladies in the Indian fashion dress their hair behind I cannot say ; but those out of that fashion that I have seen, and who do not wear wigs, have

six or eight curls in their neck and turn up the rest and curl
the ends, which, I think, look very pretty when well done."

And as closing proof of the universal wearing of
wigs by women of social standing and fashion, we

Mrs. Susannah Rowson.

find Mrs. Randolph and Mrs. Eppes, daughters of
Thomas Jefferson, preparing for their assumption
of duties at the White House, when their father
became President, by writing to Mrs. Madison,
ordering wigs of the most fashionable shape, to be
ready for their wear upon their arrival. "They are

universally worn," wrote Mrs. Randolph, "and will relieve us of the necessity of dressing our own hair, a business in which we are not adepts." Mrs. Eppes had a glorious crown of auburn hair, but her father made no remonstrance against the wigs, though he was duly informed of them in advance.

The curiously dishevelled mode which succeeded the very ornate wigs and the close-cropped Titus style had as its most prominent feature long locks brought down untidily over the forehead and cheeks. This was a mode adopted by both men and women. It was deemed elegantly negligent, and, with beautiful hair and eyes and complexion, may have been tolerable — as every mode is with such accompaniments. But in many cases it is certainly ugly, giving to every dark-eyed and dark-haired woman a bewhiskered look, which is most unalluring. It seems to have been adopted by old and young, however, at the time the empire fashions were in vogue. Sometimes the back hair was tied in a tight knot ; sometimes it was braided ; and sometimes it vanished — disappeared so com-

Mary Abby Willing Coale, born 1789.

pletely, save at the very roots to cover the scalp, that I know not what became of it. Every one, men, women, and even little children, to judge from portraits, suddenly seemed to have scant hair ; if

the hair were heavy and long, it was certainly ruth-
lessly cut; for the locks always seem meagre and
straggling.   It was a trying fashion; and for many
years women went from one ugly mode to another;
some of these were very mean, and others grotesque,
and all were unbecoming.

A high coiffure of loops of hair standing out stiffly
and surmounted with a comb was known everywhere
as *à la girafe*.   This has been attributed in a recent
book on modes to the year 1810.   Now, these
giraffe fashions were named (hair, caps, kerchief,
and hat) in honor of the arrival of the first giraffe at
the *Jardin des Plantes*; this was in the year 1827.
I have a portrait of a kinswoman painted by her
brother at the time of her wedding, in December,
1830, in which her hair is dressed *à la girafe*.   The
splendid, great tortoise-shell combs which are found
in many country houses are seldom a hundred years
old, — though I have half a dozen such, of beautiful
carving, which I bought in a New England village,
with a solemn assurance that they were two hundred
years old, — and one, prettily inlaid with silver in
workmanship of about the year 1850, was proudly
labelled, " Brought over in the *Mayflower* as a gift
for Priscilla Alden."

The precise date of the first wearing of these high
combs seems in some doubt.   In 1773 came " Tortoise Shell Poll Combs, Ivory Tupee & Tail Combs,"
and then " Bent combs "; proving that they had —
as I saw advertised in the *Connecticut Courant* —
" combs of every denomination."   The Saint Memin
pictures of the year 1808 many of them display

combs.   All are straight, plain combs, such as this
on Miss Wilson.

There was in 1805–1807, and perhaps later, a
decidedly one-sided effect to ladies' dress.   Let me
quote a few sentences to illustrate this effect on the
modes of hair-dressing.

" The hair is worn on the left side of the forehead in a
cluster of small plaits ; large flat curls on the other side.
Hair in plain band in left
with loose waves on the
right, two large cork-
screw curls on the right.

" Double diamond
straw Jockey bonnet has
a full quilling of lace
over right eye.   Lilack
silk handkerchief tied
on left side.   Hair must
be irregular in form ;
combed flat on left side
with one ringlet far be-
hind the ear.   On left
a long ringlet hangs in
front of left eye.

Miss Wilson.   1808.

" Drapery of pale blue and purple shot gauze with wreath
of silver grapes and vine leaves.   Drapery is suspended at
right side of head and reaches to the ground with tassel
of blue and silver at foot.   Combs are worn capriciously.

" Capote sky blue velvet trimmed with squirrel fur of
Tyger skin worn to expose right ear.   Under the right side
of brim white fur is intermixed.   A curl hangs at one side."

We are apt to idealize those we love.   It is one
of the tender and beautiful tributes paid to the dead,

that they are to us ever beautiful. The story of Washington Irving's despairing young love for Matilda Hoffman, and his life-long mourning, have been a romantic delight to young girls of many decades. " Beautiful and more beautiful " did Irving

Matilda Hoffman.

call her till the day of his death, and I have never doubted her beauty, which has been told by all who knew her. But I have always regretted that I ever saw her miniature. The eyes are fine, but the triangular `contour of the face, the shape of the head, even the placing of the ear, are all trying to a degree, as may be seen on this page, where the engraver has much modified the ugly lines of the miniature. An angular aspect is given largely by the one-sided hair-dressing. The dark hair is parted on the right side, varnished down tight across the forehead over the left temple to the ear, where a conspicuous curl is laid out on the cheek. This is much lessened in the print I give. The hair is knotted askew at what seems a wrong spot on the back of the head. The left side of the hair is cut short and frizzed out in forced contrast to the smooth expanse on the other temple. This is called "a most lovely miniature" by Charles Dudley Warner and by many others; indeed, it seems universally admired.

Her friend, Rebecca Gratz, is also heralded to us as a wonderful beauty by Irving in his conversations with Sir Walter Scott. Her disappointing miniature displays heavy features, a protuberant ear, and her dark hair is drawn over her cheek in straggling locks which in front of the ear bear an ugly suggestion of a side whisker; this, with the masculine heaviness of feature, renders it far from a joy forever. There are two companion miniatures in the group of four young girls who were intimate friends. These are of Rachel Gratz and of Eliza Fenno, who became Mrs. Gulian C. Verplanck. These two are truly exquisite in expression and beautiful in feature, and the hair is not disagreeable, though it has the same careful carelessness.

CHAPTER XX

COMMODES, MOBS, AND PINNERS

"*There is not so variable a thing in nature as a Lady's head-dress; within my memory I have known it rise and fall above thirty degrees.*" — "The Spectator," ADDISON, 1718.

" Give Chloe a bushel of horse-hair and wool,
    Of paste and pomatum a pound,
Ten yards of gay ribbon to deck her sweet skull,
    And gauze to encompass it round.

" Of all the bright colours the rainbow displays
    Be those ribbons which hang on her head,
Be her flounces adapted to make the folks gaze,
    And about the whole work be they spread.

" Let her flaps fly behind, for a yard at the least;
    Let her curls meet just under her chin;
Let these curls be supported, to keep up the jest,
    With an hundred, instead of one pin.

" Thus finish'd in taste, while on Chloe you gaze,
    You may take the dear charmer for life;
But never undress her — for, out of her stays
    You'll find you have lost half your wife."

"The Ladies' Head-dress," 1777.

CHAPTER XX

E have seen that all Puritan women, and indeed all Englishwomen in 1620, closely covered the head in public. Some head-tire was universal, and it appeared worn under many names and shapes — the earliest being a head-rail.

It is difficult to draw exact lines between hoods and caps, between bonnets and head-dresses — and some head-tire may be included in this chapter which might by other rules of classification be deemed a bonnet. It would be easier, perhaps, to group all "head-clothes" together, but I prefer to separate that worn to dress the head within-doors from that worn as an outdoor covering.

The head-rail of the Anglo-Saxon and Norman women was very simple, scarce more than a veil folded into a few set shapes. Then came the astonishing "horn," the "crescent," the "steeple," the "chimney," the "bossed" head-dress, each exceeding the other in size and grotesque shape. Soon was seen the curious diamond-shaped head-dress, as in the portraits of several English queens; this took numerous allied forms.

The caps of married and unmarried women differed by law under Henry VIII; no unmarried woman could wear "white or any other coloured caps." Girls must wear a kerchief or a caul or network which was not a cap.

A manuscript of about the year 1460 says distinctly : —

"Maidens wear callis of silk and of thred
And damsels kerchiefs pynned on their head."

In the inventory of Richard Lasthead of Virginia, in 1642, I find a special entry of a caul for women's

Edward Hyde Lord Cornbury
afterwards 3rd Earl of Clarendon

wear. The word had been applied to a net and to a flat-netted head-dress; but the head-dress and word thus used were out of date by 1642. It referred, doubtless, to a certain shaped cap, for the name remained in use for the back portion of a woman's cap until the nineteenth century. Possibly some elderly person made out the inventory, and used a word commonly employed in his youth.

A certain "lattice-cap" worn by English women

in the sixteenth century was allied to the caul.
Both were made of metal threads or cords or of
beads. These lattice-caps also are named in Virginia inventories. English maidens were married
with their hair flowing free. Anne Boleyn wore her
hair thus as she rode through London streets to
meet her royal bridegroom. White knit caps were
enjoined by law during several reigns as the wear of
all English folk of low degree.

I find the words "coif," "quoife," "quoyf,"
"quoiff," "ciffer," "coifer," "quiffer," and "quiff,"
all used in New England, New York, and Virginia,
to refer to a close-fitting head-dress or cap.

The first women settlers wore coifs of varied
forms and materials. The excessive use of cut-
work embroidery was forbidden to the Puritans,
yet cut-work coifs were seen in the new land.
Christopher Youngs, of Wenham, Massachusetts,
owned them in 1647; and one writer complained
of the vanity of the Pilgrims in sending to England for cut-work.

References are made in early letters to a head-tire
which is simply termed a "dressing" and another
called "cross-clothes." A sentence from a letter
written by Mary Downing, a niece of Governor
Winthrop's, in the year 1632, will show the use of
the words; and also the keen supervision of the
Puritan fathers over fanciful dress: —

"I writt to my mother for lace, not out of any prodigall
or proud mind, but only for some crosse cloathes, which is
the most allowable and commendable dressinge here. Shee
would have mee weare dressings, wch I did soe as longe as

they woulde suffer mee; whilest the elders with others in-
treated mee to leave them off because they gave great
offence; and seeinge it hath pleased God to bringe mee
hither amongst His people I woulde not willingly doe
anything amongst them that shoulde be displeasinge vnto
them."

Taylor's *Prayse of the Needle*, 1640, names cross-
cloths and chin-clouts together; both seem to have
been bands to hold the coif in place. " Coyfes and
cross-cloths" are constantly classed together in lists.
A line describing prizes at a lottery ran, " This coife
and cross-cloth will become you best." A dressing
is hopelessly vague. Elizabeth Cook of Plymouth
had, as late as 1687, six dressings worth two shillings
each; squares and head-bands worth a shilling each;
also silk hoods, hair-laces, a hat, and a hat-lace —
ample head-covering. The executors of the estate
of her neighbor, Desire Gorham, called all her head-
covering caps. All these varied caps and coifs were
worn under the black French hood or the beaver
hat when the wearer " walked abroad."

Very rarely in the earliest inventories appears the
word " bongrace." It was the frontlet of a coif or
hood; and its first function was plainly to preserve
the complexion, the " bon-grace." In Beaumont
and Fletcher this line proves its duty, " My face
was all spoiled for want of a bongrace when I was
young." A second quotation shows that the word
was applied to the frontlet which was so much worn
with the French hood. " Her bongrace which she
ware with her French hood." I have been told
that the curious frontlet shown under the French

Children of James II of England.

hood on the Puritan wife, Mrs. Clark, pictured in the second chapter of this book, is a bongrace.

The frontlet still was worn in 1630 by sober, middle-aged or elderly women. It sometimes was made by turning the back fold of the head-dress to the front, then sharply folding it back again. It thus made a stiff projecting roof-eave. These frontlets could be of rich stuffs ; but plainly dressed women had simple frontlets of some substantial stuff, apparently plain silk. The frontlet was often made separately and fastened to the coif.

In the reign of Charles II came the sole period of our two centuries when women were capless and without head-dress. It must have been a great shock to the sensibilities of these English

Mary Marshall, Mother of Chief Justice Marshall.

women, habituated for centuries to the thought of absolute impropriety in the sight of an uncovered head in public. The sense of bareness was broken at first by the fashion of " a pair of perukes," which I have described in the chapter upon Women's Hair ; these perukes or heart-breakers were so openly artificial that they might just as well be classed as a head-dress. We have a fashion to-day of tying the side curls or side locks of little girls in little bunches with knots of ribbons back of either temple or just above the ear. This is precisely the way in which these seventeenth-century perukes or the knots of natural curls were tied on women's heads. Sometimes the ribbon was interwoven and knotted in a more elaborate fashion. Sometimes the false knots were held in place by a frontlet or top-piece. This may be seen on Madame de Sévigné.

The head-covering was of much importance in New Netherland, as it has ever been in Holland. We

Mary Philipse.

find that Dutch headdresses were costly. In 1665 Mistress Piertje Jans of New Amsterdam sold a " fine little ornamental headdress" for fifty-five guilders to the young daughter of Evert Duyckinck, a sturdy schepen of the little town. It seems that Missy bought this " genteel head-clothes " without the knowledge or permission of her parents; and on its arrival at the Duyckinck homestead Vrouw Duyckinck promptly sent back to the milliner the emblem of extravagance and disobedience. Summoned to court by the incensed milliner, who wished no rejected, second-hand headdresses on her hands, and who claimed that the transaction was from the beginning with full cognizance of the parents, Father Duyckinck took refuge in pronouncing the milliner's bill extortionate; and

furthermore he said gloomily, with a familiar phrase-
ology of New York fathers, that " this was no time to
be buying and wearing costly head-dresses." The court
sympathized, but decided in the milliner's favor.

I have described in my third chapter the cornet-
cap which was worn by Dutchwomen. Some coif
or close cap always covered their heads. They
wore netted cauls, like
English women.

About the year 1680
a favorite of King Louis
XIV of France — the
Duchesse de Fontanges
— had the misfortune
— or good fortune —
to have her hat blown
off by the wind. To
confine the curls thus
disarranged she tied a
ribbon around her head
in such a way that the
ribbon loops fell over

Priscilla Webb Ropes. 1761.

the brow, and the hair stood up behind them. This
accidental head-dress was a mode so becoming that
it was universally adopted by the court, and was
given the name " fontange." The ribbon was replaced by larger loops and bands of lace ; and then
formal plaitings of gauze and silk were added, still
standing stiffly up from the bow, but the name became changed to the very unsuitable title " commode," and under that name grew in height till
Saint Simon wrote in his *Memoirs :* —

"The fontange became a structure of brass-wire, ribbons, hair, and baubles of all kinds about two feet high which made a woman's face look as if it were in the middle of her body."

In its perfected state and in its highest altitude it was made of tubes or rolls of gummed linen which stood up from the head, leaning a bit forward, and to which all the rest of the "stuff" was attached. Under the openly expressed detestation of King Louis, commodes were expelled from the French court. French women in private life persisted in wearing them until a rollicking English woman, wife of the English ambassador to France, succeeded, where the king had failed, by ridiculing them until they were extinct.

Writing in 1719, Saint Simon tells of an amusing accident which took place over a lansquenet table. An old woman gambler, Madame de Charlus, was dressed in a commode, which, says the chronicler, "was not fastened in the hair, but was all put on or taken off like a wig or night-cap. It was worn very high." She would not leave the gambling-table to eat, but seized an egg and bent over for salt, setting her commode into a candle-flame. The Archbishop of Rheims, a fellow-gambler, snatched off the blazing head-dress, and threw it on the ground, revealing to all the hoary, bare head of the old woman, who, in her anger, not knowing why she had been thus uncovered, threw her egg in the archbishop's face. He, *en omelette*, tried to explain his act, but her anger prevented her listening with understanding for a long time.   Oh! what a picture of French life.

I have never seen a portrait in an American family where the subject wore a commode or a " fontange," nor have I ever found a reference to this head-dress in letters written to or by persons living in America at the time it was worn.   This is not strange, perhaps, for I never saw an English family portrait in which the subject wore a commode, nor did John A. Repton, Esq., that acute observer and able limner and writer upon English costume (when writing in 1838), find a commode depicted in any family portrait, though he notes the

Sarah, wife of Captain John Hampson, Virginia.

prints of Queen Mary wearing this lofty head-dress.

A reason for this is given by Horace Walpole, when writing of Sir Godfrey Kneller, the court painter, who painted in England from 1674 to 1723, during the reign of the commode.   Walpole says : —

" His airs of heads have extreme grace ; the hair admirably disposed, and if the locks seem unnaturally elevated, it must be considered an instance of the painter's art.   For he painted in an age when women erected edifices of three stories on their heads.   Had he represented such preposterous attire, in half a century his works would have been ridiculous.   To lower their dress to a natural level when the eye was accustomed to pyramids would have shocked their prejudices and diminished the resemblance.   He took

a middle way, and weighed out ornament to them of more
natural materials.   Still it must be owned there is a great
sameness in his airs."

I cannot agree with Walpole that any painter's
work becomes ridiculous if he paints the real thing.
We have seen an equally preposterous head-dress in
the day of Marie Antoinette, and the artists of her
day perpetuated it without making their work absurd.   The effect of Kneller's gratuitous hair-dressing is simply a " sameness in airs," and a knowledge
that we have the Countess of Essex, of Dorset, the
Duchess of Grafton and of St. Albans without the
commodes they really wore.

I give in this chapter a commode of moderate
size, worn by the little princess, the daughter of James
II of England.

In the plates of the coronations of James II and
of William and Mary, none of the ladies wear the
fantastic commode.   Nevertheless, commodes were
earnestly preached against by the English clergy ;
and Addison (who died in 1749) refers to their wear,
saying they rose an ell above the head, were like a
steeple, and had long, loose pieces of fringed crape
hanging down the back.   The only tradition of a
commode in America is curiously enough not as-
cribed to the wear of a woman.   On a preceding page
is a print from an old portrait of Lord Cornbury,
who was governor of New York in the year 1708.
He was a cousin of Queen Anne (whose mother
was a Hyde), and is said to have resembled the
queen.   Vain of that resemblance, and through a

Mrs. Samuel Bishop.

half-crazy whim in his always foolish head that, as her representative in America, he must dress like her, he used to appear upon the ramparts of the fort dressed in hooped petticoats and rich gowns, wearing a commode and carrying a fan. The disgust of honest American citizens can well be imagined. Lewis Morris wrote to the Secretary of State that Cornbury had "a peculiar and detestable magot" in his head; namely, this absurd masquerading in women's attire. This portrait, to my disappointment, is not in a commode.

In the lists of wedding garments of wealthy brides the "linen" was a separate list. In one case it comprised these articles: —

" A Brussels laced head, ruffles, handkerchief, and tucker.
A Sute of Brussels drest night-cloaths and rufels.
A Macklin-face lase-drest night-cloaths, and hankerchief.
A Paris Cap, double hankerchief, and ruffles.
A Dormorzein mobb and tucker edged.
A pinner and quoiff of fine lace, Macklin double ruffles, handkerchieff and hood of muslin edged with lace.
A plain cambrick head, ruffles, tipett and tucker.
A laced cambrick apron, a spoted cambrick apron.
A plain cambrick apron, a lawn apron."

Lace " heads " were a costly item of dress. Heads of Brussels lace cost £30; a French point or Flanders head and ruffles could easily cost £80. They could, of course, be worn only by the wealthy. When Princess Mary, daughter of George II, was married, she had only four lace heads, two being of Brussels, two of point lace. She had also six French caps.

We find George Washington ordering for his wife a lace-head, ruffles, and lappets worth over $500.

A lappet was the lace pendant of a lady's cap or head-dress.   Horace Walpole called them "unmeaning pendants."   In 1758, Jane Eustis advertised

Mrs. Elias Boudinot.

"Blown Lace Lappet Heads."   In 1772, came "Very Neat Flanders and Brussels Lappet Heads."

I have examined, with attention devoted to that special subject, the laces displayed in at least two hundred portraits of Americans, of dates previous to the Revolution.   Where the lace is carefully and distinctly delineated, they are nearly all Flemish, Brussels point, and Mechlin laces.   A few look like Valenciennes.   For many years all the laces of Flanders, except those of Brussels and the point double, were knôwn under the general name of Mechlin lace. Ben Jonson tells us that ruffs and cuffs of Flanders lace were the fashion in England.   Francis Bacon writes, " Our English dames are much given to the wearing of costly laces ; if brought from Italy, France, or Flanders they are in much esteem."

The laces in these old American portraits seem often rich and costly.   I sometimes look upon them with a troubled suspicion which was placed in my head by one of the English essayists.   He says : —

" My friend was drawn in a full-bottomed periwig, a laced cravat, with the fringed ends appearing through the buttonhole Steinkirk fashion.   Indeed, one would wonder how and where people managed to afford so rich a selection of lace in their days, did it not call to mind the demand of the Vicaress of Wakefield to ' have as many pearls and diamonds put into her picture as could be given for the money.' "

In one or two American portraits, a lace like heavy guipure is seen ; in another, a lace precisely like our modern point appliqué laces.   A few cap-ruffles and cap-lappets seem to be some of the old French point-laces, but Italian laces appear rarely.

On page 64 (Chapter II) is given a fine old piece of Venice point-lace, which has been in the De Peyster family for centuries.   It is one of the simple monotonous designs found in the ancient pattern-books of Venice laces, some of which still exist.

" The Netherlanders," wrote Fynes Moryson, who visited Holland in 1589, "wear very little lace and no embroidery ; " and the first Holland emigrants to America wore little lace. But the Edict of Nantes sent many lace-makers to Holland, and the far-famed Haarlem thread offered wonderful opportunities for

Mrs. James Duane.

lace - making ; soon a strong point-lace was made, and in large amount. Travellers relate the curious custom of tying up Dutch door-knockers with this point-lace, to announce the birth of an infant within-doors.

The " pillow - lace," constantly recommended for caps, is easily defined, for it has not varied for three centuries ; nor has the lace pillow and method of making the lace. The pillow is a circular baseboard stuffed to form a cushion, round, ovoid, or cylindrical. When in use, it is held upon the knees. On this pillow a piece of parchment is fixed, and on this parchment a pattern is pricked in small holes. Through these holes pins are stuck into the cushion. Bobbins are pieces of wood or bone about as large round as a pencil and two to three inches long, having a deep groove around the upper end, which

forms a thin neck to the bobbin and leaves room
for the thread to be tied round it.   Sheep's trotters,
called "bones," were used before bobbins.   Each
bobbin has but one thread.   By the interlacing of
these threads around the pins, the lace ground is
made, while a thicker thread is used to form the
more solid figure.

Let me define a few of the terms used by old
lace-makers of cap laces.

Campane lace is a narrow, fine edging of pillow
lace, often sewed upon other laces to widen them or
to replace a worn-out purl or picot.   Originally of
white thread, this campane lace was varied by being
made of gold thread and colored silks.   Evelyn, in
his *Fop's Dictionary*, 1690, gives " Campane, a kind
of narrow picked lace " (picked means peaked).

Purl, spelt also pirl, pirle, pearl, perll, or pufle, is
difficult of precise definition.   It was likewise a narrow trimming, either a lace or a galloon.   It was
never a solid strip, but whether of worsted, silk,
thread, or gold wire was always of openwork design
— a lace.   It was used as an ornamental adjunct to
other laces, and was often simply a succession of
tiny points or twists.   In the New Year's gift of
Queen Elizabeth were "sleeves covered all over
with purl."

A light little lace of small lozenge pattern, about
an inch and a half wide and with a narrow purl edge,
a lace known as a " four-penny-spot " was much
used as an edging for kerchiefs and cap-ruffles.   It
is a bobbin lace of fine flaxen thread, often worn soft
with many washings.   It was known as " baby lace,"

and was used much on infants' caps.   Trolly-laces,
everywhere advertised, are difficult of description.
The sole difference which distinguishes them from
other narrow thread laces is that they have a double-
patterned mesh, not a simple net background.
Trolly-net was used to make caps like the queen's
nightcap, or any cap of large size and substance.

Mignonet lace, called also minonet, minuet, men-
uet, never exceeded two or three inches in width ;
it was a light, fine pillow-lace, a sort of blond lace,
extremely favored for head-dresses.   It was made in
France, Normandy, and Switzerland, and Americans
often called it Swiss lace or Swiss thread lace.   It
is now obsolete, though it is such a graceful, becoming lace.   Fine real laces were for a time supplanted
by gauze.   " Gauze heads are now the top mode,"
writes Mrs. Delany in 1729.   Gauze was a poor-
looking material, and a sorry substitute for the
beautiful Brussels lace.   Mrs. Delany adds : " I
will send you one exactly in the fashion.   You
will think it strange, coarse stuff, but it is as good
as the Queen's."

Mr. Felt quotes a letter written from Cape Cod,
Massachusetts, in 1720 : —

" Mobs are now worn but not so long by a quarter of a
yard as mine.   I was forced to cut mine half a quarter from
each end to make them short enough for the fashion."

The mob-cap was also called the Ranelagh mob,
because it was so much seen in those celebrated
gardens.   The Ranelagh was made of stiff gauze,
twisted about the head, crossed under the chin, and

Mrs. Dorothea Lynde Dix.

fastened behind with the ends hanging down. Some of the market-women, who sold green stuff in Covent Garden, used to wear silk handkerchiefs wrapped round their heads in this way, and a certain fair one took a fancy to this head-gear, and made herself a mob like it in fine lawn. Others followed her. The mob-cap had a checkered career. At one time it was deemed over-light in character. It closed its career with a reputation of prudishness.

There still exist letters written in 1724 by Edmund Quincy to his daughter, " Dorothy Q.," while she was visiting in Springfield, Massachusetts. In one he writes : —

Mrs. Samuel Stringer Coale.

" Half a yard of Muslin being too little for 2 Headdresses your sister has sent you one yard wanting half a quarter which cost her ten and sixpence, and the 2 head (dresses) cost fourteen shillings — so much I paid for and tis the best thread and muslin for the price."

A mercury was a cap worn in 1755 to 1765 ; the *Boston Evening Post* had " gauze net, bugles, lace, &c. for Mercuries." It was said to have wings on either side, set around with beads, bugles, or paste jewels of many colors.

Mrs. Delany told one year of caps " with vast winkers"; and in 1756 she recounted this headdress : —

" Heads are variously adorned, pompons with some accompaniment of feathers, ribbons or flowers; lappets in all
sorts of *curli wurlis*; little plain cypress gauze, *trolly* or fine
muslin caps; long hoods are worn close under the chin and
tied behind, the earrings go round the neck, and tye with
bows and ends behind. They curl and wear a great many
tawdry things, but there is such a variety in the manner of
dress, that I don't know what to tell you is the fashion."

In 1766 the cap was rather mean and small in
comparison with some of the past modes, and also
in the companionship of the great hoop. Some did
not wear a cap at all, but " in room of a slip of cambric or lace, planted a whimsical sprig of spangles or
artificial flowerets."

> " Now dressed in a cap, now naked in none,
> Now loose in a mob, now close in a Joan ;
> Without handkerchief now, and now buried in ruff ;
> Now plain as a Quaker, now all of a puff."

The close caps, ridiculed as nightcaps, worn by
ladies in 1773, are described by contemporary observers as odious, unbecoming, and frightful. " If
the ladies could see themselves," says one writer,
" thus hood-winked in a proper light, they would
immediately throw off the disguise, and carry what
is far more becoming — an open countenance."

In the year 1772 we find Anna Green Winslow
writing to Miss Caty Vans about a cap which Miss
Vans had offered to make for the little girl — a
" Queen's Night Cap." Anna's aunt thought " it
was a black skull cap lined with red which Miss
Vans meant, which she thought would not be be-

coming to Miss Green's light complexion," and she declined it.   But learning what the cap really was,

Mrs. Faith Savage Waldo.

the materials were sent to Miss Vans, the cap was made, and after a few days this entry appears in the diary : —

"This Minute I have rec'd my Queen's Night Cap from Miss Caty Vans. We like it. Aunt says, if the material it is made of were more substantial than Gauze it might serve occationally to hold anything mesured by $\frac{1}{2}$ peck. But it is just as it should be, & very Decent. & she wishes my Writing was As Decent. But I got into one of my frollicks at sight of the Cap."

And well she might, dear, happy child! for on the head of Martha, wife of George Washington, painted by Savage, is her favorite cap, and it is this very queen's nightcap. We can picture a child of twelve wearing that cap — a great frolic truly. Madam Dorothy Lynde and Madam Daniel Waldo both wear forms of the queen's nightcap. These two clever, intelligent women were neighbors in Worcester; and I am sure the same milliner made both of these magnificent caps. Mrs. Oliver Ellsworth wears a similar one.

Wonderful variety was given to millinery in the last quarter of the eighteenth century by the sudden introduction of the black laces of Chantilly. Chantilly lace is silk, but is not glossy; it is what is called "grenadine," and is often and wrongly deemed a thread lace, and is known as "black thread lace." The original pattern-books of one establishment exist, with autograph letters of Marie Antoinette, the Princess of Ligne, and other ladies of the court, giving orders for laces, or commenting on past purchases, etc. Du Barry was a large buyer.

The Chantilly manufactories fell in 1793; it was deemed a royal lace, and hated accordingly. Some of the unhappy lace-makers perished with their patterns on the scaffold. All lace-making suffered. Over thirty kinds of lace were abandoned, and their manufacture has never been revived; it is extinct. Valenciennes lace-making was transferred to Brussels. The nearness to Paris had proved anything but a blessing in those terrible days. With the empire came again lace buying; and soon were

Mrs. Daniel Waldo.

revived some of the old laces, and there appeared the black blond lace known now as Spanish lace. This went largely to Spain and the Spanish colonies in America. The beautiful Cuban mantillas of those days we all have seen; they have become family heirlooms. It was not till 1835 that black lace took a permanent place in woman's dress as fixed as white lace. Chantilly lace is now made in many places, chiefly in Bayeux; but it has retained deservedly the name of the place of its creation.

It would be idle to enumerate the various designs which were borne on the heads of women at about the time of the American Revolution. There were "garden" styles with flowers; "kitchen-garden" modes with vegetables fastened to the side curls and heaped on top; "rural" styles had windmills, which turned in the wind, a sportsman and deer, a shepherd and sheep. The "peal of bells" was a headful of ringing bells; the "treasurer" showed the hair dangling with coins. The "naval battle" displayed a French ship of war in full sail, in spun glass. This might have been worn by the Duchess de Chartres, a most unusual woman, whose intimacy with and appreciation of John Paul Jones is one of the most fascinating and romantic side-lights of American history. But this forceful, intelligent, and thoughtful woman chose to wear instead a perfect museum of little figures of spun glass, silk, silver wire, and human hair. Among them was a figure of her son (afterward Louis Philippe) in his nurse's arms; also a little negro, a parrot nibbling a cherry, and figures made in the hair of her kinsfolk and friends. Truly we may say of this rigging, in Carlyle's words, —

"Here assembled from all the four winds, came the elements of an unspeakable hurly-burly."

Many examples of the work of Charles Willson Peale appear in this book, for he was a most prolific

Mrs. Robert Morris.

artist.   One of his most marked portraits is that of
Mrs. Robert Morris.   She wears, in this picture, the
extreme of high head-dressing; and that in Philadelphia, the home of Quakerism.

There was a Philadelphia cap worn in France, and
named, of course, during the great popularity of
Franklin during his visit to France.   One almost
disgusting name was the *pouf à l'inoculation,* named
in honor of the discovery of inoculation for small-
pox.   This great *pouf* bore a crown, emblematic of
the king; a serpent and club representing medicine,
the wisdom which had destroyed the terrors of the
disease; the olive branch meaning peace and tran-
quillity, which came after the operation.

The *Times,* in 1794, says, " The ladies' feathers
are now generally carried in the sword-case at the
back of the carriage."   A little later came a paragraph as follows : —

" There is to be seen on Queen Street a coach on a new
construction.   The ladies sit in a well, and see between the
spokes of the wheels.   With this contrivance, the fair pro-
prietor is able to go quite dressed to her visits, her feathers
being only a *yard and a half high !* "

I give an old print showing a sedan-chair open
at the top to make room for the peaked roll of a
macaronic head.

A new word appeared in the latter half of the century — pennache.   You will find it constantly used
for a number of years in describing head-dressing.
The pennache was a " bristle-plume," a stiff bunch
of feathers standing stiffly up in front of the head-

dress or hat. It was held to be part of a Grecian coiffure. The word "pennache" appears in other and unusual places. At one time it seemed to be used in the sense of chenille.

Mrs. Abraham Redwood Ellery.

The beautiful embroidered collars, capes, undersleeves, caps, and ruffles, which every "old American family" cherishes so faithfully and in such numbers, are haloed with a tradition of vast age. Their beauty, delicacy, and marvellous workmanship are reason enough for their preservation, without any question as to their antiquity. Few are very old. These fine embroideries nearly all owe their existence to the revolt of Marie Antoinette against formality and ceremony, with their incidental accompaniment of heavy and rich dress. She could not show this revolt at public functions, but in private life she gave up the rich laces of heavy point, and wore fine, embroidered India muslin and mull.

" The ladies of the Court look like cooks and convent porters, in their muslin aprons and ker-chiefs," wrote the indignant Maréchale de Luxem-bourg, and she sent to her granddaughter in derision aprons and fichus of sail-cloth. The well-known portrait of Madam Ro-land shows that the plainest neckerchiefs were worn.

The accounts of the famous Rose Bertin, the queen's favorite milliner, give little lace. Some of the portraits of the day show spotted blond capes and caps, like Mrs. Rudd's and Lady Ac-land's caps. Tulle ap-peared in the French dictionary in 1765, as a kind of lace like that called entoilage — which

Mrs. Armira Wilson Tyler.

is the plain net upon which the pattern is worked. Tulle was originally made on a pillow.

In 1768 net was first made by machinery ; bobbin-net was invented in 1809. Pin-net, spider-net, bar-leycorn, all are advertised by that year. They mark the introduction of lace-making machines.

These simple nets were used with the domestic embroideries, which were being made so happily in every household of English-speaking girls and women.   Cowper writes in *The Winter Evening* : —

> " Here the needle plies its busy task
> The pattern grows, the well-depicted flower
> Wrought patiently into the snowy lawn
> Unfolds its bosom ; buds, and leaves, and sprigs
> And curling tendrils gracefully dispos'd
> Follow the nimble fingers of the fair —
> A wreath that cannot fade."

A constant reference in fashion notes of the early years of the nineteenth century is to "urlings lace" and "urling."   In Ackerman's *Repository*, samples are given.   It is net, like tulle, but much stronger, being apparently of a very fine linen thread ; but it is not as stiff as trolly-lace.   Sometimes sprigs and dots were woven in it.   The color was yellowish, not pure, bleached white.   Its effect in festoons, knots, folds, and puffs was not unlike tulle or a very fine net.   Whole robes were made of urlings, to be worn over silk or satin slips.   It was employed as a substantial ground or foundation for tambour-work, which was then greatly admired for caps.

Mrs. Hesselius wrote in 1788 a sketch of the Primrose household, entitled *The Family Picture*. In it she said of her daughter Charlotte : —

> " To tambour on crape she has a great passion
> Because here of late it has been much the fashion."

Of Caroline : —

> " She loves to tambour on muslin as misers love pelf
> Sometimes for her friends but still more for herself."

Charlotte's pretty face is shown on a later page. Her mother wrote other lines of her : —

" Good humoured and thoughtless she can't be called vain,
Though she loves a craped head and is fond of a train.
In the morning her features she will not expose,
For the flounce of her cap almost covers her nose.
Her handkerchief's crimpt and up to her chin,
But generally partial for want of a pin.
When dressed still her head has a great deal of trash on,
If her gown is pinned crooked 'tis made in the fashion."

A favorite mode of hair ornamentation in 1797 to 1810 was through the use of squares or scarfs of gauze.

This fashion was invented and elaborated by the celebrated Leonard, coiffeur of Marie Antoinette, who alternated locks of hair with strips of gauze. He is said to have used over fourteen ells of gauze in dressing a head.

Mrs. Adam.

Embroidered silk, or fringed crape, or even soft handkerchiefs were also knotted in the hair. Sometimes the fringed edge was tufted in among the many curls. At other times the embroidered edge was folded diagonally into a jabot at the side of the head.   Sometimes the gauze scarf was twisted with a lock of hair ; or even was braided with the hair into a Cadogan loop at the back.   Broad sash ribbons were twisted into turbans ; heavy cords and tassels were twined among the hair.   Long bands of rather wide ribbon were tied around the head, and curls and loops of hair were pulled out in the interstices, as in the portrait of Lady Johnson.   Narrow Greek fillets were worn ; and nets confined the long loops at the back and small nets held the side buckles in place.

Trumbull painted nearly all his women sitters, except in extreme old age, with these gauze fillets and kerchiefs.   Gilbert Stuart was equally devoted to their portrayal.   It was a pretty picturesque mode, sure to please an artist's taste.

Stuart's charming portrait of Mrs. Robert Eglesfield Griffith, whose maiden name was Maria Thong Patterson, was painted in the year 1797, when she was twenty-three years old.   Her father was a major in the British army, who, in 1758, had married Catryna, the daughter of Robert Livingstone. Their daughter was therefore by birth, education, and station in the best social circle, and her dress was doubtless that of a woman of fashion.   The painting is one of Stuart's best.   It faces this page. Her abundant hair is curled all over the head, and falls on the neck.   A soft, silken ribbon a few inches wide is twisted into a fillet which passes low twice on the left side of the head (once over the ear), and is tied high on the right side in a most graceful and coquettish knot.   The dress has a simple sur-

Mrs. Robert Eglesfield Griffith.

plice body, long, plain sleeves with a shoulder-cap which is short at the top of the shoulder, and is edged with a slight lace or ribbon. The gauze fillet on Mrs. James Greenleaf varies in form slightly. A fashion-note of the year 1815 ran thus : —

" No caps are seen in full dress on young women ; but the hair in full curls, or otherwise fancifully disposed in the Grecian and Eastern style, and ornamented with gems or flowers. To the morning dress, however (and, indeed, with the intermediate order of costume), they must ever be considered a becoming and appropriate appendage. The old English mob, the Indian feather cap, French foundling, and Grecian nightcap, are the only wearable articles admitted by us fashionable females."

A certain head-dress worn early in the century showed Oriental influences — the turban. Nine-tenths of the portraits of women in the years near 1820, women in youth and women in old age, display a turban. It may be called the characteristic head-dress of a quarter of a century. It was so loved that many women thought it would always be worn — an everlasting mode. The well-known one of Madame de Staël is a popular example. A most charming one made of an Oriental shawl is upon the lovely head of the beautiful Mrs. Gilmor.

Mrs. Erskine of Philadelphia writes with high praise of turbans of soft muslin, " with Bird of Paradise feather put at the side and drooping low over one eye."

The noble face of Mrs. Porcher has a simple fillet or turban with a Bird of Paradise plume drooping at one side.

Soft orange-colored gauze or silk was a favorite
in turbans.   I can imagine no greater trial or triumph of beauty than to wear an orange-colored
turban; and it must have been a trial not worth

Mrs. Porcher.

the chance of triumph.   The picture is amusing,
of a score of women's heads at an assembly surmounted by orange-colored turbans; it is like a
field of cheerful, hearty pumpkins.   It is strange
to account for their popularity.

CHAPTER XXI

HATS, BONNETS, AND CALASHES

" *That build of bonnet whose extent*
Should like a doctrine of dissent
Puzzle church-goers to let it in.
Nor yet had reached the pitch sublime
To which trim toques and berets climb.
Leaving, like lofty Alps that throw
O'er minor Alps their shadowy sway
Earth's humbler bonnets far below
To poke through life their blameless way."

—THOMAS MOORE.

" *Hail great Calash! o'erwhelming Veil*
   By all-indulgent Heaven
To sallow Nymphs and Maidens pale,
   In sportive kindness given."

— "Rivington's New York Gazette," 1780.

CHAPTER XXI

AVING written of the hat of Madam Pocahontas and Puritan dames, and having given a chapter, as its due, to the venerable hood, and another chapter to head-gear such as cauls and cornets, coifs and ciffers, cross-cloths and chin-clouts, commodes and towers, veils and dominoes, lappets and liripipes, fontanges and shades, mobs and night-caps, poufs and pennache, there would seem to be little else to chronicle as to woman's head-gear; but beaver hats were not the only hats our grandmothers wore; nor must we be silent upon that comparatively recent acquisition, that delight of delights, a woman's bonnet.

A letter written in Dorchester by a lover to his lass, in 1647, tells of "thinking upon you for a hat & chose out ye comelyest fashion hatt yt they could find avoiding fantastick fashions. Ye hatt was a demi-castor the priz was 24s." This plain beaver hat, like the ones worn by Pocahontas and the Tub-Preacher, were succeeded by the Cavalier hat, or the Van Dyck hat, as it is called. It was in shape just like the man's hat of that day; the ostrich plumes may have been a bit gayer in color. But I am not

sure even of that.   Here is a picture by Pepys.
Can you not see it?

" 1663, The Lady Castlemaine rode among the rest of
the ladies; she looked mighty out of humor and had a
yellow plume on her hat which all took notice of, and yet
is very handsome but very melancholy.   I followed them
up to White Hall and into the Queen's presence, where all
the ladies walked talking and fiddling with their hats and
feathers, and changing and trying on one another's by one
another's heads and laughing.   But it was the finest sight
to me considering their great beautys and dress that ever I
did see in my life.   But above all Mrs. Stewart in this
dress, with her hat cocked and a red plume, with her sweet
eye, little Roman nose, and excellent taille is I think now,
the greatest beauty I ever saw in my life."

And pray who would not have followed the gay,
laughing, careless group, with solitary, sulky my
lady; I warrant *she* did not let Mrs. Stewart try on
her hat and yellow plume.

It is given to few authors to be able so to stimulate
and illuminate the brain of the reader that he is able
to see, to visualize, the scene which the author describes.   Often this is accomplished with very few
words, and with most simple words.   Pepys has for
me this power.   Long descriptions by many authors
naturally afford to us every detail, and thus form a
picture; but Pepys, Hardy, and Besant can accom-
plish it with half a dozen lines, with a few phrases.

The word "bonnet" is found in English literature used in the sense in which it is now employed
in Scotland; that is, applied to the close-woven caps

Charlotte Hesselius.

worn by men.   These have various names, "glen-
garrys," "kilmarnocks," "balmorals," etc.   But
the term "bonnet" applied as to-day to a woman's
outdoor head-covering does not appear in America
to my knowledge till 1725, when Madam Usher's
wardrobe was sent to England; two silk bonnets are
on that list.   By the middle of the century, milliners
in New York and Boston all advertised and made
bonnets.   "Quilted bonnets, Kitty Fisher bonnets,
Quebeck bonnets, Garrick bonnets, Ranelagh bonnets, French bonnets, Queen's bonnets, Cottage
bonnets, Russian bonnets, Drawn bonnets, Shirred
bonnets,"—all these names appear.

After a period when French hats were fashionable
bonnets came again into popularity; and we may
deem them as a whole the head-covering of women
of the nineteenth century.   In the twentieth century
we have once more turned to hats, and a real bonnet
with strings is harder to find than the poke-bonnet
of the Quakers.

Working in straw has ever been an industry of
women, as was also its invention.   Mrs. Isabel
Denton of Beeston, Leeds, England, invented straw
hats in the time of Charles I, and maintained herself and a large family thereby.

In a work written by a Pennsylvania Quaker in
1685 he urges that schools be provided where girls
may be taught among other arts and mysteries "the
making of straw works, such as hats and baskets."
His useful hint was not carried out in any fulness
till a century later, when many Americans awoke
to simultaneous consciousness that the costly and

intricate straw bonnets made of the beautiful Italian braids could be successfully imitated at home.

It is curious that the first recorded effort to manufacture straw in America should be through a patent awarded to a woman, Mrs. Sybilla Masters of Philadelphia, and that this woman was the first American ever awarded a patent in England for anything; and that the first patent issued by the United States was to a woman, and for an invention for straw-plaiting.

A Connecticut girl, Sophia Woodhouse, took out a patent for a new straw material for bonnets, a new way of preparing the upper stalks of spear-grass and redtop grass. This girl took a prize in America for a hat she plaited in a single piece, like a Leghorn hat; and a prize of twenty guineas for a straw hat, from the London Society of Arts. The wife of the President, Mrs. Adams, wore one of Miss Woodhouse's bonnets, and it was "much admired" by the President, who, I believe, admired everything that rested on Mrs. Adams's head.

A young girl named Betsey Metcalf, of Providence, Rhode Island, started the manufacture of straw head-gear in this country. She wrote late in life an account of her venture, which I give in part: —

"In compliance with your request I will write an account of my learning to braid straw. At the age of twelve I commenced braiding. My father, Joel Metcalf, brought home some oat straw which he had just mowed in June, 1798. I cut the straw and smoothed it with my scissors and split it with my thumb-nail. I had seen an imported bonnet but never saw a piece of braid, and could not tell

Mrs. Abigail Adams Smith.

the number of straws. I commenced the common braid
with six straws and smoothed it with a junk bottle, and
made part of a bonnet, but found it did not look like the
imported ones. I added another straw and then it was
right. An aunt who resided in the family encouraged me,
while most of my friends said I should never learn. She
would sit and hold the braid while I braided many yards,
thus keeping it straight and in place. We bleached the
braid with fumes of sulphur."

Claims are made for several other young women
who lived at this time, that each one is the pioneer
straw-braid maker in this country. The truth is,
they all began at the same time. Like many more
important inventions, — the steamboat, for instance,
— the idea of the thing came to several inventive
minds at the same date, because conditions were
ready for it, and also because, in this case, conditions
forced it; for during the embargo no foreign hats
came to American women, so they had to braid their
own straw hats or live without them.

Another simple reason may be given for the simultaneous making of straw braid in America. Straw
work was vastly fashionable that year in England.
In 1783 the manufacture came to perfection, and
under the protection of the Duchess of Rutland
"straw-works" became the rage.

Paillasses, or "straw coats," were worn; they were
made of sarcenet, calico, fine linen, trimmed and
ornamented profusely with straw. A correspondent
of the *European Magazine* bursts forth, "Straw!
straw! everything is ornamented in straw, from the
cap to the shoe-buckles; Ceres is the favourite, not

Ancient Leghorn Hat and Bonnet.

only of the female but the male part of the fashionable world, for the gentlemen's waistcoats are ribbed
with straw." A caricature called "a bundle of
straw" was published to ridicule the taste. But it
was not easy to destroy the liking for straw trimmings, for the simple reason that they are, as we all
know (though they are not now worn), extremely
becoming. The soft, pale yellow tint suits almost
all complexions.

The making of straw braid was a pleasant home
employment for young women of small incomes
who wished to earn pocket-money. I recall that
when I was a child, in driving through country villages with my father, I often saw young women
sitting at their doorsteps, on a sunny summer afternoon, braiding straw. It was clean work too, which
recommended it. All straw braids are now bought
in Italy in vast wholesale bales.

Leghorn hats were sold in America as early, certainly, as 1730.

In 1731 these Leghorn straw hats were lined with green, and had, in that guise, much popularity; it being a time of "pride that apes humility."

In 1732 a writer in the *Weekly Rehearsal* speaks thus of "High-Croun'd Hats": "After being confin'd to Cots & Villages so long a time, they have become the Mode of Quality & the politest Distinction of a Fashionable Undress."

These hats were named Churchills after the beautiful sisters of the Duke of Marlborough. Then came the Leghorn chip worn by the beautiful Miss Gunnings. Leghorn hats were costly. I recall one of my childhood that cost $25. Others were said to cost $50. They would last for years, with annual cleaning and re-pressing into new forms. Hats made of shavings were worn in the year 1800.

Lavinia Hat.

In 1751 Harriot Paine had for sale in Boston "Saxon blue silk and Hair Hatts, black horsehair & Leghorn hatts," and in 1753 "Black & White & Black Horsehair Hatts emboss'd and stampt Sattin Hatts." "Fine beverett hatts with tabby linings," "tissue sattin & chipt hatts," were sold in South Carolina as in the more northern states. We gain

a little suggestion of contemporary historical events
and persons by such names as " Quebeck Hats and
Garrick Hats."   We know prices also, " Womens
chipt Hats 60s. O.T. per doz." in 1764, and "4s. 6d.
apiece, O.T." in 1767.   The Salem *Gazette* advertised, in July, 1784, "Air Balloon" and " Princess"
hats.   These were French fashions.

In 1796 Sally McKean (afterward Marquise
d' Yrugo) wrote thus to the sister of Dolly Madison,
of the fashions of her day : —

" The hats are quite different shape from what they used
to be; they have no slope in the crown, scarce any rim,
and are turned up at each side and worn very much on the
side of the head.   Several of them are made of chipped
woods commonly known as cane hats; they are all lined.
One that has come for Mrs. Bingham is lined with white
and trimmed with broad purple ribbon put around in large
puffs, with a bow on the left side."

Never were fashions more varied than under
Marie Antoinette.   Straw and chip bonnets were
worn, then great beaver hats.   Susannah Reed,
writing to Mrs. Rutherford in 1787, said that "a
Scarlet Great Coat and black beaver hat with
feathers was the most elegant morning dress worn."

In 1784 to 1786, inclusive, only two years, the
shape of women's hats changed seventeen distinct
times, — hat-caps, close shapes, large bonnets, pouf
hats with military trophies, black gauze hats without
crowns, and other odd forms.

I show, on the following page, three broad-
brimmed hats known as riding-hats.   These came

into fashion in 1786, and were worn for four years. They were a bit too wide and heavy for comfort, but are certainly graceful and becoming. Usually they were trimmed with a scarf or ribbon or feathers. A French taste brought in 1792 a pointed-crowned felt hat, with a narrow tricolor ribbon laced around

Riding Hats, 1786–1790.

the crown in lozenge shapes; also a hat of the year 1794, shaped from the bonnet of the French peasantry, and called "The Duke of York's nightcap." This usually had an enormous round crown. Riding hats also were trimmed with a deep lace frill, such as is worn by Mrs. Abigail Bromfield Rogers.

A curious custom arose of hat-wearing withindoors by ladies; they danced wearing hats. And they carried muffs in evening dress also.

I present in this book two portraits of Mrs. William Smith, who was Abigail Adams, daughter of President John Adams. One is with a muff and in a curly wig; the other in a picturesque feathered hat. Her mother wrote in 1786 a lively description of her in full dress : —

" A small white Leghorn hat, bound with pink satin ribbon; a steel buckle and band which turned up the side and confined a large pink bow; large bow of the same kind of pink ribbon behind, a wreath of full-blown roses round the crown, and another of buds withinside the hat, which being placed at the back of the hair brought the roses to the edge — you see it clearly? One scarlet one, one black feather and two white ones complete this head dress. A gown and coat of Chamberi gauze with a red satin stripe over a pink waist; coat flounced with crape and trimmed with broad point and pink ribbon, wreaths of roses across the coat; gauze sleeves and ruffles."

Bonnets of 1810.

These bonnets are the four common shapes worn in 1810; they were called the Gypsy, the Beehive, the Polish fly-cap, the Cottage. The latter is worn over a foundling cap.

The poke-bonnet appeared for general wear in 1804, and was at once attacked. The *Portfolio* called it repulsive. It was then called a coal-scuttle bonnet.

The *Philadelphia Repository* of the year 1802 reprinted fashion-notes from London. These are the modes given in hats: —

" The Bonapartian hat is coming into vogue. It consists of white or salmon colored satin, in the form of a helmet, surrounded with a wreath of laurel, and worn much on one side.   Plain white hats in the gypsy style, without any ornament whatever, are tied carelessly under the chin with pea-green or pink ribbon."

Bonnets of 1815.

Many of the contemporary fashion-plates display this Bonapartian helmet set askew in a rakish air most unsuited to the classic helmet shape and laurel wreath.

The "Lavinia" hat, 1805–15, was a broad-brimmed hat like the gypsy hat.   It is given in this chapter, with a feather.   Often it had no trimming, not even a ribbon.   A very dispiriting advertisement is of an artist-milliner who, in 1798, "makes up worn out umbrellas into gipsy bonnets." I am glad I never saw one of these horrors, and happier still am I that I never wore one.

We learn from the newspapers of 1800 what headgear was for sale; "straw, vellum, cane, willow, and chip bonnets, maids' village straw bonnets; women's and dames' bag, gipsy, volney, Leghorn, Tuscany, Norway, and Oatlands straw bonnets."   These straw bonnets were worn in winter as well as summer; and in 1800 were generally tied on the head with a crimson silk kerchief.   This seems to have been a universal mode assumed without any regard to the color of the bonnet-trimming; for one description is of a " green willow-bonnet" trimmed with orange-colored gauze ribbons, and black and white feathers, "tied down with a crimson silk handkerchief."

Sometimes it was tied down with a rich half-handkerchief of lace, or a folded veil of silk and lace. This was in 1807 called the Agrippa hat. The "Troutbeck" was a flat straw hat worn in 1803. The hat on this page was very popular, and was known as the military, and also as the Polish casquette.

The Polish Casquette.

A constant item in advertisements of about 1800 to 1820 is roram hats. A Romany maid stole her mistress's " Gray Roram Hat with Purple and Green Feathers and gold band." Roram was the first step toward an imitation of the old and well-beloved beaver hat. Roram was a wool or felt, with a facing of long beaver fur felted in. It was in a sense a false beaver. Beaver was growing scarce, and imitations were sure to be made.   The letters of Eliza Southgate Bowne to her sisters in Maine give glimpses of metropolitan fashions in 1803.

" Caroline and I went a shopping yesterday, and 'tis a fact that the little white satin quaker bonnets, cap-crowns, are the most fashionable that are worn — lined with pink or blue or white; but I'll not have one, for if any of my old acquaintance should meet me in the street they would laugh, I would if I were them.   I mean to send sister Boyd a quaker cap, the first tasty one I see; Caroline's are too plain, but she has promised to get me a more fashionable pattern."

One of the most charming portraits I have ever seen is the beautiful Gainsborough of Captain Ricketts, his wife, and child (the frontispiece of this volume).   The colors are perfect, and the whole composition beautiful.   But the chief interest it has for us now is in the young mother's dainty dress — especially her hat.   For the hat she wears in this portrait is, by tradition, the shape declared by Gilbert Stuart to be the most graceful, most becoming, most altogether charming hat ever worn by woman.   It is held to be good in outline, adequate in trimming, and perfect in poise.   We seldom can have the pleasure of seeing the most beautiful hat ever worn.

There were many country devices for covering the head; slat sunbonnets were universal.   One is given in this chapter; also another of green silk.   Shaker bonnets were small pokes made of straw-board.   A quaintly ugly bonnet was the calash.

This is said to have been invented by the Duchess of Bedford in the year 1765, though it is claimed that similar head-coverings may be seen on English effigies of the sixteenth century. It is found in English woodcuts of the year 1770, and I believe was worn before 1765. It was also called the "bashful bonnet." The calash was usually made of thin green or brown silk shirred on strong lengths of rattan or whalebone placed two or three inches apart, which were drawn in at the neck by a cape. These lengths when bent into hoop shape by the cape had a diameter some-

Green Silk Sunbonnet.

times of twenty inches. The calash was extensible over the face like the top or hood of an old-fashioned chaise or calash, from which latter it doubtless received its name. It could be drawn out over the face by narrow ribbons, or bridles, which were fastened to the top edge. It could also be pushed flatly to the back of the head. Thus,

standing well up and touching only at the neck,
the calash formed a good covering for the high-
dressed and powdered heads of the date when it was
worn,—from 1765 throughout the century,—and for
the great lace caps worn in the beginning and even
the middle of the nineteenth century.   These were

Calash or Bashful Bonnet.   1790.

frequently a foot and a half in diameter.   Madam
Dorothy Lynde Dix wears one which would have,
as said Anna Green Winslow, "the capacity of a
peck measure."
    Calashes were worn by old-fashioned ladies until
fifty years ago; chiefly for an informal call or a stroll
down the garden border.   Last summer I saw an

old lady standing in a calash by the roadside, near Lexington, Massachusetts, waiting for a friend to alight from one of the electric cars which have penetrated into every New England township. Before these cars, and the automobiles, will soon vanish all we have had left of the quaintness and reserve of the olden time.

Slat Sunbonnet.

One singular thing may be noted in this history, — that with all the vagaries of fashion, woman has never violated the Biblical law that bade her cover her head. She has never gone to church services bareheaded. The wife of an English naval officer was recently excommunicated because she had persisted in thrice attending church without bonnet or hat.

CHAPTER XXII

THE POCKET

" *Here's to budgets, packs and wallets,*
Here's to all the wandering train."

— Burns.

" *Lucy Locket lost her pocket,*
Lucy Fisher found it."

— "Old Nursery Rhyme."

CHAPTER XXII

THE POCKET

THAT Lucy could lose anything so distinctly an inherent part of a dress as a pocket was a puzzle to me as a little girl until I saw the detached pocket of the child we called "our milk girl." She was the daughter of the farmer who provided the folk of our neighborhood with milk; her name was Apolline. I have told of her brilliant beauty, of her more brilliant mind, in my book, *Old-time Gardens*. She wore by her side, strongly fastened with tapes to a belt wrought in crewel-work, a pocket of strong-figured chintz worked in with silk in the high lights of the flowers. It would contain very nearly, perhaps fully, a peck of country goodies, such as apples, pears, checkerberries, pippins (the young, tender leaves of the checkerberry plant), pop-corn, nuts, sweet flag-root, sassafras bark, slippery-elm bark, wild ginger, and its contents were a constant surprise and delight.

Varied in form and name, attached and detached, these pockets were worn till the present day. As "a pair of pockets" they appear in colonial inventories as early as the year 1650, and I cannot find that our modern dress-pockets sewn in the skirt of a gown were in general wear until fifty years ago.

585

These pockets were worn under the gown in Cromwell's day. There is a satirical contemporary print of Oliver Cromwell preaching. At one side in the foreground a pickpocket has raised the gown-skirt of a rapt woman listener, and is rifling her hanging-pocket.

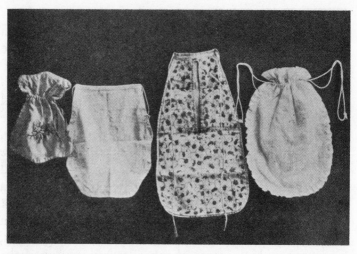

Detached Pockets of Figured Calico and Embroidered Linen.

After the pockets were worn under the gown some one invented having them sewed into the placket of the gown. The kinship of the words "pocket" and "placket" is not very well known. At first, apparently, a placket was this pocket sewed into the gown or petticoat. We read in an old play, "For fear of cut-purses she'll sweep it into her plackerd." Then the word "plackert" was applied as now to the opening, not the pocket.

These pockets were a favorite gift. We often read in letters of "working a pocket" for a friend. They served to display the varied and beautiful sampler stitches learned by every little girl.

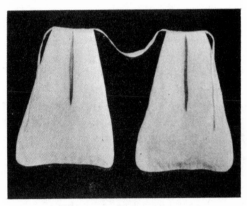

A Pair of Pockets.

Here is the copy of the clause of a letter from Esther Duché in London to her aunt, Mrs. John Morgan in Philadelphia, Pa., April 19, 1782.

"It is with great pleasure, my dear Aunt, that after such a length of time I have now an opportunity of writing to you. My Sister is sitting by me writing also. I am sure you would be very much diverted to see her; she is so proud of having it to say that she has wrote a letter to her grandmama. She has just finished a pair of Pockets for her which she is to send by this opportunity."

One pocket of fine white linen, a foot square, bears these unpleasant and ill-spelled lines, worked by a little girl ten years of age: —

" Jesus, the Saviour was a Child like thee
Save the Foul Nature in thy Bosom bred.
But oh! how much thy Blessings Disagree
With his coarse Swaddling Clothes and Manger Bed.

" Like Him, a child, approved by Earth and Heaven
Mays't thou in Wisdom as in Stature grow.
And chearful deferance to thy Parent given
His filial Love exemplefy anew."

Eleanor Wortley of Yorkshire married in succession Sir Harry Lee and then three old gentlemen, — all earls, — Sussex, Warwick, and Manchester. As Lady Sussex she kept up a lively correspondence with Sir Ralph Verney and his father (in whose cipher correspondence she was known appropriately as " Old Men's Wife "), and many of her letters have been preserved. Nothing was too petty to bring forth a letter from her, and she revelled in making her correspondents go shopping for her. She gives thus a commission for the material for what she terms " a swite bage," which was, I am sure, a perfumed pocket. The spelling was that of her day : —

" If you woulde plese to employ somebody to chuse me out a lase that hath but very littell silver in itt, and not above a spangell or two to a peke I think would do well; I would not have it too hevy a lase; about the breth of a threepenny ribinge, very littell broder will bee enofe; and desier Mrs. Verney I pray you to chuse mee out some ribinge to make stringes; six yardes will be enofe; some shadoed sattin ribinge will be the best, of fourpenny breth; and I would fain have some littell eginge lase as slite as may be to ege the strings and but littell silver in it; ten yards will be enofe."

In 1787, in the will of Hannah Lord of Ipswich are named dark calico pockets, white dimity pockets, a patch pocket, a pair of pockets, left each to some friend.   Pockets are constantly named in wills; Mrs. Morgan bequeathed hers to a friend — possibly the very pockets made by " Sister."

When a sedate New England dame left to her lifelong woman friend her "embroidered dimity pocket with the pocket-glass, comforter, and strong-waters-bottle kept within it," the bequest bore a convivial aspect which it did not really deserve. For the pocket-glass was a tiny folding mirror ; the comfortier but a hand-warmer, a little box to hold within a muff; the strong-waters-bottle was

Mrs. Stewart.

frankly what its name bespoke, namely, a goodly sized barrel-shaped flask of strong Bristol glass, flowered with red and yellow, and used for holding New England rum. It could be carried with the glass and comfortier in the muff or in the pocket. There were distinct provisions in many wills for ample liquor for feminine use, as in a will of a respected Concord gentleman that his widow have ample cider and New England rum supplied her each year; that she "may treat as she has been accustomed to do."

The word "pocket" is the old French *pouchet*. Allied words are "poke," "pouch," "pucker." In *Piers Plowman* it became "palke." Chaucer tells of "two pigs in a poke"; here a poke is a bag. Chaucer also used the words "poket" and "pouch." Shakespere's shepherd "drew a dial from his poke," a sun-dial from his pocket.

Pocket and purse form a word-study. When there was little circulation of coin, there was no need of purses. When purses became necessary, pockets were evolved to hold them.

The reticule and balantine were part of the attire of the *Merveilleuses*. Balantine was the old name for a bag like the hussars' sabretache, and this form was worn like the hussars' bag hanging at one side. Some of the first reticules were woven of horsehair. Then they were made of the same material as the spencer or pelisse, the outer garment.

The time of their constant wear was during the empire fashions. The scant, gauzy garments, the tunics and peplums, gave no opportunity to wear a pocket, and they were too frail to sustain one, so women were forced to carry a pocket in their hands, or to go without one. That would never please the arbiter of fashions, the Empress Josephine, for she must always have a fine handkerchief at hand, of fine lace, or embroidered in gold; for she had an awkward habit — the only awkward act of her life — of holding a handkerchief before her

Mrs. William Jackson. By Gilbert Stuart.

mouth when talking or smiling, for her teeth were poor.

Another word for a reticule was "cabas"; the *New English Dictionary* calls this an Americanism, and gives as an example a use in the year 1885. Of course, this is wholly inadequate, for the word is

Bead Chain.

used by Charlotte Brontë. It is in *Villette* (1853): "the patterns for the slippers, the bell-ropes, the cabas were selected; the slides and tassels for the purses chosen." In Lady Morgan's *Dramatic Scenes from Real Life* (1833), a cabas is described as a novelty in England. The word meant originally a rush basket for figs or dates. It was made familiar to Europeans through Napoleon's campaigns in

Egypt.   For a time cabas was always a work-basket frilled with ribbons; then it was a bag — small — of any material.

Another appropriate term for a reticule was "indispensable."   Eliza Southgate's sister sent her a pretty silk indispensable in 1805.   We read that in 1806 the rows of pretty peeresses brought sandwiches in silk indispensables to eat in court during Lord Melville's trial.   It is said that they were bags with long strings, by which strings they were hung on the back of a chair if the woman seated herself.

The charming bead bags which are now so fashionable are not novelties; they are in many cases literally old.   New bags are made to imitate the old ones; these are worked on canvas, or made of purse silk and beads with knitting-needles or crochet hook; but the beads of the new examples are seldom of as fine kinds or as varied or rich in color as those of the old bags.   These new bags are costly, but not as high priced as the ancient ones; indeed, the old ones were never low priced.   In 1800, $5 was the regular price paid for knitting a bag, and the many-tinted beads were costly.   The stringing alone was a matter of much work, as it was done by rule; if the number of beads varied from the rule, the design would be knit awry, and when horses, barns, houses, churches, trees, and flowers formed the picture, such mistakes were grave ones.   Some women raised silkworms in small numbers, and wound, twisted, and made their own strong purse-silk.   Besides the pouch-shaped bags, long, narrow purses with a slit in the middle held coin at each end. Watch-chains were also knitted, bearing initials, dates, and tiny checker designs.

A handsome pattern for knitting a bead bag was a treasure beyond price; its written rules were given only to nearest and dearest friends. Simple designs could be counted out from existing bags. Many a tale of domestic jealousy and social envy centred around these bags. In one New England town Matilda Emerson reigned a queen of bagmakers; her patterns were beyond compare; one of a Dutch scene with a windmill was the envy

Bead Bags. 1810.

of all who beheld it. She was a rival with Ann Green for the affections of the minister, a solemn widower, whose sister kept house for him and his three motherless children. Matilda gave to the parson's sister the written rules for a wonderful bead bag (the design having originated in Boston), a bag which displayed when finished a funereal willow tree and urn and grass-grown grave, in shaded grays and purple and white on a black ground; a properly solemn bag. But when the pastor's sister essayed to knit this trapping of woe, it proved a sad jumble of unmeaning lines, for Ann Green had taken secretly the rules from the knitter's work-box, and had changed the pencilled rules in every line. When the hodgepodge appeared where orderly symbols of gloom should have been seen, the sister believed that Matilda had purposely written them wrong in order to preserve her prestige as a bag-knitter; and she so prejudiced her brother that he coldly turned from Matilda and married, not Ann, but a widow from another town. Disappointed of her desired husband, Ann tormented herself with her New England conscience until she revealed her wickedness to poor Matilda, whose reinstatement in the parson's esteem could not repay her loss of his affections.

CHAPTER XXIII

DRESS OF THE QUAKER

" *Though stately the ostrich-plume gracefully throwing*
  Its feathery flashes of light on the eye ;
Though tasty and trim the straw bonnet when glowing
  With its ribbons so glossy of various dye ;
Yet still must I own, although none may seem duller
  Than a simple drab bonnet to many a gaze,
It is, and it will be, my favourite colour
  Around which my fancy delightedly plays ;
And it well suits my muse with a garland to wreathe it
  And echo its praises with gratefullest glee,
For — knowing the goodness that oft lurks beneath it —
  The bonnet of drab beats a turban with me."

— "The Bonnet of Drab," BERNARD BARTON.

" *Dear Sisters, These things we Solidly recommend to yor Care*
and Notice, in a degree of y^t Divine Love wch hath previously
manifested itself for ye Redemption of ye Vain Conversations,
Customs and Fashions y^t are in y^e World ; that we might be
unto y^e Lord, a Chosen Generation, a Royal Priesthood, an Holy
Nation, a Peculiar People."

— "Women ffriends at Yearly Meeting at Burlington, 21st of 7th Mo.,"
HANNAH HILL, 1726.

CHAPTER XXIII

DRESS OF THE QUAKER

HE letters and journals of good old Quakers, the abuse of them by their enemies, the accounts of their many legal difficulties, the records of their meetings for sufferings, have all been consulted by me whenever and wherever possible for several years with a view to writing an extended study of Quaker dress. A far more exhaustive and sympathetic study has been made by one whose knowledge came from within, by Mrs. Amelia Mott Gummere, and published under the title *The Quaker*. Of the motives and spiritual history of the Friends Mrs. Gummere knows far more than any outsider could hope to learn, though I have studied carefully their transactions and have ever been familiar with their meetings.

A Quaker meeting-house set in a large grassy lot and shaded with tall cedars and whispering pines and hemlocks was my neighbor from earliest childhood in my New England home. Thirty years ago a drab-coated and drab-hatted congregation of wealth and influence came each First and Fifth Day, went within the leaden-hued walls, opened the heavy shutters, and sat sometimes for hours on the hard,

narrow benches; the rows of broad-brimmed hats on
one side of the house, and rows of white net caps
and rich gray silk bonnets on the other; the older
and sedate members were on the higher seats in a
gallery raised in the background, overseeing the
meeting literally as they did spiritually.

> "In gown of gray or coat of drab,
>   They trod the common ways of life ;
> With passions held in sternest leash,
>   And hearts that know not strife.

> "To yon green meeting-house they fared
>   With thoughts as sober as their speech ;
> To voiceless prayer, to songless praise,
>   To hear their elders preach."

Substantial carriages and good horses bore them
to the door and filled the horse-sheds, from which
an occasional impatient whining and stamping
mingled with the sound — monotonous and dron-
ing, yet pleasing — of inspired testimony or accepta-
ble teaching from visiting minister or home teacher
which floated out — half-chant, half-speech — on the
sweet summer quiet.   At other and far more meetings the spirit did not "move"; and after a sitting
of hallowed thought they rose, shook hands and
departed. To one not of Quaker birth or faith
these hours of stillness and rest bestowed a balm
and blessing for the closing years of his life, as he
sat each First Day among the rapidly thinning ranks
of Friends. As long as any Quakers would meet,
the meeting was held; but here, as in other communities, young lives wearied of Quaker restraint,

and the meetings dwindled. In Wickford, Rhode
Island, for some years two Quakers only attended
the meeting. Beriah Brown and Holland Vaughan
came each First Day, shook hands, sat with their
hats on side by side in solemn silence through a
proper term, then rose, shook hands again, and
parted.

To the Worcester meeting came another fate than
dwindling by death, or desertion to other folds. In
their houses, as in their meetings, Quakers had no
pianos, and no songs were heard; and ever plain of
speech were they. But, alas! times have changed
since that fatal May meeting at Lynn when music
was "approved." The Worcester meeting-house has
been painted yellow and white, and has new green
window-blinds, — a sight to make one weep, — and
every Sunday the shrill notes of Moody and Sankey
hymns with parlor-organ accompaniment rend and
pierce the air; and the pine and hemlock trees have
died. I know not why, but I can guess the reason.
Few who enter these walls speak with "thee" and
"thou," and the Quaker men and women in Quaker
garb, save a few aged Friends, have vanished with the
pines and hemlocks. Among the Sunday-school
children there is not a Colton, Hadwen, Earle, Chase,
or any of good old Quaker name; but people say
with great satisfaction that it is no longer a dull old
Quaker meeting, but "a hustling mission."

Well do I recall the serenely tranquil faces of
those Quaker mothers, women dressed in the dignified, substantial garb worn by Elizabeth Fry, a dress
whose rich material and ample folds combined a cer-

tain beauty, the effect of which was curtailed by the ugly Quaker bonnet.

I am sure the person of intelligence is yet to be found to whom the figure of Elizabeth Fry, shown in this portrait by Richmond, is not the personification of womanly dignity and beauty in old age. Nor have I ever known any one to deem her dress other than becoming. Of course in this we are much influenced by the great elegance of her figure, her fine proportions, and erect carriage, and her indescribably winning face. It influences us in the portrait as she influenced in life all who saw her.

Among the most interesting pages in Mrs. Gummere's book are those which, to use her own words, "attempt to show that the typical Quaker dress has been, in the case of the men, a survival of the original dress of Charles the Second, while that of the women has been an evolution, having its continuation one hundred and fifty years later in the costume of Elizabeth Fry." The dress is shown of George Fox, the Quaker preacher and founder of the faith and order of Friends. His hat was that of Charles the king, minus the feather. Both men wore the hair cut across the forehead, hanging in curls on the shoulder. Plain linen bands take the place of lace ties. The cloth doublet of Fox is shaped like the king's silken coat. Knee-breeches, stockings, low shoes, both wear. Fox's breeches have no points; his stockings are homespun; his shoes have no ribbon roses. The long cane is common to both. This is all. "The Dress of the Quaker was simply the Dress of everybody, with all extravagances left off."

Elizabeth Fry.

This dress of Elizabeth Fry's was not at all the dress of the original Quakeress. Drab and gray and brown had not been selected as Quaker colors. At first all Quakeresses wore colored aprons of green or blue, but preferably of the former color. The quarterly meeting at Lincolnshire in 1721 said distinctly, " We think Green aprons are Decent and Becoming to us as a People."

In 1698, Aberdeen meeting said : —

" Let none want aprons at all, and that either green or blue, or other grave colors, and not white upon the street or in public at all, nor any spangled or speckled silk or cloth or any silk aprons at all."

But few details are known of the dress of Margaret Fox, the wife of George Fox. Her son-in-law sent her a white mantle and a white sarcenet hood in 1670; and we know that her sisters had all the worldly garments of their times — black hoods, ala-mode whisks, sky-colored stockings, red petticoats, masks. Fox bought a scarlet mantle for his wife, but he denounced " unnecessary buttons," " short sleeves," and " vizards," — though his sister-in-law wore one, — and he was wrathful over " long slit peaks behind in the skirts of your waistcoats." One young woman, ordered by George Fox to sew up this slit, answered that she saw no evil in it, and had been advised by another Quaker that she should be sure herself that it was evil, and not think so because others said so. This slit was the placket-hole, and it was the fashion of the day to draw the petti-coat out through it.

I cannot find that any of the early Quakeresses
wore what we call Quaker dress. The two wives
of William Penn differed much in dress. I have
noted that both wore black hoods, as did every
other woman of that day. One was a fair, young
creature, Gulielma Springett, to whom Penn wrote
that beautiful love-letter which is one of the most
exalted and exquisite examples of English composition known in our language. Her dress has

Quaker Hats of Leghorn and Beaver.

not a suggestion of Quakerism. See page 240.
Hannah Callowhill, the second wife, is plain of face
and dress, as may be seen in her picture on page
242, but her collar is laced, and her dress is not
that of a Quaker. A copy of a Dutch print called
"The Quaker Meeting" is shown in this book.
Therein it may be seen that the Quaker "Tub-
Preacher" wears a beaver hat and dress like other
women of her day; while her woman-hearer is in a
hood.

George Fox hated the "skimming-dish hat"; *his*
Quaker women all wore hoods shaped like the French

hood. These were known by the various names that
"the world's people" used, cardinals, capuchins,
riding-hoods. In 1707 the Southwark meeting in
London had to enter in their records that "several women Friends do usually hang their riding-
hoods on the rail of the gallery so low that Friends
that sit under the gallery are incommoded."

I suppose the first step taken to set the skimming-
dish hat in place was to wear it over the hood. But
at last it outlived the hood ; and by the years of the
American Revolution, Watson, the annalist of Philadelphia, could write that the Quaker women of that
Quaker city wore large white beaver hats with
scarcely a sign of a crown, which were confined to
the head by silk cords tied under the chin.

In a painting of a Quaker meeting in 1778, the
older women wear the old hood ; others the "skimming-dish hat," or the modern Quaker bonnet. It
is a great surprise to be told that the "bonnet of
drab" known irreverently as the sugar-scoop, the
poke-bonnet, the stiff-brim, the coal-scuttle, is comparatively a new thing. This sentence is found in
*A Memorandum Book belonging to Ennion Cook, of
Birmingham, Chester County, Pennsylvania,* dated
1820. Ennion Cook was the village schoolmaster,
and the old memorandum book is in possession of a
descendant. It runs : —

"Martha Routh, a Minister of the Gospel from Old
England, was at Goshen (Pennsylvania) Meeting the 11th
day of 11th mo. 1798 ; was a means (if I mistake not) of
bringing bonnets in fashion for our leading Frd's, and hoods
or Caps on the Cloaks in the Galleries, which of Latter

time the Hoods on the Cloaks of our overseers and other
active members have increased to an alarming hight or size:
— how unlike the dress of their grandmothers!"

The Quaker bonnet is indeed a solemn subject;
to the chosen people it could speak of distinctions
of belief. The wearer, by its folds and plaits and
flare, was known to be Hicksite, Gurneyite, or Wilburite. The crown of the Gurneyite bonnet tipped
up an eighth of an inch more than that of the Wilburite, which is the Philadelphia plain bonnet, and
was rounded down at the ears. The crown had a
plait at each side, while the Wilburite was plaited on
the top. The English Quaker bonnet had a cape,
and was gathered, not plaited, and flared out at the
face, and had a smaller front. It is said that the
stiff-plait bonnet was regarded as rather gay when it
was first worn. Ann Warder was reproved for wearing a whalebone bonnet instead of one of pasteboard.
A doll model dressed like the Quaker Rebecca Jones
of Philadelphia· (who died in 1817) had a bonnet
with soft, gathered crown while the large cape had
three points, one at the back, one hung in front of
each shoulder.

The "pinched cap" seems to have been assumed
at an early date, though Quaker women are constantly being warned against "long lappets" and
"fair pinners at a side," with other frivolities. Long-
eared caps were worn by some, round-eared caps by
others. The prevailing modes of women's dress
always were reflected in a faint tinge of alteration in
Quaker dress. Thus when all world's people wore

empire gowns, Quaker maids and some of the elder
women had shorter waists than of old.   When mut-
ton-leg sleeves appeared, Quaker sleeves swelled out.
If cap-crowns rose high on Martha Washington when
her husband was President, so they did on her pretty
Quaker neighbors in Philadelphia.   Even the big,
flat, beaver hats were worn by world's people and
the chosen ones alike; and bonnets were assumed
as general wear by all together.

In 1786 an English Quakeress named Ann Warder landed in New York.   She wrote some most
entertaining letters which we are fortunate enough
to have to-day.   She was a quick-witted, quick-
sighted, quick-tongued woman, and her letters reveal
all these qualities.   Her first letter to England says:
" The women all wear short gowns, a custom so truly
ugly that I am mistaken if I ever fall into it.   Notwithstanding they say I shall be glad to do it on
account of the heat."   The short gown was simply
what we would now term a dressing-sacque, and
doubtless was comfortable in hot weather.   I cannot understand why such a very shapeless and
meaningless dress could ever have been worn in
public as it was both in America and England.

The short gown seems to have been made of cotton or linen stuff, lawn or calico.   A bed-gown was
a similar garment of woollen, and corresponded with
a man's nightgown.   These, too, for a time were
worn without-doors.

It is amusing to an outsider to read the articles
of dress over which Quaker saints were " exercised."
Suspenders caused an Ohio meeting many anxious

moments; umbrellas at various times were offensive.
Yet Edward Shippen had an umbrella in 1738,
eighteen years before Jonas Hanway carried his in
London.

Excess in red cloaks was one of the exaggerations
of dress deplored by sober Quakers, in spite of
George Fox's wife; and trollopees were most offensive, though they did not mind the short gown.
Caricatures of both articles forced them into disuse.
In Philadelphia a woman felon was led to the gallows
in a scarlet cloak; and the wife of the hangman
paraded the town dressed in derision in a great
trollopee.

Ann Warder wrote thus in 1788 in Philadelphia:—

"I put no cloak on this forenoon, but was obliged to
afterward, not to look singular, for some had long ones
lined with Baize down to their toes, but no hoods, instead
of which a lay-down coular (collar) which would look very
disagreeable to me but for the Cape to their Bonnets, hid-
ing the neck.   Black are worn more here than with us;—
no Brown except Cloth."

The "immodest fashion of hooped petticoats"
grieved all Friends sorely.   Thomas Chalkley was
moved to deep abjurations of its horrors.   Rilston
meeting specified "Quilted Petticoats sett out in
Imitation of Hoops; some wearing two together."
Some of the lamentations read almost amusingly
to "world's people" of to-day.   Mrs. Gummere
gives these extracts from the diary of Ann Whitall,
a Quakeress of Red Bank, New Jersey, written in
1760:—

" Oh will there never be a Nehemiah raised at our Meetings to mourn and grieve ! Oh the Fashions and running into them ! The young men wearing their hats set up behind and next its likely will be a ribbon to tie their hair up behind. And the girls in Pennsylvania have their necks set off with a black ribbon — a sorrowful sight indeed. There is this day Josiah Albertson's son — all the son he has — and his hat is close up behind ! O I think my eyes could run down with tears always for the

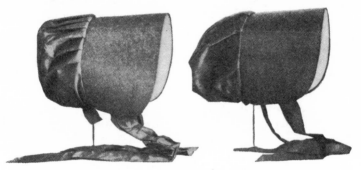

Quaker Bonnets.

abomination of the times ! So much excess of tobacco ; and tea is as bad, so much of it, and they will pretend they can't go without it. And there is the calico ! Oh the calico ! I think tobacco and tea and calico may all be set down with negroes, one as bad as the other."

In another world Samuel Sewall and Ann Whitall now have met, and understand at last why they were so afflicted with hair and hats, and tobacco and tea, and ribbons and wigs. Strange is to learn that while Ann Whitall mourned like Nehemiah over the black ribbon on the young girl's neck, she herself wore a straw bonnet lined with pink silk. Silk seems to have been all right, so it was not in the form of ribbons.

Much testimony as to dress has been preserved in the records of the actions taken at the various Friends' meetings. Thus, in 1695, Philadelphia yearly meeting advised : —

"That all that profess the Truth and their Children, whether young or grown up, keep to Plainness in Apparel as becomes the Truth and that none wear long-lapped Sleeves, or Coats gathered at the Sides, or Superfluous Buttons, or broad Ribbons about their Hats, or long curled Periwiggs, and that no Women, their Children or Servants dress their heads immodestly, or wear their Garments indecently as is too common; nor wear long Scarves; and that all be careful about making, buying or wearing (as much as they can) strip'd or flower'd Stuffs, or other useless & superfluous Things, and in order Thereunto, that all Taylors professing Truth be dealt with and advised Accordingly."

Women Friends of Burlington, New Jersey, issued this specific warning : —

" Dear and Well-beloved Sisters :

"A Weighty Concern coming upon many ffaithful ffriends at this Meeting, in Relation to divers undue Liberties that are too frequently taken by some yt. walck among us & are Accounted of us, We are Willing in the pure Love of Truth wch. hath Mercifully Visited our Souls, Tenderly to Caution & Advise ffriends against those things which we think Inconsistent with our Ancient Christian Testimony of Plainness in Apparel &c., Some of which we think it proper to Particularize.

" As first, That Immodest ffashion of hooped Pettycoats, or ye. imitation of them, Either by Something put into their Pettycoats to make ym sett full, or Wearing more than is Necessary, or any other Imitation Whatsoever, Which we take to be but a Branch Springing from ye. same Corrupt root of Pride.

" And also That None of Sd ffriends Accustom themselves to wear their Gowns with Superfluous ffolds behind, but plain and Decent.   Nor to go without Aprons, Nor to wear Superfluous Gathers or Pleats in their Capps or Pinners, Nor to wear their heads drest high behind, Neither to Cut or Lay their hair on ye fforehead or Temples.

" And that ffriends are careful to avoid Wearing of Stript Shoos, or Red or White heel'd Shoos, or Clogs, or Shoos trimmed wh. Gawdy Colours.

" Likewise, That all ffriends be Careful to Avoid Superfluity of Furniture in their Houses, And as much as may be to refrain Using Gawdy floured or Stript Callicos and Stuffs.

" And also that no ffriends Use ye Irreverent practice of taking Snuff, or handing Snuff boxes one to Another in Meetings.

" Also That ffriends Avoid ye Unnecessary use of ffans in Meetings, least it Divert ye mind from ye more Inward & Spiritual Exercise wch. all ought to be Concern'd in.

" And also That ffriends do not Accustom themselves to go in bare Breasts or bare Necks."

Friends were quick to adopt any simple forms of dress; for instance, the shawl.   The plainness of outline of this article of dress at once pleased them, and soon every Quakeress wore a pretty square of gray cashmere cloth folded shawl-fashion.

Mrs. Gummere notes the great variability in the

dress of Quakers, but she gives one rule of dress which is rather surprising. These are her words : —

" Through the latter half of the eighteenth and the beginning of the nineteenth century all plain Women Friends wore gowns with low necks and short sleeves. This, I think, may be taken as an universal rule. The neck was protected by a dainty muslin or lace handkerchief folded across the bosom and pinned at the waist at each side. Over this was worn a soft silk shawl."

Yet the portrait of Elizabeth Fry, which was painted in 1824, is not with short sleeves, nor do her sisters wear short sleeves.

An excellent picture of the dress of a Quaker gentleman about the time of the Revolution is given of Jonathan Kirkbride. It reads thus : —

" During his preaching expeditions, he went out mounted on a pacing horse, a pair of leather saddle-bags, containing his wardrobe, hung behind the saddle, a silk oil-cloth cover for his hat, and an oil-cloth cape over the shoulders, which came down nearly to the saddle, as a protection from storms. Stout corduroy overalls, with rows of buttons down the outside to close them on, protected the breeches and stockings. A light walking-stick did double duty, as a cane when on foot and a riding whip when mounted. . . .

" He wore a black beaver hat, with a broad brim turned up at the sides so as to form a point in front, and rolled up behind ; a drab coat, with broad skirts reaching to the knee, with a low standing collar ; a collarless waistcoat bound at the neck, reaching beyond the hips, with broad pockets, and pocket-flaps over them ; a white cravat served for a collar ; breeches with an opening a few inches above and below the knee, closed with a row of buttons and a

silver buckle at the bottom; ample silver buckles to fasten
the shoes with; fine yarn stockings. . . .

"In winter, shoes gave place to high boots, reaching to
the knee in front, and cut lower behind to accommodate
the limb."

Another Quaker minister is described thus by
Ann Warder in 1789 : —

"His dress unstudied, a Cocked Hat, Clumsy Boots,
Brown cloth large Breeches, Black Velvet Waistcoat, light
old Cazemar (cassimere) coat, handkerchie instead of stock
which is tied on without much pains. Conceive J. W.
(her husband) with his suit — Nankeen Inexpressibles and
white silk stockings, much more resembling an English
gentleman."

Miss Hill, in her *History of English Dress*, states
that Quakers did not wear wigs. I would she could
read the minutes of Quaker monthly and yearly
meetings during wig-wearing years. One is the
meeting of Massachusetts Friends in 1719, when
"A Concern is lying on this Meeting Concerning of
Friends wearing Wigs." Sandwich quarterly meeting indorsed the wearing of a small decent wig.
As early as 1700 Philadelphia desired testimony as
to "Long Periwigs," and "extraordinary Powdering," and they warned their younger members against
extravagance in wigs. London Quakers yielded to
small wigs — they could not stem the tide. Many
English prints exist of Friends' meetings; some are
caricatures, a few are not; in these half the Quakers
are pictured with wigs.

There were other sects that advocated a dress much like the Quaker's. In Pennsylvania the Mennonites and the Dunkards wore plain drab or brown garments, and condemned buckles and buttons. Indeed, the Mennonites were known as " Hookers " from the hooks and eyes which fastened their garments. The Amish brotherhood in our western

The Gallery of the Meeting-house.

states still wear them, and are called Hookers. Shaker women wore plain Quakerish dress and close cap, and the excellent cloak called by their name. This originally was made solely in russet-colored and dull-blue homespun cloths. But as the "world's people" have discovered the utility of these cloaks, the Shakers (being above all things else money-getters) make them of all kinds and grades of cloth, and sell them for a goodly profit.

CHAPTER XXIV

THE HISTORY OF THE RIDING-HABIT

" *Some Women (Oh the shame !) like ramping Rigs,*
Ride flaunting in their powder'd Perriwigs ;
Astride they sit (and not ashamed neither),
Drest up like men in Jacket, Cap, and Feather ! "

— " A Looking Glass for the Times," THOMAS ELLWOOD, 1670 (circa).

" *Walking here in the galleries I find the Ladies of Honour dressed in their riding garbs, with coats and doublets with deep skirts, just for all the world like mine ; and buttoned their doublets up to the breast, with periwigs and with hats ; so that only for a long petticoat dragging under their men's coats nobody could take them for women in any point whatever ; which was an odd sight, and a sight that did not please me.*"

— " Diary," SAMUEL PEPYS, June 12, 1666.

CHAPTER XXIV

THE HISTORY OF THE RIDING-HABIT

IT can be seen plainly that in America, though coaches, chaises, chairs, and carriages were found in all the large cities as soon as there were roads for their use, and often before there were suitable roads, and sedan-chairs were also known, still the general travelling was on horseback. Nor was it for travelling only that a woman rode. She needed a horse for the everyday outdoor events of life; for going to a friend's house or to market; she needed it above all for going to church. In rough roads women rode astride in America until Revolutionary times, just as women had ridden over sorry English ways.

Queen Anne, consort of Richard II, had ridden sitting sideways, but found few to follow her fashion. The first illustration of a woman's saddle with a crutch may be seen in a portrait of the Countess of Newcastle, painted about 1650; the second crutch did not appear till a century later, and then rarely. After all, very few women rode alone on horseback; nearly all sat on a pillion behind a man rider. We pulled down an old pillion from an ancient garret two summers ago. It was a leather cushion about a foot and a half long and ten inches wide; the edge of the leather was cut in a pattern; a foot-board hung on the off side; and there was a metal handle to which the rider could cling. We had it beaten fiercely to try to shake from it the dust of a century; sewed a fresh heavy linen cover over the worn moth-eaten cushion; and had strong leather straps replace the crumbling ancient ones. It was done in jest to amuse a young girl who was slowly convalescing from a fever; and the exercise of riding around the farm - lanes

Foot-mantle.

(and the laughter over the ride) were important factors in her recovery.

In ancient days the fair wearer often held fast to a stout leather belt worn by her male companion. She was usually lifted into the pillion after he had mounted; but in an ancient book upon horsemanship, written by one Stokes, is an absurd picture of a gentleman vaulting into his saddle *after* the lady was in her place. In Mexico the woman used to ride seated in front of the man. This is said to be very wearying to the horse; for the man's seat is not on the croup, and is scarcely changed from its ordinary position; while hers is necessarily well up on the horse's withers.

There would appear to be little in the dress of Elizabeth and her gentlewomen that was masculine, though there was much in men's dress that was of feminine aspect; yet there were complaining critics who thought women too eager to assume men's fashions. We have read Stubbes's wails over doublets and jerkins; another complained: —

> "With her long lock of hair upon one side
> With hat and feather worn in swaggering guise
> With buttoned bodice skirted doublet-wise,
> Speak! Could you judge her less than be some man?"

There was, however, special dress for riding, as we learn from the inventory (still existing) of Queen Elizabeth's garments. We know thereby that the queen had in the year 1600 thirty-one cloaks and safeguards; thirteen safeguards; and forty-three jupes and safeguards. The safeguard was a heavy petticoat of wool or linen stuff, worn as its name indicated to guard women's other garments from mud and mire while riding. It was worn by Elizabeth with a cloak or a jupe; or apparently simply over the petticoat of a formal gown with no other waist-covering. Another name for a safeguard was a weather-skirt; and Chaucer called it a foot-mantle

or foot-cloth.   The Wife of Bath rode in one.   A
very old woodcut of a "fote-mantle" such as she
wore is reproduced on page 616.

Men also wore foot-cloths.   Aubrey wrote of the
great Harvey, discoverer of the circulation of the
blood, thus : —

" He rode on horseback with a foot-cloth to visit his
patients, his servant following on foot as the fashion then
was.   The Judges rode also with their foot-cloths to West-
minster Hall; which ended at the death of Sir Robert
Hyde, Lord Chief Justice.   The Earl of Shaftesbury
would have revived it; but several of the Judges, being old
or ill-horsemen, would not agree to it."

The substantial figure of William Cecil, Lord
Burghley, faces page 618.   A sensible old gentleman
in furred robes of office and a foot-cloth, mounted
on a steed such as received everywhere the significant title of a "foot-cloth nag," he trundles along in
a secure confidence which finds fitting expression in
his carrying in one hand a nosegay of "coronations" and honeysuckle — the sweetest of sweet
flowers.   His long-eared nag scarce needs so pon-
derous a curb.   The coat-of-arms hanging on "the
honeysuckle tree," and the carved motto on the
trunk beneath, are as quaint as the rest of the sedate
figure in coif with citizen's flat-cap over all.

Safeguards were worn in America as long as
women rode universally on horseback.   In 1654 a
Salem woman, Ellinor Tresler, had "a Sad-collered
Cloak, Wascote, Safeguard and Gouene to goe
together."   Governor Winthrop sent to his grand-

William Cecil, Lord Burghley, in a Foot-cloth.

daughter "a gown peticote and safeguard." Another woman had "a safeguard cloak and hood suitable." Thus we see that these formed a complete riding equipment. In Pennsylvania, in 1771, the English visitor, Ann Warder, found Quaker women riding to meeting in safeguards : —

"They are very shiftable; they ride by themselves with a safeguard, which, when done, is tied to the saddle, and the horse hooked to a rail; standing all meeting time as still as their riders sit."

Some of these Quaker "safeguards" have not been destroyed. They are of heavy linen. Another name given them in Pennsylvania was "riding petticoat."

No special riding-dress for women seems to have existed until the times of Charles II; this the Quaker Ellwood angrily reviled in verse, as quoted at the head of this chapter. He said further : —

"The Women wear the Trowses and the Vest
While Men in Muffs, Fans, Petticoats are Drest."

This wail of women's trousers was wholly imaginary unless English women wore a garment that had been devised in France in the time of the conflict of Catholic and Huguenot, when women had to fly from their homes and make long journeys on horses or mules. These were drawers, *calençons*, a sort of long hose, to be worn with doublet and petticoat. The *calençons* were the forerunner of the trousers of women's riding-habits of to-day.

Frequent allusions in contemporary plays and poems show the general annoyance and suspicion that women were going a step too far. *Will Bagnall's Ballads*, 1655, has this stanza : —

> " Doublets like to men they weare
>   As if they meant to flout us ;
> Trust round with poynts and ribband fayr。
>   But I pray let's look about us,
> For since the doublet so well doth fit 'em
> They'll get the breeches if they can get 'em."

It is believed that doublets were first adopted by women as a riding-dress ; then they became general wear. So was it with the garment called juste-au-corps by Pepys in 1667, when he met Lady Newcastle riding in one. Of course Mrs. Pepys had to have one, though she wore hers as she walked afoot.

The juste-au-corps was a jupon or jacket which came into fashion in Paris about 1650. The word was soon corrupted to justico in English speech.

The ladies of the court are described in a newsletter of the year 1682 as taking the air on horseback "attired very rich in close-bodied coats, hats and feathers with short perukes."

A lady's riding-dress was advertised in *The Spectator* of June 2, 1711, as of blue camlet laced with silver. Like Pepys, Sir Roger de Coverley had to look to the heels of the wearer to find out by petticoat or boots whether he should say Sir or Madam. When George II reviewed the Guards in 1727, he wore gray cloth faced with purple with a purple feather in his hat (such an ugly unmilitary

Riding-dress of 1784.

dress), and the eldest three princesses accompanied
him in "riding habits with hats and feathers and
periwigs" — this being the earliest use of the word
riding-habit that I have found.   In France ladies
wore hoods on horseback — hence the riding-hood.

A writer of the year 1731 says thus of riding-
dress : —

"The hat and peruke, which has been some time made
part of a lady's riding equipage, is such an odd kind of
affectation, that I hardly know under what species to range
it.   It adds such a masculine fierceness to the figure, and
such a boldness to every feature, that neither decency nor
elegance can justify it.

"The riding habit simply, with the black velvet cap and
white feather, is, in my opinion, the most elegant dress
that belongs to a lady's wardrobe; there is a grace and
gentility in it that all other dresses want.   It displays the

shape and turn of the body to great advantage, and betrays
a negligence that is perfectly agreeable.   This fashion was
certainly invented by a woman of taste, and I am pleased
to see the ladies in general so well reconciled to it."

These riding-habits were called Brunswicks, and
various names were given in quickly succeeding years.
The Brunswick was introduced into England about
1750.   Brunswick was a name agreeable to English
ears at this time, and in 1758 had a glory of popularity
when Prince Ferdinand of Brunswick regained Hanover, which had been lost by the Duke of Cumber-
land in 1757.   " Prussian cloaks " were popular at
the same time, for they marked the Seven Years'
War wherein England sided with Prussia.

Brunswicks had collars, lappets, and buttons like a
man's coat.   Of course Boston dames had to follow
English fashions; so Boston milliners had Brunswicks for sale and Brunswick buttons and loops and
Prussian cloaks likewise.

The surtout is almost as puzzling as the doublet.
It was worn both by men and women, and is defined
in the notes to Gay's *Trivia* as a joseph or a wrap-
rascal.   Now Sir Walter Scott in *The Heart of
Midlothian* describes a wrap-rascal very distinctly as
" a close-buttoned jockey-coat with large metal buttons, worn with coarse blue stockings called boot-
hose because supplying the place of boots, and a
slouched hat."   Such garments were worn by the
drivers of our American stage-coaches, with the
addition in winter of a fur cap and gloves and a
great scarlet sash.   But I have never known a woman

Mrs. Thomson in Riding-dress.

to wear a wrap-rascal. The *London Chronicle*, 1762, describing the dress of "spruce smarts," says that men's surtouts had four flaps on each side like dog's ears. They had buttons and buttonholes for ornament only, so they were wrapped around the wearer like morning-gowns; "a proof," says the writer, "that dress may be made too fashionable to be useful." Certainly surtouts were women's wear as well as josephs.

Jamieson's *Scottish Dictionary* gives this definition; "Joseph, a kind of surtout, generally made of duffle and worn by females when riding." It was a garment shaped much like a man's greatcoat, buttoned closely down the front, and with capes or collars like the greatcoat. It was certainly worn on horseback, but in walking as well, whenever warmth and protection were needed. Goldsmith in the *Vicar of Wakefield* says, "Olivia would be drawn as an Amazon, dressed in a green joseph richly laced with gold and with a whip in her hand." The word would seem to be derived from Joseph's coat of many colors. In Rev. Zacharie Boyd's *Flowers of Zion* (he died in 1653) we read: —

> "Jacob made for his wee Josie
> A tartan coat to keep him cosie.
> And what for no ; there was nae harm
> To keep the lad baith saft and warm."

The words "joseph" and "josie" were in common use in America from 1750 until almost our own day. In the advertisements of runaway servants and slaves we often read that they were

"dressed in a blue cotton Josie," or "wore a peni-
stone Josey." In 1750 one Simon Smith of Boston, a "Taylor from London," made in addition to
"all sorts of Men's and Boys' Cloaths, laced and
plain," feminine garments which he termed "Ladies
Habits and Riding Josephs in the newest Fashion."

About 1790 a longer riding-coat came into fashion,
and was called the "artois." It was much like the
joseph, having lapels and revers like a box-coat, but
it had also several capes. It resembled the riding-
coats of men at that date.

Two prints are given on page 621 of riding-dress
in 1784. These were illustrations in a scurrilous
London magazine called *Town and Country*, and
form a part of a series of portraits of women, of
note in England either for their beauty, rich dress,
or extravagant or scandalous behavior. It was a
record both of the gossip and costume of the
day. These two riding-habits show the simpler
form of the very jaunty English riding-dress which
so charmed Frenchwomen. The coats and waistcoats were worn in France with much larger hats,
and these great hats were perched on top of Cadogan braids, or plaits, which either hung to the waist
or were turned up in a mode familiar to us to-day.
A vast pouter-pigeon puff or necktie filled out the
chest. This dress was called in France appropriately the *Amazone*. Moreau, in a fine series of
engravings, has shown us "life" in his day, its fêtes,
pleasures, ceremonies, functions; "life" in the
salon, boudoir, country house, opera, court; "life"
in the *Bois de Boulogne*, with women garbed in this

Amazone dress. And very becoming the dress was, far more gay and more attractive than riding-dress to-day in the same place.

A very interesting habit and riding-hat is shown facing page 622 on the portrait of Mrs. Hannah Harrison Thomson. She was of the Norris and Lloyd families of Philadelphia, and had been married according to the ways of the Quakers, but this habit is not a Quaker dress. It is of rich brown satin trimmed with braid and white satin frilling. The hat is a silky beaver, very long of nap; of "natural" color, but deeper in tint than usual. The satin ribbon is beaver colored. This was a costume of very good shape and cut, I feel sure. It was certainly the very top of the London mode. The countenance looks much older than Mrs. Thomson really was.

These riding-habits were not the only English fashions which invaded France. English driving-coats, cropped hair, pudding cravats, two watches with fobs, riding-whips, and walking-canes became favorite French wear.

Riding-habits were worn with full white petticoats when the skirts became full. Riding-trousers have been worn less than fifty years; white ruffled petticoats are seen at the lower edge of many of the riding-habits in *Godey's Lady's Book* and *Graham's Magazine*, as late as 1855.

When the short-waisted scant-skirted empire fashions prevailed, there were empire and classical riding-habits. The wives of Napoleon's generals wore such a dress as the *Amazone* of 1808, shown here, which was a scarlet habit, short waisted, with onesided cap; the Glengarry, light blue, trimmed

with lace and frogs was also much admired. (See page 627.) The hat is of cork, which must have been light in weight and very suitable. It is over-weighted, however, with a great tuft of feathers nodding over the nose.

It must be remembered that riding-dress fashions had not yet fixed on dark colors. Every tint of bright color was used, even figured materials. The Quakeress Elizabeth Fry and her six sisters, in girlhood, all had scarlet riding-habits, in which they dashed over the country, and ranged themselves across the road in high frolic to hold up the mail-coach. Cloth was, of course, the general material, but velvet was also used, and even silk.

The Amazone. 1808.

Skirts, as we know, were very full and absurdly long, until our own day.

There seemed to be no limit to the equipments and trimmings of habits. Where undersleeves were worn in full dress they appear on the habits; if fichus were the mode, fichus were worn on horse-back while artificial flowers decked riding-hats, as well as long feathers. Necklaces even appear, and frequently chatelaines with watches and various trinkets. I have seen several old French and English fashion-plates in which the rider carried a carefully spread fan.

If ruffs were worn in full dress, ruffs appeared on horseback. If embroidery was worn, the habit was embroidered. A snip-waisted, soft-whiskered father wore a vast plaid waistcoat on horse-back, while his little son is in pantalets and high stock on a pony.

Glengarry Habit.

The young wife has a Scotch cap and long veil with her full habit. For many years, certainly fifty, a long, floating, blinding veil vied with a long ostrich plume for adornment of the riding-hat.   A bird of paradise was also eulogized as "quite the *jante* for the riding hat," though a wreath of weeping-grasses was called also "tippee."

The head-gear of a woman rider was often most absurd.   Even in treatises as late as 1860 ladies were advised that riding in a bonnet was injudicious. I have seen a French print where a mounted dame was clad in a very trim habit with fairly short skirt and long-skirted coat much as is worn to-day; but her hat was a great heavy beaver with feathers over her eyes, and she carried an open parasol.

All these appurtenances indicate very mild horsemanship; and doubtless few women riders were very bold.   I have a book of advice to equestriennes in which many words are given about choosing a "gently-ambling" horse, and one sentence says curtly, "For a woman to ride a trotting horse is indecent."   Great stress was placed upon never riding fast.   Therefore it was possible to hold an open parasol or to spread a fan with ease, instead of carrying a riding-crop.

CHAPTER XXV

BRIDAL DRESS

" *The Gardener stands in his bower door*
  Wi' a Primrose in his Hand.
And bye there came a leal Maiden
  As jimp as a Willow wand.

" *O Ladie! can ye fancie me?*
  For to be my bride;
You'll have all the Flowers in my garden,
  To be to you a Weed.

" *The Lily white sall be your smock,*
  It becomes your body best;
Your head sall be busk't in Gellyflower
  Wi' the Primrose on your brest.

" *Your gown sall be the Sweet William,*
  Your coat the Camovine;
Your apron of the Sallets neat
  That taste baith sweet and fine.

" *Your hose sall be the braid Kail-blade*
  That is baith braid and lang;
Narrow, narrow, at the cute,
  And braid, braid, at the brawn.

" *Your gloves sall be the Marigold*
  All glittering to your hand;
Weel spread owre wi' blue Blaewart
  That grows in the corn-land."

— " Old Scotch Ballad. "

CHAPTER XXV

BRIDAL DRESS

THERE existed in colony, province, and state, certainly for over two hundred years, a simple, neighborly, homely custom known as "Coming out Bride." In New England and in the central provinces, and in the South wherever the segregated plantation life made it possible, on the first Sunday after a wedding and usually for the four Sundays of the honeymoon month, bride and groom, whether old or young, gentle or simple, went to the church services dressed with as much pretty, and distinctly bridal, finery as was their good hap to possess. The bride might, if a fortunate sister, be able to wear a new gown each of the four Sundays. Judge Sewall writes with frank pride in his diary, after his daughter made what was deemed a very good match, that bride and groom and the bride's parents and the bridal attendants all walked together on the Sabbath morn through narrow Boston streets, a proud, happy, and pious little procession, to the Old South Meeting-house. I should have loved to see the bridal party when his granddaughter, Mary Hirst, was married to Sir William Pepperell; she would wear, of course, the great hoop which was one of the groom's bridal gifts, given with a splendid ring, just as to-day a groom would give a string of

pearls with a ring. I should love to see her with her vast swaying hoop and brocade, happy and smiling in her close cap and little hat, with the groom in his rich flowered-velvet suit, and the old judge sombre in black satin, and his third wife in her " striped Persian," walking proudly behind them. Carlyle amused himself with the fancy that he would like to have a clear vision of all the suits of clothes he ever had worn. I am sure I shouldn't. Many of mine I barely tolerated in life, and I should abhor them in a vision. I can think of nothing more depressing than to have them recalled when I thought myself well rid of them, — even of the

Wedding Gown of Mary Leverett. 1719.

memory of them. And the fact that I should find many of them with full evidence of having been very little worn would not make them any more cheerful.

But I should like to have a clear vision of the attire of all who have " come out bride " in the Old South Church in Boston.   The first maid-servants of Winthrop, godly young women " help," the children of his old English neighbors, were speedily married in the New World, where bachelors were

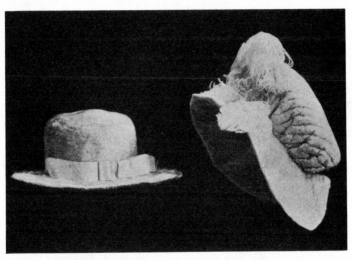

Bridegroom's Hat and Bride's Bonnet of Pink Silk Plush.

not only most forlorn but most restricted and most despised.   From their simple substantial dress down to the satin gown and point-lace veil of the fashionable wedding of later years — what a Cyclopædia of Costume !

The decorous little procession arm in arm to the meeting-house was not all of the harmless and happy little Sunday show.   In many country communities the bride and groom were not placed in the seats rigidly assigned to them, which might be of no great distinction or prominence, but, in that dignity which ever haloes the newly-married, were seated side by side in the most prominent place in the house. This might be in the front row in the gallery, or perhaps in the front seat of the body of the house. They usually arrived a bit late, in order to have their full meed of attention; and proceeded slowly arm in arm down the broad aisle to seats of honor, in the hushed attention of the entire congregation. One bride, a hundred years ago, attired in fawn-colored watered silk walked by her proud husband in what was then the newest fashion — trousers; and his were made from the same piece of fawn-colored silk, and his silken left leg rustled well against her fluttering silken petticoats. At a certain point in the services, usually after the singing of the second hymn, the happy couple, in agonies of shyness and pride, rose to their feet, and turned slowly twice or thrice around before the eyes of the whole delighted assembly, thus displaying to the full every detail of their attire. In the diary of a young Medford girl she tells of her sister's determination not to marry in April lest April showers spoil her " coming out bride." She therefore waited till the last Sunday in May, and had such a violent thunder-storm that she could not go to church at all. The splendid yellow brocade gown shown on page 632 was worn to church by Mary Leverett after her marriage in 1719. Here are also parts of the dress worn by young Salem folk as they came out bride in the year 1810. Her bonnet was of pink shirred plush,

Pink Silk and Plush Wedding Coat.

his hat is of the same plush. (See page 633.) The accompanying coat (see facing page 634) is the groom's, of pink figured silk trimmed with pink plush, and the groom's waistcoat was of the same material.

In the diary of a young girl, Betsey Heath, kept in Brookline in 1783, she tells of her sister's marriage on Thursday. "The Bride was drest in a Lilock colour'd Lutestring gownd and coat." On Sunday she "came out Bride drest in strip'd Lutestring Negligie, three white waving plooms in her hat; wore her new short Polanees flounced and trim'd with Blue."

William Livingstone, in his *Philosophic Solitude*, 1747, gives proof that the stage for the display of fine clothes was the church, in such lines as these : —

> " Polly avers that Sylvia dressed in green
> When last at church the gaudy nymph was seen.
> Chloe condemns her optics, and will lay
> 'Twas azure satin, interstreak'd with gray.
> Lucy invested with judicial power
> Awards 'twas neither — and the strife is o'er.
> At length equipped in Love's enticing arms,
> With all that glitters and all that charms
> The ideal goddesses to church repair
> Peep through a fan, or mutter o'er a prayer ;
> Or deeply studied in coquettish rules
> Aim wily glances at unthinking fools."

The wily Abbé Robin, a close observer, wrote just after the Revolution : " Piety is not the only motive which induces American women to be constant in their attendance at church. Having no places of public amusement, no fashionable promenades, they

Wedding Gown of Mrs. John
Sparhawk. 1736.

go to church to display
their fine dress. They
often appear there
clothed in silks, and
covered with superb
ornaments."

There was much for-
mality in the dress worn
by those coming out
brides, even at a later
day. One of my kins-
women was married
when seventeen to a
young husband who
died in a few weeks.
After more than ten
years of widowhood, but
still young, she married
a second time. She wore
"coming out bride" a
silver gray satin gown,
and a gray pelisse of
uncut velvet with a
silken stripe; this was
lined with cherry-col-
ored satin and trimmed
with marabout plumes.
Her bonnet was of
shirred gray velvet with natural gray feathers and
cherry-colored face trimmings of very full ruches of
ribbon loops. This seems to me a charming costume, but she was exceedingly unhappy because,

having been a widow, she could not in etiquette
appear in a white bonnet and feathers and veil.
And she felt that coming a stranger to her new home
it was so unfortunate to appear in a gray bonnet;
that it made her seem like an old woman, and was
"so conspicuous."

White Lace Wedding Veil. 1810.

No special color was chosen for a bride's dress,
as white is worn to-day. The bride wore the
most costly gown she could afford, and often that
the market could supply. The favored silk for
many years was a thick brocade such as is shown on
page 636. This was worn by Mrs. Sparhawk, of
Salem, Massachusetts, both at her wedding and to
church services the succeeding Sunday. This dress
is a rich white silk, brocaded — to use Dante's words
— "in flowers of noble colours."

This splendid dress might well be the one ordered from England by Sir William Pepperell for his daughter to wear upon her marriage to Nathaniel Sparhawk. It was, in his words, "*Silk* to make a woman a full suit of Clothes; the Ground to be white *Padusoy* and flowered with all sorts of Coulers suitable for a young woman."

He also ordered for her wedding outfit another gown of "white watered *Tabby*, with *Gold Lace* for trimming of it;

Bridal Hair Combs.   1820.

twelve yards of Green Padusoy; thirteen yards of Lace for a woman's Head Dress 2 inches wide as can be bought for 13 shillings a yard." As its purchasing power would be to-day, this sum for lace was equal to about £40. Other bridal finery was a handsome fan mounted in leather for twenty shillings; two pair silk shoes, with clogs a size bigger than the shoes.

A piece of the yellow brocade wedding-gown of Cornelia de Peyster is shown on page 375. The gown itself has eight straight breadths in the skirt, and it measures four and three-quarter yards around the bottom. The waist has one square tab below the waist-line in front. There is an open space left from neck to waist-line for a lace tucker and stomacher. The back is cut a low, square neck. The back is laid in plaits, stitched perfectly flat and very closely down to the waist-line; there it is left loose in princess shape all in one piece, making the back breadths of skirt very full at back. The dress has never been altered. The sleeves are plain, elbow length, with a small turned-back cuff. At bottom of each sleeve there is sewn in a round piece of lead (covered with linen) the size of a half-dollar, for a weight, to keep the sleeves hanging down straight. The sleeves had lace ruffles or engageants at elbow.

The earliest wedding-veil and all-white bridal gown, made distinctly for a wedding-dress, which I have known was worn by Mrs. James H. Heyward, of Charleston, South Carolina. She was Decima Cecilia Shubrich, a lovely creature, married at nineteen. Her portrait was painted by Malbone, who was in Charleston in the year 1800. She wears a tulle wedding-veil placed on the head as would be a similar bridal veil to-day. Also a splendid tiara of pearls, and ear-rings of pear-shaped pearls. These rich jewels were sent her from England by her godmother, Mrs. Rutledge, as a wedding-gift.

These pearls were rivalled by those of another Charleston bride, whose marriage is thus written about by that lovely young creature, Eliza Southgate Bowne. This was in 1804, in New York:—

" Miss Pell was married last week to Robert MacComb; they are making a prodigious dash. I went to pay the bride's visit on Friday; they had an elegant ball and supper in the

Three Nightcaps and Dress Cap of a Salem Bride.

evening, as it was the last day of seeing Company; 7 bride's-maids and 7 Bride-men, most superb dresses; the bride's pearls cost 1,500 dollars; they spend the winter in Charleston."

The "seeing company" took the place of our present wedding-tour. Every one who knew bride, or groom, or their parents, called upon the bride. Sometimes she received one day, and her husband had men callers the next day. At other times ladies and gentlemen visited her in one parlor, then went to another room and drank to and with the groom, who, as one chronicler said, generally got "reasonably pleasant."

Anna Green Winslow writes in her diary in Boston, in 1771 : " On the 6. Mr. Sam Jarvis married Miss Suky Pierce; on the 11 I made her a visit in company with Mamma and many others. The bride was dress'd in a white Sattin night-gownd."

I have turned to the illustrations of old books thinking I might learn therefrom when brides began to be pictured with wedding-veils. The earliest veil I have found is in a little book of crude rhymes entitled *The Courtship and Marriage of Jerry and Kitty*, London, 1814. In this the bride wears a bridal veil over her hair and face, hanging to the hem of her gown. Further evidence of later date is in *The Dandy's Wedding*, London, 1823.

Wedding Dress. 1818.

In this the bride wears a veil hanging from her comb over her face, and the accompanying verse reads : —

> " The handsome veil of Mechlin lace
>   A sister's love bestows.
>   It adds new beauties to her face
>   Which now with pleasure glows.
> Friends, brothers, sisters, cousins, meet
>   To attend the happy bride ;
> And Queer's joy is all complete,
>   The nuptial knot is tied."

I should add, however, that I have found at least a hundred pictures of brides of these dates without veils. The earliest fashion-plate I have found with a conventional white wedding-dress is given on page 641. It appeared in 1818. It has no wedding veil.

I know not at what date orange blossoms became closely associated with bridal attire. In 1848 Thackeray wrote in *Vanity Fair* : —

" Had orange blossoms been invented then (those touching emblems of female purity imported by us from France) Miss Maria would have assumed that spotless wreath."

I cannot find when orange blossoms " were imported from France "; but it would seem as if English brides had worn them before *Vanity Fair* was written. T. Haynes Bayly, who died in 1839, wrote a song which was popular in the early thirties, entitled, *She Wore a Wreath of Roses*. The second stanza of this begins : —

> " A wreath of orange blossoms
>   When next we met she wore,"

and goes on with references to the orange blossoms on her brow in a way implying that the custom of wearing them was well known.

A list of wedding shopping is preserved in a tiny satin-covered book at " Little Rest," Kingston, Rhode Island. Madam Randolph was married July 4, 1802, at Newport. Her husband, a young Virginia planter, came North with his own carriage and horses; and after the wedding returned to their plantation on the James River, Virginia, driving all the way from Newport. This was some of her wedding finery: —

" Necklace & Case . . . . . . $52.
  8 yds. muslin 14/ per yd. . . . . 20.
  5½ yds. lace 5 dolls. per yd . . . . 27.
  5¾ yds dimity a 5/ per yd 4.9
  1 doz Stockings a 9/ . . . . . 18.
  4 yds of Calico a 5/6 . . . . . 4.
  Dressing Case & Comb . . . . . 3.
  Piece of Linen . . . . . . 25.
  3 yds of Cambric . . . . . . 7.
  Piece of Cambric . . . . . . 22.
  6 yds of muslin . . . . . . 20.
  4½ yds. of figured cambric 5.1
  5 prs stockings at 8/ 5.1
  4 yds of Dimity 9.4
  9 yds of Cambric 2.4
  Money sent to Antwerp . . . . 150.
  Ditto for Furniture making . . . 150.
  Money carried to Boston . . . . 110.
  26 yds of Diaper at 3/6 . . . . 15.
  5 yds of ditto a 2/ . . . . . 2.
  Tea set of China . . . . . . 15.
  Dinner set ditto . . . . . . 69.
  Tea trays . . . . 7.
  Bill of Geoffroy . . . . . . 100."

The last $100 was for silver, as Geoffroy was an old silversmith, and there are spoons still in the family with his mark. This bride also received from her father (he gave the same to his six daughters) a full set of Canton china, of which a few pieces, such as water-plates, deep dishes, pitchers, etc., still remain.

It will be noted that not a yard of silk was bought. Dimity, organdy, lawn, linen, are the material of the gowns. The $150 sent to Antwerp was probably for Flemish lace, which was so fashionable.

Bridal Parasols. 1810.

In 1817, in November, a gallant commodore was married; General Scott and Captain Kearney were two of the groomsmen. The bride wore white Canton crape; and her travelling dress, in which she drove off to the station at Sackett's Harbor, was a dark blue habit trimmed with three rows of frogs on the front; a black Leghorn hat with black satin bows and three great ostrich feathers. These habits were a close-fitting, short-waisted garment, which were soon used as a walking dress as well as a habit. This bride's pretty wardrobe was wholly of Canton crape and India mulls, not a silk gown among them all.

Mrs. Gummere gives a beautiful picture of Quaker bridal attire : —

"In the month of May, 1771, Isaac Collins, of Burlington, N. J., married Rachel Budd, of Philadelphia, at the 'Bank Meeting,' in that city. His wedding dress was a coat of peach blossom cloth, the great skirts of which had outside pockets; it was lined throughout with quilted white silk. The large waistcoat was of the same material. He wore small clothes, knee buckles, silk stockings and pumps — a cocked hat surmounted the whole. The bride, who is described as 'lovely in mind and person,' wore a light blue brocade, shoes of the same material, with very high heels — not larger at the sole than a gold dollar — and sharply pointed at the toes. Her dress was in the fashion of the day, consisting of a robe, long in the back, with a large hoop. A short blue bodice with a white satin stomacher embroidered in colors, had a blue cord laced from side to side. On her head she wore a black mode hood lined with white silk, the large cape extending over the shoulders. Upon her return from meeting after the ceremony, she put on a thin white apron of ample dimensions, tied in front with a large blue bow."

This gay-colored raiment will surprise all who know not the true history of Quakerism and Quaker costume. The black hood is a curious detail of this bridal garb; it appears to confirm what is told by Watson and other annalists, that in the eighteenth century a certain black silk hood was worn always by a Pennsylvania bride. It was deemed as much a part of the wedding outfit as a lace veil is to-day. It seems to have been originally a German fashion.

CHAPTER XXVI

MOURNING ATTIRE

" *Ask not why hearts turn magazines of passions,*
And why that grief is clad in several fashions,
Why she on progress goes, and does not borrow
The smallest respite from extremes of sorrow ;
Her comfort is — if any for her be,
That none can show more cause of grief than she.
Ask not why some in mournful black are clad ;
The sun is set ; there needs must be a shade."

— " Dirge for the Tenth Muse, Anne Bradstreet," REV. JOHN NORTON, 1678.

CHAPTER XXVI

MOURNING ATTIRE

BLACK, the emblem of Death, was in early times the ordinary mourning color in Europe. Froissart refers distinctly to the custom of placing a whole family in mourning when he tells that the Count de Foix clothed his whole family in black at the death of his son Gaston. Chaucer in 1379 wrote —

> "Cresyde was in widowe's black,"

showing there was then a distinct widow's dress. We find often that at the death of persons of dignity and note in that century, persons and houses were dressed in black, and persons who attended the funeral were furnished mourning, which they were given to carry home with them.

Testimony has been gathered to show that mourning wear was not necessarily black; but ample lines from Shakespere give proof to the contrary : —

> "'Tis not my inky cloak alone, good mother,
> Nor customary suit of solemn black,
> . . . The trappings and the suits of woe."

These lines would clearly indicate that black was English mourning in Shakespere's day — the "cus-

tomary suit." Strutt says that Henry VIII wore
white for mourning after he beheaded Anne Boleyn;
scarlet would have been more appropriate.

We have seen in our own day a vast change in
the customs of mourning wear. Thirty years ago
heavy crape was donned for every relative; thick
crape veils were worn in periods of several years.
Often after the death of a cousin or uncle or aunt,
unrelieved black would be worn for two or three
years. Now, little crape is seen on gowns; in nearly
all cases a "nun's veiling" veil has replaced the
crape, and in many cases the veil is not assumed at
all where formerly it would have been worn for
years. The wearing of mourning in colonial times
was a part of that sentiment, that regard of friends
and neighbors, which was so strong in those days.
We find Judge Sewall putting a black ribbon on his
cane because a friend had recently died; we see him
donning his "mourning rapier." We read of others
putting on mourning-rings at the anniversary of the
death of a friend.

When Lady Andros, the wife of the governor,
died in Boston in 1690, six "mourning-women"
sat in front of the pulpit, and the hearse was drawn
by six black horses with scutcheons on their sides
and death's heads on their foreheads. They must
have been absurd! Scutcheons were placed around
the room; hatchments were hung in front of the
house. But four of these old hatchments are known
to be now in existence in America. One hung in
Christ Church in Philadelphia and may be there
still; one is of the Izard family in Charleston,

South Carolina; another in Kentucky; the fourth, the Browne hatchment, still is owned by one of the family residing in Massachusetts.

Ribbon, "corle," or caul, crape, white linen in varying amounts were given to mourners. Cyprus, a kind of crape, and "hood mourning" were ordered from England for funeral purposes, in large amount.

The funeral expenses of a Baltimore citizen in the eighteenth century included these items: —

Coffin . . . £6.10s.
41 Yards Black Crape.
32 Yards Black Tiffany.
11 Yards Black Crape.
5½ Yards Black Broadcloth.
7½ Yards Black Shalloon.
8½ Yards Black Callamanco.
16½ Yards Linen.
3 Yards Shirting.
3 Dozen Pairs men's black Silk Gloves.
2 Dozen Pairs Women's black Silk Gloves.
6 Pair Men's cheaper black Gloves.
6 Pair Women's cheaper black Gloves.
Black Silk Handkerchiefs.
Mohair Buckram.
13 Yards Black Ribbon.
47 Lbs. Loaf Sugar.
14 Dozen Eggs.
Ten ounces Nutmegs.
1½ Lb. Allspice.
21 Gallons White Wine.
12 Gallons Red Wine.
10 Gallons Rum.
Coffin Furniture.

Not only the dress of the sorrowing ones, but the household surroundings, were made deeply black. Mirrors and pictures were covered with cloth. The window shutters were slightly bowed and tied together with black, and were left thus for months. In England was still deeper gloom.

Throughout the *Verney Memoirs* there looms up

a black bed, which all adown the centuries goes like
a Car of Juggernaut from house to house, killing
all cheerfulness in its route.   It figured in all the
family bereavements, and was lent (and with alacrity,
I suspect) to friends in affliction.   In those days of
speedy remarriage, it proved not always a welcome

Duchess of Cleveland in Widow's Weeds.

sojourner.   For instance, on the death of Lord Sussex, Ralph Verney at once despatched "our black
bed" to his widow; and no doubt she solemnly
enjoyed its gloomy pomp and elegance of grief for
a few weeks.   But she speedily found another old
earl for her third husband; and when writing to announce her approaching marriage she says: " The
Black Bed and Hanginges your aunt never sent for.

If you would have me deliver them anywhere I will,
or keep them — whichever you desier I will do."
The Black Bed was not always welcome to mourners.   One young widow was made so ill by its trying
gloom that her sister apologized for drawing a white
coverlet over her, and over the black silken sheets.

Carriages of course were hung in black, and black
liveries were worn.   Even saddles and pillions were
covered with black.
Ralph Verney did not
have the use of his
own " Black Bed,"
for he was on the
continent when he
was bereft of his wife
— his bright " Mis-
chiefe," his gentle,
laughing, brave, loyal
Mary, whose nature,
so sunny, so sweet,
so endearing, is fully
revealed in her own
and her husband's

Lady Russel in Widow's Dress.

letters.   No wonder that by her death her husband's
life was wholly shattered.   Being methodical and
conventional even in grief he ordered due mourning
— this not only in garments for outer wear but " black
taffety Night-cloathes, with black Night-capps, and
black Comb and Brush, and two black Sweet-bags
to it and slippers of black velvet; and a black needle-
case with a great gold bodkin, blew thred, shirt buttons, cap-strings and tapes."   One wonders that

the thread was not also black.   It tells his sincerity of grief to know that he never married again; this at a time when all men remarried.   And yet his marriage to this wife had been almost a matter of sale and purchase.   She was a ward in chancery, and was disposed of to him to good advantage when she was but thirteen years old.

An inky picture is that of old Lady Bute sitting up in her " black bed," the room lighted but by one taper, while her grandchildren stood in silence at the foot of the bed, and all the acquaintances, friends, servants, tenants, passed through the room a con- tinuous procession, speaking not a word, but by their presence showing complimentary condolence on the death of Lord Bute.

The funeral usually took place at night; and the rank and station of the deceased was known and marked by the flambeaux.   At the funeral even the soles of the shoes were sombrely blackened. Mourning lasted for a wearisome time.   As it was assumed even for remote relatives one might readily pass all his days in mourning.   Often it was worn for life.   We know the unkempt-looking, almost "seedy" portrait of Sir Kenelm Digby after the death of his fair wife, Venetia.   He wears his own plain hair and an ill-shapen beard, a suit of black cloth, a black cloak, and a black slouch hat.   This dress he never changed.

Mourning dress was not always a great expense to the wearer, for it was supplied liberally by the family or through the will of the deceased person.   Often several hundred pounds' worth of black garments would be given to friends, servants, clergymen, doctors. Black gloves were sent broadcast to friends, " None of 'em of any figure but what had gloves sent to 'em." At the funeral of the wife of Governor Belcher in Boston, in 1736, over a thousand pairs of gloves were given away. At the funeral of Andrew Faneuil in Boston three thousand pairs were distributed; often several hundred would be given.

Mrs. Stephen Sewall in Widow's Weeds. 1726.

By Liberty Days, in 1769, mourning-gloves showed the influences of the times, and were made in America of American materials, and it was proposed that they be stamped with a suggestive design such as the Liberty Tree.

Mourning-rings were a great expense likewise; two hundred gold rings were given at one Boston funeral in 1738; these rings cost over a pound each. These rings bore sombre mottoes, such as : —

" Prepared be
To follow me."

" Death parts
United hearts."

Mourning-jewelry was popular, especially when made of the hair of the lost friend, or put in locket form to hold the hair. Often the hair was mounted with a miniature or with a mourning-design.

There is shown on page 657 a locket and a pair of bracelet clasps done in what is known as hair-painting. I have examined these hair-paintings with a microscope, but I cannot find any proof of the tradition which accompanies them that they were painted with human hair ground into a powder and mixed with the sepia color. I have been shown a score of such articles, all with the same tradition. One bracelet had a letter accompanying it telling the name of the person whose hair had been thus introduced. An associated tradition is that "the art is lost." An ancient lady told me what seemed much more probable; that they were painted with a paint-brush made of human hair. However they may be made, they form a pretty trinket, of a decoration common at that day on china, where it was called by various names, such as "black-line china," "India-ink china," "pencilled china," etc.

Human hair was also woven in many intricate plaitings into rings, bracelets, brooches, watch-guards, etc. Sometimes a bracelet would contain the hair of a score of persons, members of one family. Other times a design in basket-work was woven of human hair into a flat disk and then framed with gold and pearls. This was usually a memorial jewel. A lock of hair was a favorite gift of affection, and the slightest bit of hair from the head of some distinguished person, as Washington, would be richly framed in a locket and proudly worn.

It would be difficult to fix the exact date when a

band or armlet of black around the upper sleeve became an emblem of mourning. We have seen a
black scarf thus worn in the time of James I.   In a

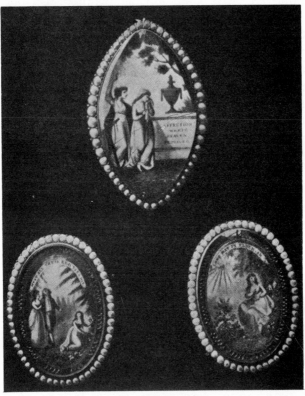

" Hair-painted " Jewelry.

play dated 1826, written by E. Lebrun, a knavish
notary, a widower, described as in mourning, is pictured in a colored lithograph in a brown coat, blue
knee-breeches, white waistcoat and tie, with a flat,

black band on the right arm as the only symbol of mourning.   I know no earlier example.

When Mrs. John Morgan died in Philadelphia a hundred years ago, she had women pall-bearers; and Sarah Eve recounts a similar sad service which she rendered, dressed in white, with a white veil.

Catilina de Peyster's funeral was held to be specially solemn since six of her young girl friends, dressed in white gowns, with hair powdered and tied with white ribbon, served as pall-bearers.   The coffin and pall were both white.   The funeral was held in Trinity Church, New York, and the following Sunday these young maids sat in a pew near the parents of the dead girl while the clergyman preached the funeral sermon.   Within two or three years we have seen another group of women serve as pall-bearers at a funeral in Trinity Church.

Several of the early illustrations in this book show widows' weeds; Lady Mary Armine, Mrs. Clark, Mrs. Beekman, wear widows' caps and dominoes.

Though the following definition of the word *domino* is not given in the *Century Dictionary*, there is ample evidence that the black veil or hood which was thrown over the white cap or coif as a mourning veil by widows, was called a domino.   Cotgrave says a domino is "a kind of hood or habit for the head worn by canons, and hence also a fashion of a veil worn by some women that mourn."   The *Ladies' Dictionary*, 1694, also defines *domino* as a woman's mourning veil.

Heavy black veils were always worn by widows, no matter what their age — and there were some very youthful ones.   One of the most charming pictures of King Charles shows him with Mary Villiers, the daughter of the Duke of Buckingham ; her portrait is on page 126.   At her father's sudden and appalling death this daughter and her brother and sister were taken by the king as his wards.   " Pretty sweet Moll " was married in childhood to the young son of the Earl of Montgomery and Pembroke, and was by his death left a widow at nine years of age.   Not at all quieted by her widow's weeds, she romped and played with her companions, and one day climbed a tree in the palace garden to gather fruit.   The king, walking with his gentleman in waiting, Mr. Endymion Porter, spied the black veil fluttering in the branches, and called out that there was a strange bird in the tree ; for Mr. Porter to fetch his gun and bring it down.   So Mr. Porter went under the tree, only to be pelted with fruit.   He called up, " What shall I do?   I am to kill you and bring your feathers to the King."   " Be as good as your word," cried down to him the happy young widow.   So a fruit-hamper was brought, and Mr. Porter shut down the cover, and with the gardener carried her to the king.   " Here," said Mr. Porter, " is the bird, which I have had the good fortune to catch alive."   And out sprang " pretty Moll," and threw her arms round the king's neck with no more ceremony than if he had been a playmate of her own age.   Such anecdotes as this make us know why the king was loved.

CHAPTER XXVII

FASHION DOLLS AND FASHION-PLATES

" *Frontenac tells me that you desire patterns of our fashions in dress. I send you therefore some model dolls.*"

— " Henry IV of France to Marie de Medicis," 1600.

" *To be seen at Mrs. Hannah Teatt's, Mantua Maker at the Head of Summer Street, Boston, a baby drest after the newest Fashion of Mantuas and Nightgowns & everything belonging to a Dress. Latilly arrived on Captain White from London. Any Ladies that desire to see it may either come or send, she will be ready to wait on 'em; if they come to the House it is Two Shilling & if she waits on 'em it is Seven Shilling.*"

— " New England Weekly Journal," July 2, 1733.

•

CHAPTER XXVII

FASHION DOLLS AND FASHION-PLATES

WO existences as widely remote as the spread of the vast world seem those of great Henry and humble Hannah Teatts; yet their lives swing on closely together in a common circle when there comes to them a very simple force, a dressed doll baby showing the fashions of the day.

These "babies" were no novelty even in Henry's time. Similar ones had been shown in Venice at the annual fair upon Ascension Day for many centuries; and in France at an equally early date. Indeed, it is asserted that in the list of royal expenses for the year 1391, in France, are so many livres for such and such a doll sent to the queen of England. A hundred years later another was sent to the queen of Spain, and at the close of another century one to the duchess of Bavaria. Thus early had France led in the fashions. In those centuries what scores, what hundreds of these little puppets had been sent on their pleasant journey. A happy existence they had; garbed in all the daintiest and prettiest of garments, complacent with the fact of being leaders and arbiters in their orbit of life, free from care, from hunger, from want,

from pain; sent forth with loving attention, welcomed with an eagerness which never varied or
waned; handled gently; cherished religiously; the
companion of the young, the beautiful, the rich,
the gay; truly a life to be envied had the fashion
baby of past centuries.

The custom of dressing these dolls originated in
the salons of the Hotel Rambouillet, where one,

Doll dressed like Mrs. Bowditch.
1770.

called *la grande Pan-
dore*, was exhibited in
full dress at each change
of the modes. *La petite
Pandore* was in the
" politest undress." In
1764 similar dolls had
been made the shape
and size of a full-grown
human being, and were
landed at Dover dressed
in richest laces. When
English ports were
closed in war times,
they were open to an
alabaster doll four feet
high called the *Grand
Courrier de la Mode*. In the war of the First Empire
this privilege was not given; and from that time
"English women deprived of French aid for a whole
generation began to dress badly. Pitt has much to
answer for." These are not my words but those
of an English woman, Mrs. Bury Palliser.

Similar puppets were also employed by hair-dressers. The notorious hair-dresser Legros had exhibitions of dolls coiffed in his latest dreams in hair-dressing, in forty varied styles. English milliners also dressed these dolls. In 1727 one was sent around among the Ladies of the Bedchamber in Queen Caroline's day. It was "a little young Lady dressed in the Court dress," and when all had studied it, Mrs. Tempest, the court milliner, was to have it to keep.

The fashions were at one time borne from place to place by an amusing toy which was in every one's hand. In a letter of the day, we read : —

"Pantins, pasteboard figures moved by strings were in 1748 in every lady's hand in France and England, and used in caricatures in France."

Churchill called it a pantine; others a pantini; but under any spelling it is not found in our dictionaries. W. T. Cooke says : —

"A Pantini was a figure made of pasteboard in imitation of the human form; by the least touch of the finger it might be thrown into a variety of antic and ridiculous postures; it was in high vogue among the beau-monde and deemed a most diverting plaything for gentlemen as well as ladies. Madamoselle Pantine, one of Marshall Saxe's mistresses, was the ingenious inventor from whom it received its name."

I have found a number of advertisements of fashion babies in American newspapers. In New York newspapers in 1757 two modish mantua-makers were announced for some weeks as "just arrived from the kingdom of Ireland," as are nine-tenths of the fashionable " Madames " of the gown-making world to-day. These two Irish mantua-makers announced that they " have furnished themselves

from London in patterns of the following kinds of wear for Ladies and Gentlemen, and have fixed a correspondence to have from thence the earliest fashions in miniature." These fashions in miniature were doll babies.

American women setting out for England were implored " to send back babies "; letters of request for them were constantly being despatched.

Sally McKean wrote to the sister of Dolly Madison in June, 1796, " I went yesterday to see a doll which has come from England, dressed to show the fashions." And even her Qua-

French Fashion Baby.

ker neighbors in Philadelphia had their babies. We fancy so little change in Quaker dress that " new fashions " were never known; but it is plain that Vanity can lurk in the plait of a Quaker bonnet or in the flap of a Quaker coat. Why, even the pinning of a Quaker shawl has its rules and modes. Mrs. Gummere tells of two " babies " dressed in the exact miniature of Quaker dress. In Independence Hall in Philadelphia is " Patty Rutter," a doll dressed by Sarah Rutter in 1782, and sent to Mrs. Samuel

Adams of Massachusetts.   This doll has a complete
little equipage by her side, with watch, pencil, etc.

At the time of the French Revolution Stephen
Grellet, a French gentleman of birth, took refuge in
America and became a Quaker.   In 1816 he returned to England, and was there given a perfectly
dressed baby in Quaker garb which he was to take
to France to a struggling little community which
was trying to become a Quaker settlement.   The
visit was not made, for
Grellet returned sud-
denly to America, where
the doll, which he had
wholly forgotten, was
found in his trunk.
He wrote to the Eng-
lish baby-maker, asking
how he should dispose
of the doll ; and the
answer came, "Give her
to thy little daughter."
The little daughter lived
till 1901, to be ninety
years old, and always
preserved her doll Ra-
chel.

Two Empire Fashion Babies.

These   dolls   were
called "little ladies," and "babies," but not dolls
until the middle of the eighteenth century.   The
old Danish name for maid-servant was daul ; it also
meant a doll.

In the *Gentleman's Magazine*, London, September,

1751, is an early example of the word: "Several dolls with different dresses made in St. James Street have been sent to the Czarina to show the manner of dressing at present in fashion among English ladies."

The finest ones came from the Netherlands; they were called "Flanders babies." To the busy fingers of Dutch children, English and American children owed many of these dolls. It was a rhymed reproach to the latter that —

"What the children of Holland take pleasure in making
The children of England take pleasure in breaking."

Fashions changed, and the modish raiment grew antiquated and despised, but still the "Flanders babies" had a cherished old age. They were graduated from milliners' boxes and mantua-makers' show-rooms to nurseries and playrooms, where they reigned as queens of juvenile hearts. There are old ladies still living who recall the dolls of their youth as having been the battered fashion dolls sent to their mammas.

The fact that these fashion babies generally closed their days as the beloved play-child of real children did not add to their longevity. And in one case known to me intimately, a fashion baby which had successfully eluded the destroying hands of one generation perished in the loving clasp of a grand-child to whom nothing could be denied. Mrs. Vanderbilt, in her charming memories of her child-hood in Flatbush, Long Island, gives a like instance. Old letters written by Americans abound in allusions to these babies.   I have found at least a score of such references.   Here is a part of a letter written by the vivacious Jewess Rebecca Franks from New York just before its evacuation by the British : —

"I shall send a pattern of the newest bonnets : there is no crown, but gauze is raised on wire, and pinched to a sugar loaf at the top — the lighter the trimming the more fashionable — and all quilling.   Nancy Van Horne and myself employed yesterday morning in trying to dress a rag baby in the fashion, but could not succeed ; it shall go, however, as it will in some degree give you an opinion on the subject."

In 1797, a young Norwich girl, Rachel Huntington, wrote thus to her sister Lucy from New York : —

"I send a doll by Brother George, which I intended to have dressed in a neater manner but really could not find time — it, however, has rather a fashionable appearance, the cap is made in a good form but you would make one much handsomer than I could, the beau to Miss *Dollys* poultice neck cloth is rather large but the thickness is very moderate, — there is a large pattern for two train gowns of the muslin, which should be made three breadths wide two breadths to reach to the shoulder straps forward, & one breadth to be cut part of the way down before, to go over the shoulder & part of it to be pleated on to the shoulder straps, meeting the back breadths, & some of it to go around the neck, like the *doll's*."

A truly unique mode of transporting fashions was by what may be called paper dolls ; cut-paper figures. It is so simple, so clever, and so correct a means

that I wonder it was not frequently employed. I
know of but one instance where it was done, and
the name of both sender and receiver are wholly
lost. The little fashionable cut-paper figures, how-

Cut Paper Pattern.

ever, exist; they are preserved in a shallow box,
with the written words of explanation of each detail
of dress that originally accompanied them. Our
grandmothers were so skilful in this cut-paper work
that it was natural they should employ it in sending

fashions. The art was called papyrotamia; teachers of it advertised in newspapers, and *Ackerman's Repository*, a fashion magazine of the early years of the nineteenth century, published copies on " Bath post " of landscapes and many fanciful designs for cut-paper work. A part of one of these patterns is here given (page 670). It can be seen that fine lace could be readily represented. The whole of the black work was laboriously cut away with finest scissors, knives, and pins, and the white figure was then mounted on colored paper.

Pin-pricked pictures were another accomplishment. Pins of different sizes were used. A little toothed wheel was employed for outlines. In opening recently a handsome book of copperplate engravings of the year 1815 of the Keepsake family, I found one of the very fashionably dressed London beauties entirely outlined, — and her garments pricked out also with tiny pin pricks. I feel sure the copy thus pricked had been sent somewhere as a fashion-plate, and warmly welcomed.

Had we no books of the modes, no magazines of fashions, and indeed no portraits, our descendants would know well what we wore to-day from the descriptions in our modern novels. But we have few detailed accounts of costumes in early English novels, and I know of no English fashion magazines prior to 1799, when the *Ladies' Monthly Museum* appeared. In America our well-beloved *Graham's Magazine* and *Godey's Lady's Book* were the earliest comers. Angels of the household we might well term them when we think of the gratification, the satisfaction, the diversion, the instruction, the occupation they brought for so many years to so many families, to so many eager women. What innocent amusement, what harmless entertainment, what varied employment came from the closely printed pages! There was never a word of evil, a suggestion of wrong, in any of these pages, and among all the flat tales and silly poems and vapid sketches were some gems of literature; and it is agreeable to know that these gems were promptly recognized by the entire community, though they appeared in the same settings as the paste jewels. We should not be satisfied nowadays with *Godey's Lady's Book* of 1840, nor would our grandmothers in 1840 have been satisfied with *The World's Work*, or *Success*, or the *Century Magazine*.

I have used few fashion-plates in this book, and only for the last twenty years of my history. I can say of these illustrations, in the words of Paul La Croix, the historian of institutions and customs in France: "The imitative and fanciful compositions now current have been carefully excluded, and the original contemporary works of many faithful artists have been chosen."

The *European Magazine* was one of those several miscellanies of English publication, in the closing years of the eighteenth century, which were so very lofty in their asserted intents and so very low in reality. One series of papers is from "The Man-Milliner," but he confines his fashion notes chiefly to recitals of court dress. We learn nothing of everyday garments. He tells of a grand ball given in 1782, by "The Kiddies," a club composed of young men under twenty-five; a costly ball of fifteen hundred tickets at two guineas each. It proved, however, but "a dull scene of unanimated grandeur." The dress of the men was almost entirely "velvet with fur linings" — fur for ball dress! If the coats were embroidered on the seams, they were called "gala-suits." The prince wore a velvet coat, its color, "Dauphin's blush." One of his dukes, velvet "gris de Daricé"; Carmelite color was a favorite; and "air-balloon" tint. "The ball was crowded at 9," he writes. All the

Miss Jane Butterfield
Drawn from the Life.
Publifhed by G. Robinfon as the Act directs Sep.r 1. 1775.

"vanitees and balls" seem dull in the recital. At the queen's birthnight ball, one of the princesses dropped her slipper, and this was deemed most for-

tunate, because so " very lively an event " gave great
" go " to the affair. A long poem was evolved, a
great flame from the tiny spark of the dropped slipper. Such accounts as this, and many of the pictures,
even the caricatures of the day, show so much excite-
ment over trivial events, find such mild wicked-
nesses so astonishing, that we really wonder whether
there was any very great vice in " Life " at that time.

There was a scurrilous miscellany or magazine,
published in London in the latter half of the
eighteenth century, called *Town and Country*. It
was one of the poorest of the class of which the
Gentleman's Magazine was the best. All of them,
in response to the taste of the times, gave résumés
and sometimes extended accounts — reports they
were termed — of recent crimes and current trials.
Town and Country, and the *European Magazine*, and
the *Ladies' Miscellany*, had scant illustrations, usually
but one to a number.

In *Town and Country* were copperplate portraits
of persons in some prominence or notoriety. A
famous set were the Tête-à-têtes, which ran for
twenty-seven years; and in that time gathered in
much social refuse. These were simply kit-cat
portraits, monotonous in form; a man and a woman
facing each other, sometimes labelled with explanatory
titles (often ill-spelled), as " The Fair Inconstent; "
" The Famous Orater; " " A Young Pennitent; "
" A Princes Favourite; " " A reproveing Moni-
toir; " " The Aged Seduser." Sometimes initials
were given, with that transparent guile by the help
of which our sapient editor ancestors managed

to afford infamous information without incurring suits for libel or challenges to duels. If the features of " The Frail Amerecan " were placarded beside a scant-chinned British officer entitled " General W—fe," it did not require extraordinary perspicuity to know that General Wolfe was indicated ; I presume every reader in London and many in New York and Boston at that time could name the " Frail Amerecan," but her name is now to us as dust and ashes.

Town and Country found in the criminal court, as well as in the

Mrs Rudd

Drawn from the Life. Sep.18, 1775

royal court, subjects for illustration ; in the year 1775 two women were portrayed who shine, not only as noted criminals, but as the very " Glass of Fashion." Their portraits can well be copied now, as they were studied then, as patterns of the prevailing modes. They are far more distinctive than any French fashion-plates of that date.

One of these women was Miss Jane Butterfield. The plate showing her fashionable dress is reproduced on page 673. She was a beautiful young creature who was arrested and put on trial on the accusation of poisoning a gentleman named Scawen. This man had been her greatest friend and her greatest ill-doer ever since she was fourteen years of age. He had given her an extraordinary education and a beautiful home, as well as rich carriages and superb attire. This she recounted in the appeal she made to the jury, in which she told her overwhelming grief at his death, and her great reason to desire his life. The simplest mind could discover from the evidence that the man had died from reckless overdoses of a violent quack medicine administered by himself, and the jury in fifteen minutes returned a verdict of " Not Guilty," which was received with great applause.

The pretty prisoner's hat with its studied folds and graceful puffs seems to me of elegant style ; and her polonaise most refined and graceful ; the whole outline of her dress is good. But her glory pales before a more shining star of suspected womanhood, namely, Mrs. Mary Caroline Rudd, who was tried for forgery in the Old Bailey, London, in 1775. She was acquitted ; it was told frankly that her great beauty and wonderful style, her well-simulated agitation, and even " the tremulous flutter and rustle of her elbow laces," all told upon the susceptible jury, to whom early in the day she turned "in perfect confidence," so she clearly and cleverly stated, "in their judgment, intelligence, and honor."

The accounts of the trial show a wonderfully active brain and "astonishing composure," while other testimony was given, some of it plainly damaging. She kept a constant relay of notes of advice flying out to her lawyers, and she turned every incident to her account and benefit. Her accomplices, two brothers named Perreau, who were tried at the same court, were hanged; and it is impossible to see why they were convicted when she was acquitted. They were picturesque rogues, too, being twins of exact likeness, very handsome, very tall, very agreeable, very fashionable both in dress and equipage.

Ruffled Levite on Mrs. Rudd.

They were reputed to be wealthy — as was Mrs. Rudd, who passed as the wife of Charles Perreau. These brothers solemnly declared their innocence; but Mrs. Rudd was plainly anxious that they should not escape, for up to the day of their being "turn'd off" she sent a series of letters to those in authority

in the court, eagerly offering proof of the guilt of
the Perreaus.   She plainly feared they might be
pardoned.   Among others who asserted their admiration of her grace and style was little Boswell;
and even the great Dr. Johnson proclaimed his
interest in her agitation and her cunning.

   She wore at her trial, says a contemporary account,
"elegant second mourning," which was black and
white.   A drawing of her "from life," as she stood
in the witness-stand with her pendulous ruffles fluttering in her modest agitation, appeared in *Town and
Country*.   It is reproduced on page 675.   If I had
never seen any presentation of the dress of the year
1775, I should know by instinct that this costume
was the height of good style.   It has that indescribable "good form"; that air of complete fashion which
can be felt at times even in viewing a carved effigy
on a tomb.   Every detail of the dress, its hang, its
pretty and fashionable robings, the poise of the
figure, the set of the little mantle, the exquisitely
dressed hair, the wonderfully elegant "head" with
its graceful spotted trimmings,—all are perfection.

   Her story and her style did not fail to catch the
attention of Bartolozzi; I have his drawing of her,
but have not reproduced it here.   He was so anxious to present the criminal with the striking contrast of the Old Bailey pen, that he failed to catch
the elegante.

   Another drawing of Mrs. Rudd, also from life, is
on page 677.   We may study every detail of these
portraits of her with perfect confidence that therein
we have the very best modes of her day.   Her head

in an undress cap is given on this page ; and a beautiful spotted " head " on page 680.   I feel really grateful to Mrs. Rudd for her attention to her dress at

Mrs. Rudd.

these trials, and I am even willing to believe her
beautiful.   But if her real face was as sly as her picture, it was well she was tried by a jury of men, for
no woman would trust her or believe in that sleek,
treacherous, Becky Sharp countenance.

It is easy to obtain a complete presentation of

French modes for the nineteenth century. From 1799 to 1829 that truly important and powerful publication, *Journal des Dames et des Modes*, was owned and carried on by an ecclesiastic named La Mésangère, who had been professor of philosophy in the college of La Flèche. In

the pursuit of his last-chosen and most unecclesiastical and unphilosophical calling, he became so deeply imbued with a purely personal love of dress that at his death he had in his wardrobe, for his own wear, two thousand pairs of shoes, seventy-five coats, a hundred round hats, and uncounted breeches. Every fifth day for the thirty years of his reign this reverend philosopher and mode-

Spotted Lace Head.

maker issued a colored plate of a fashionably dressed dame; and on the fifteenth of each month, two larger and more important plates. The official organ for description of those fashions was *Le Bon Genre*.

To English-speaking folk, the presence of priest or parson in such a calling is unspeakably ill fitting, but it was neither shocking nor even surprising to French folk. Madame had turned for many years to Monsieur l'Abbé for advice and information on matters of dress. While the hair-dresser built up her hair and curled and frizzed in a great pouf, and until both lady and friseur retired for a final touch in a powdering-closet, an idle, sneering, or cringing priest whispered in madame's ear accounts of the gowns of her friends; scandal about the debts of her rivals; secrets he had bullied or wheedled from milliners and tailors or from ladies' maids. He often brought to her boudoir pawned jewels and smuggled or even stolen laces for her purchase. The French priest of those days has been called a tame cat, but the comparison is not wholly a true one. There was an element of jackal, of vulture, in his nature. He fattened in purse and person on the spoils and misfortunes of others. He carried scandal, foul truths, and foul lies just as he disposed of cast-off jewels and finery.

CHAPTER XXVIII

ARMOR, ARMS, AND UNIFORMS

" *There was a steel head-piece, a cuirass, a gorget and greaves with a pair of gauntlets and a sword hanging beneath; all, especially the helmet and breast-plate so highly burnished as to glow with white radiance. This bright panoply was not made for idle show; it had been worn by the Governor on many a solemn muster and training field; and had glittered moreover at the head of a regiment in the Pequod War.*"

— "The Scarlet Letter," NATHANIEL HAWTHORNE, 1850.

" *Stand to it noble Pikemen*
And look you round about.
And shoot you right, you Bowmen,
And we will keep them out.
You Musket and Calliver men
Do you prove true to me.
And I'll be foremost in the fight,
Says brave Lord Willoughby."

— "Ballad of Brave Lord Willoughby," 1588 (circa).

CHAPTER XXVIII

ARMOR, ARMS, AND UNIFORMS

N the " List of Apparell" furnished in 1624 to the emigrants of the Massachusetts Bay Colony were ample arms and armor. It is interesting to know how the Colonial militia and the heroes of the Indian wars were equipped and garbed, so I will recount their outfit : —

" 3 Drums and to each two pair of Heads.
2 Ensigns.
2 Partisans; one for the Captain & one for Leftenant.
3 Halberds for the 3 Sergeants.
80 Bastard Muskets with snaphances, 4 foot long in the barrel; without rests.
6 long fowling pieces, musket bore, $6\frac{1}{2}$ feet long.
4 long fowling pieces, musket bore, $5\frac{1}{2}$ feet long.
10 full muskets, four foot barrel, match cocks, and rests.
90 Bandoleers for the muskets, each with a bullet bag.
10 Horn Flasks for the long fowling pieces to hold 12 pounds powder apiece.
100 Swords and belts.
60 Corselets.
60 Pikes.
20 Half Pikes."

Heavy arms such as culverins, sakers, drakes, shot and powder, were also supplied.

Of course these articles formed precisely the arms, armor-uniform, and accoutrements which were supplied to English soldiers; and the simplest way to view the dress of one of these first American militiamen is to turn to pictures of English soldiers of that day. I give on this page two rude cuts from a rare book entitled *Directions for Musters*, 1638. The

Two Cuts from "Directions for Musters," 1638.

pike-drill was comparatively simple, but the drill of musketeers was complicated by the necessary use of the gun-rest. If you will consider a moment the difficulty of holding a heavy musket, of loading it, of aiming and firing it, you will see that a soldier should have had at least four hands. He had to hold his bullets in his mouth, and twist his burning match in two fingers of the hand that steadied the gun-rest, whereby it constantly scorched him.

Among the unusual arms was the partisan, a great pike or spontoon. It had a broad crescent-shaped blade. A halberd was a long-staffed axe; a snaphance was a fire-lock musket. A bando-leer is here given. It was a shoulder-belt bear-ing bullet-bag, priming-box, and a row of little cylindrical boxes or cases each containing a single musket charge of powder. Sometimes the whole belt and its trappings was

Bandoleer.

termed the bandoleer; at other times the word was applied simply to the little cylinders containing the charges. The case was of wood or metal covered with leather and strung with a cord on the shoulder-belt. The cover was made to slip up and down on the cord, that it might not be detached and lost. The band holding these bandoleers was frequently of strong neat's leather, and was usually worn over one shoulder and hung down under the opposite arm. It will be seen that the bandoleer was a very ornamental as well as useful part of a soldier's dress. The corselet covered the body. In another entry in our colonial records it was explained that the corselet, breast-piece, back-piece, culet, gorget, tasses, and head-piece of each set of " defensive armour" furnished to the American soldier were all varnished black, as were the leathers and buckles.

Cromwell's soldiers fought in cuirasses and tassets, vambraces and pauldrons, gorgets and triple-barred helmets.   These latter named were called " lobster tailed," from the jointed flap which covered the back of the neck.   The Cavaliers, we are told, opposed them wearing only a gorget over buff-coat, and a triple-barred helmet.   If this were so, I cannot see why these same reckless Cavaliers constantly had their portraits painted in the fullest of armor; these portraits bearing also the tradition that this armor was worn at such and such an encounter with the Round-

William Penn in Youth.

heads.   However, it matters little now whether the Roundhead carefully encased himself in protective iron which gave him his name, Ironsides, while the Cavalier rode in careless attire, since of both we must say : —

> " Their bodies are dust,
>   Their good swords, rust,
>   Their souls are with the Saints, I trust."

The other pieces worn by the stern Ironsides may be described thus : the tassets were horizontal steel bands or flat hoops forming on either side a skirt below the breast-plate.   Sometimes the separate tasset had plate overlapping plate, till the thigh and leg from waist to knee were covered. These ended with ornamental knee-caps. Vmbraces or vambraces were armor for the forearm. They included a gracefully shaped shell curved out as a shield to the inner part of the elbow-joint. Pauldrons were shoulder-plates. The gorget was the collar or throat-piece of armor which protected the throat and upper neck. It is of interest because in the form of a gilt crescent-shaped trinket it appears until our own day. It was worn by officers while on duty, and may be seen dangling around the neck on many of our portraits of Revolutionary officers (Washington, General Sullivan, Greene, Benedict Arnold, and on Lord Howe). As the " sign

Sir Nathaniel Johnson in Armor.

and symbol " of active military service it was regarded with much sentiment; and one of these Continental gorgets is deemed a priceless relic. Madam Washington could bestow no greater treasure to honor a gallant soldier than when she gave the gorget which had been worn by her husband.

The Puritan's open protestation of despising gay dress showed in Cromwell's army. But one portrait is known to exist of any of his officers. This is the portrait of Colonel Nathaniel Fiennes. He wears the orange-colored scarf over his right shoulder and under his left arm; and also a breastplate over a buff-coat. This buff-coat is open on the hips, and has a curious and interesting sleeve edged with pink-ing and fastened with ties of leather.

An excellent example of a buff-coat is shown in the portrait of Sir Richard Saltonstall (facing page 18). Another is upon Captain George Curwen. (See facing page 204.) He was born in England, 1610; came to Salem in 1638, and became a prominent merchant and commanded a troop of horse, from whence he received his title of captain.

By 1663 the new English uniform was fixed. Officers wore no armor save a steel gorget; this,

Sleeve of Buff-coat.

of course, of full size. Silk armor was invented, doublet and breeches of quilted silk, thick bonnet with ear-flaps, all a dusky orange color. Roger North says of it: —

" Abundance of those silken back and breasts were made and sold, that were pretended to be pistol proof, in which any man dressed was as safe as in a house, for it was impossible any one could strike at him for laughing, so ridiculous was the figure, as they say of hogs in armour."

I was very glad when I learned of this stuffed
and quilted armor of the English soldiers; for I
had always been rather ashamed of the figure cut
by the New England colonists, who, in Connecti-

Fitz-John Winthrop.

cut, and possibly in other colonies, were ordered to
wear jackets and breeches thickly "stuffed with
cotton-wool, as defensive against Indian arrows."
I had heard in my ears the roars of laughter of
Governor Andros and his troopers when he came to

Hartford to demand the Connecticut charter, and first saw the cotton-stuffed doublets and breeches of the Connecticut soldiery. But now I know that Colonel Andros had seen the English "hogs in armour," and could not laugh at the colonists.

The armor worn by Fitz-John Winthrop in his picture is apparently mediæval. English noblemen and military men were constantly painted in such antique armor at that date, but it was not what they wore in the army. The real armor which Fitz-John Winthrop wore is much simpler; it is still owned by members of the Winthrop family. His sword, a genuine Andrea Ferrara, is now in the custody of the American Antiquarian Society in Worcester.

The square coat, cocked hat, and wig of the French army and the French court had come to England, and French influence had continued to transform the army throughout the century until the accession of Queen Anne in 1702.

Throughout the reigns of George I and II little changes came save in wigs and hats, which were, however, deemed of vast importance in dress. The Ramillies wig of the army was succeeded by the tie-wig, bob-wig, and natural pigtail. A very high German grenadier's cap was adopted — you can see it in many of Hogarth's prints, such as *The March to Finchle*y. Purple had become a favorite color. Even in 1695 the coats of drummers were purple, with gray breeches. George II, habited in gray cloth faced with purple, and purple feathers in his hat, reviewed his troops in 1727; it seems to me a most unsoldierlike dress. The cocked hat was turned up in the corner "like a minced pye," but soon gave way to a hat called the Kevenhuller. In 1770, under George III, the cocked hat was worn. This is the hat which came across seas to fight the "ragged regimentals" of our Continental soldiers. It was small, and the flaps fastened up to the shallow crown with hooks and eyes, the crown being seen above them. In the Kevenhuller, the crown had been wholly hidden, and the middle of the front brim was the highest point. In the Ramillies hat, the back flap turned up sharply, and was not only higher than the crown, but higher than the two front flaps, the middle of the front brim being scalloped out a bit. The long, narrow hat, with two flaps, which came later and had a little tassel or rosette on the two extreme points of the brim, was called the Wellington hat.

Wellington Hat.

It is here shown. This hat was worn in the nineteenth century when the United States had had for a number of years a uniform of its own for its own army; but the tradition of perfection which existed as to all relating to the British army was strong enough to place a Wellington hat on a Yankee head.

As this book is not a general history of the United States, nor is this chapter upon the war of the Revolution, there is no need to dwell upon the condition of the English army when Americans began to dream of liberty. It may be read in the letters of General Wolfe to his father. Mean, corrupt, murdering, insolent, dirty, drunken, disorderly, immoral, undisciplined, slack, demoralized, easy to disorder, hard to recover, of precarious valor, tramps, loafers, jailbirds, — all these words and phrases he applies to the soldiers, ending with " the officers are loose, the soldiers are very devils."

These wonderful English officers and these wonderful English soldiers sneeringly called Washington's army the " Homespuns." Let it stand! It was a truthful nickname — and one to be proud of. There was far deeper power and significance in that title than the English scoffers knew. Had it not been a homespun army it could never have conquered the British. There were no great contractors to supply cloth and make uniforms for the Continental soldiers in those days; there was no money to pay them had there been such firms, but when in 1775 the Provincial Congress sent out through the land an appeal for thirteen thousand warm coats for the winter uniforms of these American soldiers, there was a great army of loyal, loving, industrious women ready to supply homespun garments. At hundreds of hearthstones, wool-wheels and hand-looms were started within a day, within an hour, at work on the wool sheared from the home sheep; that order was filled almost wholly by these patriotic women. In the inside of each coat was sewn a label bearing the name of the town and the coat-maker. Many a romance sprung therefrom. Some rather

rudely shaped garments came from those homespun
tailoresses, but the coats were warm and substantial,
and when the choice was offered to each man of a

coat or a boun-
ty, he eagerly
chose the home-
spun coat. The
list of the mak-
ers and wearers
of these bounty
coats still are
saved in old
New England
towns, and
called a "Coat-
Roll."

For some
years the Eng-
lish officers who
came to Amer-
ica noted with
approval certain
details of dress
of the Ameri-
can Indians,
and they even
adopted articles

Daniel Boone in Indian Hunting Dress.

of Indian wear for occasional use. In the lists of
the attire of English soldiers in America, Indian
leggings and moccasins, and even a hunting-shirt,
appear side by side with pigtail wigs and muffs.

It had been more than hinted to Braddock that

he could learn of the Indian how to fight the Indian. Franklin said of him that his reverses came because he had too poor an opinion of the Indian. Braddock's way of carrying out a skirmish or attack was a perfect delight to the savage, who, safe behind a sheltering tree, picked off the vivid red coats at leisure. His successor, clever Lord Howe, promptly threw off the cumbersome English uniforms, cut off the troublesome pigtails, and put on Indian leggings to protect the legs from briers.

In 1775 Washington ordered Indian boots or leggings instead of stockings, "especially as the General has hopes of prevailing with Congress to give each man a hunting shirt." In October, 1776, these were assigned to each soldier : —

> " 2 Linen Hunting Shirts.
> 2 Pair Stockings.
> 2 Pair Shoes.
> 2 Pair Overalls.
> A Woolen Jacket with Sleeves.
> 1 Pair Breeches.
> 1 Leathern Cap or Hat."

A Continental uniform had taken definite form on paper — a blue or black coat with the lapels fastened back, ten openworked buttonholes done in yellow, with ten large buttons at equal distances on the lapels ; three like buttons on the cuff and pocket-flap ; the skirts hooked back showing a red lining ; the bottom of the coat cut square ; the lappets, cuff-linings and standing-capes red ; a single-breasted waistcoat with twelve smaller regular buttons ; black

half-gaiters ; white shirt, ruffled at sleeves and wrists ;
black cocked hat with yellow or red plume and black
cockade ; gilt-handled small sword and gilt epaulettes.   Such was the soldierly dress that Washington
longed to see on his men.   Few of them, alas ! ever
wore it in completeness.

Soon we learn of a company of picked Virginia riflemen, under the famous old hunter Daniel Morgan,
on their way to join the Continental army at Cambridge under the command of Washington.   Here
is a description of these Virginia marksmen : —

"They wear also a shot bag and powder horn carved
with a variety of whimsical figures and devices hung from
their neck over one shoulder ; on their heads a flapped hat,
burnt a reddish hue by the sun.   Sometimes they wear
leather breeches of Indian dressed elk or deerskin, but more
frequently thin trousers.   On their legs they have Indian
boots or leggins made of coarse woolen cloth, either wrapped
around loosely and tied with garters or laced on the outside.
These come better than half way up the thigh.   On their
feet they sometimes wear pumps of their own manufacture,
but generally Indian moccasons which are made of strong
elk or buckskin dressed soft ; drawn in regular plaits of the
toe, lacing from thence round to the fore-part of the middle
of the ankle ; without a seam in them yet fitting close to
the feet and perfectly easy and pliant."

Thus clad, with his rifle on his shoulder, the man
was "completely equipped for visiting, courtship,
travel, hunting, or war."   The dress was warmly
approved by Washington, who said tersely that the
wearer "was cool in warm weather and warm in
cold weather"; that no dress could be found

"cheaper or more convenient." He says it is a garb both "decent and light"—and he adds, shrewdly, "it causes no small terror to the enemy, who think every such wearer a complete marksman."

It is easy to gather sentences of approval of the hunting-shirt. American history and letters abound in admiring words. To the primitive articles of absolute perfection made by the North American savage, namely, the canoe, snowshoe, and moccasin, all who had worn it added the hunting-shirt.

These men of Morgan's wore a motto on the breast of their hunting-shirts,— "Liberty or Death,"— and Patrick Henry's command of riflemen carried tomahawks and scalping-knives, and

Uniform of Continental Officer.

wore bucktails in their hats. Their shirts and breeches were made of tow-cloth steeped in a tan-vat till the color of a dry leaf. When dressed, the Virginia riflemen thus bore a very good resemblance to the khaki-clad soldier of the nineteenth-century volunteers.

In the general orders of Washington, August 20, 1776, we find field officers assigned a pink cockade; captains, white or buff; subalterns, green. On July 19, 1780, the officers are recommended to have white and black cockades, a black ground with white relief, emblematic of the expected union of the armies, American and French. In 1783 it was

Cocked Hats with Continental Cockades.

called a " Union Cockade," and was to be worn on the left breast. By 1798 several persons were punished for a misdemeanor for having a red and blue cockade.

The cockades were made both of leather and silk. The chapeaux bras, which are still worn by the general and staff officers of the American army, have the same black cockade.

Much thought was given to this cockade. I have a letter written in the year 1782 by the famous John Paul Jones, the most romantic figure in the American Revolution. In it he says: —

" I have the Honour to send you the Cocade I promised, as I forgot to deliver it when I breakfasted with you.

The *Blue* in it may with Propriety be adopted as the National Cocade of America, leaving the *Black* to England, which is a true emblem of the character of that *Dark-minded Nation.* The Friendship of our illustrious Ally towards these Sovereign Independent States — as the Red may represent the glowing Friendship of Spain — I wish to see this Cocade worn by the Officers of the Navy — at least till a better can be devised. It is known in France as our Cocade of Triple Alliance, and I have on particular Desire presented many of them to the first Characters of Europe."

Two officers' hats are given on page 699 (on General Wayne and Colonel Willetts) from portraits

Major André.

by Trumbull. They show the cockade very distinctly; a circle of black ribbon loops with white ribbon caught up in the middle to two buttons at the top from one button at the bottom. We owe much to Trumbull for his portraiture of the Revolutionary times and characters.

The cut of the hair caused much thought in the army. The hair of the officers was often worn like this of André, the most becoming form of

hair-dressing ever worn by civilized men. The face
was of course clean shaved; and the hair powdered
and cued. Stores of flour and tallow for the hair of
the common soldiers were issued to each company;
each man was allowed half a pound of flour a week.

Colonel Claiborne.

Those whose hair was not long enough had false
cues of chamois leather with a tuft of hair at the
end which was spliced or fastened on in some way.
To tie a good cue was an accomplishment; soldiers tied each other's when the regimental barber
did not get around. Sometimes a whole company,
as of gunners, would wear false cues of strong

black leather which were cleaned and polished with
the shoes.   When whiskers were allowed, a string
was stretched from one ear through the lips to the
other ear ; all the beard below the string was shaved.

Short ear-whiskers were permitted, but no other
beard or whisker until the year 1853.   When the
hair was ordered to be cut, the older officers re-
belled, and some were court-martialled.

I own an original portrait by Trumbull of
General Horatio Gates.   He wears the blue and
buff uniform, and the hat with black and white
cockade ; also small-clothes and top-boots.

The greatest change in the uniform of the army
of the United States came in 1802 when standing
collars of vast proportions were enjoined.   One of
these collars is shown on page 701.   These must
not be less than three inches wide and must " reach
the tip of the ear and in front as high as the chin
would permit."   Coatees or jackets came in, also
nankeen breeches and leather caps with bell crowns,
a grotesque dress.   Soon came long trousers, and
modern times and attire.

CHAPTER XXIX

DRESS DURING THE REVOLUTION

" *Do not conceive that fine clothes make fine men any more than fine feathers make fine birds. A plain genteel dress is more admired and obtains more credit than lace and embroidery in the eyes of the sensible.*"

— " George Washington's Letter to his Nephew, Bushrod Washington,"
January 15, 1783.

" *Dress yourself fine where others are fine ; plain where others are plain ; but take care always that your clothes are well made and fit you. When you are once well dressed for the day, think no more of it afterwards ; and without any stiffness for fear of discomposing your dress let all your motions be as easy and natural as though you had no clothes on at all. So much for Dress which I maintain to be a thing of consequence in the polite world.*"

— " Lord Chesterfield's Letter to his Son," 1748.

CHAPTER XXIX

DRESS DURING THE REVOLUTION

O write a true account of dress during the years of the American Revolution seems a well-nigh impossible thing. Never was a poor historian confronted with more conflicting sources. In one letter you read of poverty, want, and privation, — the next has the story of a great and gay ball. You read that the people of Boston died of cold and inadequate food; the next sentence is the description of a theatrical entertainment in Faneuil Hall. Women on the farms pinched and almost starved to send food and clothing to the soldiers; my own great-grandmother stood in the fields directing the puny ploughing of a single ancient ox and a young Indian boy and heard the distant cannon of the battle of Ticonderoga; heard the sound with glad rejoicing, though she saw around her a wasting cropless farm where two years before a score of sturdy men had been at work, and hundreds of fertile acres had yielded plenty and comfort for her and her family. Yet here is a splendid brocade sacque that was worn by another kinswoman, the wife of an American officer, at a regimental dinner. It was a day of vast incongruities.

Without recounting all the influences which led
to these conditions, I may point out two which had
a special bearing upon dress at this time; one was
the presence in America of the English and German
officers, and occasionally of their wives.   Read of
Quaker Philadelphia when, garbed in gayest of uniforms and crowned with tallest of plumes, the army
of Howe took possession of the city.   Look at the
truly beautiful face of the unfortunate André.   Can
you wonder that Peggy Chew and Peggy Shippen
eagerly wore high head-dresses, or, indeed, any
kind of head-dress that he designed for them?   He
makes in a characteristically charming letter this
rash promise : —

"You know the Mesquianza made me a complete milliner.   Should you not have received supplies for your fullest equipment from that department I shall be glad to
enter into the whole details of cap-wire, needles, gauze,
&c.; and to the best of my abilities render you in these
trifles services from which I hope you would infer a zeal
to be further employed."

Read of the dancing-parties, the regattas (a novelty even in England at that time), the fishing-par-
ties, the horse-races, the theatrical entertainments
which André and the English officers got up for
the amusement of Philadelphia belles.   For these
plays André and Captain de Lancey painted the
scenery, and the parts were played by English officers.   Outraged and indignant Continentals, to
whom came this heartless news must have deemed it
appropriate that the play was entitled *The Duce is*

in Them. Read of the climax of gayety, extravagance and pomp in that most singular of all entertainments in times of war — the *Meschianza,* in
which The Knights of the Blended Rose con-
tended with The Knights of the Burning Moun-
tain for laurels for their fair ones in one of the most
beautiful pageants ever seen in private life. André
proved he could do more than design millinery.
He planned the cards of invitation, he oversaw the
erection of vast pavilions, he painted yards upon
yards of satin and silk with designs of festoons of
flowers for the walls and ceilings of supper rooms
and ball-rooms, he made elaborate drawings of the
costumes.

After the tournament came costly fireworks, and
a supper of " 430 Covers, 1200 Dishes, 24 Black
Slaves in Oriental dresses with Silver Collars and
Bracelets ranged in 2 lines and bending to the ground
as the General and Admiral approached the Saloon."
We cannot help smiling a little at the thought of
poor André as he drilled the average " darky waiter "
of that day — twenty-four of them — until they were
full-fledged " Oriental black slaves."

It is curious to read that a faro-bank was set
up in a pavilion, and much enjoyed by the guests.
The decorations for this gaming-room were horns-
of-plenty — a singular choice.

Naturally all this extravagance and frivolity was
abhorrent to the Quaker citizens of Philadelphia;
but in truth, it was a very orderly affair — in spite
of the faro-bank and the liberal wine; the character
of the young ladies who took part in it absolutely

insured its being a perfectly respectable affair.   It
should also be noted that it had no sentimental sequence; not one of the Knights married one of their
chosen Ladies, though several found American wives
in other cities.

It was natural that men in the American army
should resent this warm participation by American

girls in English army
festivities; and an ef-
fort towards social pun-
ishment was made in
Philadelphia after the
American army were
conquerors;   patriotic
citizens tried to exclude
from social life all the
ladies who had taken
part in the Meschianza
and other British func-
tions; but when we
know that General
Benedict Arnold, the
American commanding
officer,   soon   became
affianced to fair Peggy
Shippen, one of André's

Mrs. Anne Jones.

dearest friends, we can see that such efforts were
short and futile.

New York girls had several years in which to flirt
with gallant redcoats and to display their most modish gowns; and several important marriages were
the result of the flirtations and the gowns.

There were plentiful balls given even in that shut-in city. The King's Birth-night Ball, the Queen's Birthnight Ball, the Coronation Ball; the rejoicings over the arrival of the third son of George III, Prince William Henry — "an amiable young prince"; there was no lack of occasion for gayety.

Rebecca Franks, a Philadelphia belle who was visiting shut-in New York in 1778, wrote thus of social life at that time : —

Mrs. Rebecca Blodget.   1790.

" You have no idea of the life of continued amusement I live in. I can scarce have a moment to myself. I have stole this while everybody is retired to dress for dinner. I am but just come from under Mr. J. Black's hands, and most elegantly dressed am I for a ball this evening at Smith's, where we have one every Thursday. . . . The dress is more rediculous and pretty than anything I ever saw — a great quantity of different colored feathers on the head at a time beside a thousand other things. The hair dressed very high, in the shape Miss Vining's was the night we returned from Smith's — the Hat we found in your Mother's closet wou'd be of a proper size. I have an afternoon cap with one wing, tho' I assure you I go less in the fashion than most of the ladies — not being dressed without a hoop."

The second great incentive to dress in those Revolutionary times was the presence of our French allies. Read of Newport during these years. Count de Rochambeau was fifty-five years old, but he entered all the merrymaking in Newport town as if he had been but twenty-five; and he records

Needle-wrought Lace Veil.

the gayety in that collection of letters in which English grammar affords but a poor conveyance for French courtesy. See the pretty face of Peggy Champlin with her "creped" hair, in "the French taste"; you can fancy her dancing "A Successful Campaign" with General Washington to the rollicking tune played by De Rochambeau and his suite. Nothing old or hallowed was spared by irreverent young American lasses in their desire to fascinate the Frenchmen. What of Miss Patty Parsons, who cut up the embroidered sky-blue satin waistcoat which had been worn by her grandfather at the English court; and who fashioned therefrom a

" Jocky " which was deemed " wondrous becoming."
A trooper's scarlet coat was made into a beautiful
jacket for a fair girl, and from the little pieces cut
from the coat-tails, lapels, etc., were fashioned a
perfectly fitting pair of warm winter gloves, bound
with gray squirrel fur which also furnished a collar
and cuffs for the jacket.   With a gray homespun
petticoat to match, Miss Virginia had a truly becoming dress ; her great grand-daughter copied it in 1864,
and from like materials and in like exigencies of war.

The term " macaroni " was just as familiar to New
York as to Lon-
don — in fact, it
had a more en-
during name and
fame because
"Yankee Doo-
dle stuck a
feather in his
hat and called it
Macaroni."   I
find macaroni
buttons adver-
tised, and maca-
roni ribbons,
and a macaroni

Embroidered Neckerchief.   1800.

hat ; a " macaroni waistcoat pattern " as early as
1771, and " macaroni velvet for waistcoats."   There
was a " Macaroni Purse " at the Jamaica races — a
purse for £100, and a " Macaroni Consort " was
given in the tavern parlor.   The type and the term
originated in 1770, when a number of idle young

Englishmen formed a Macaroni Club in London after having taken a "grand tour" in Italy. The name stood for all that was grotesque and extreme. The most marked characteristic of dress was the high-pointed peaked roll of craped and powdered hair that men and women both wore; and men as well as women wore great breast-knots of flowers.

There is no doubt but the presence in America of the wives of many of the English and German officers was a certain stimulus in dress. We know what a little court was held at times of quiet in the towns by that sweet woman, Baroness Riedésel; a woman whose presence in the British camp was a God-sent blessing in times of action.

Another woman of charm, whose fortunes and affections brought her to America during the Revolution was Lady Harriet Acland, or Ackland as it was sometimes spelled.

This interesting and beautiful young woman followed her gallant husband to America, where he served his king in the war with the colonies. She was a graceful, gracious creature; most charmingly dressed, aristocratic in her features and carriage; or, as said a contemporary, "the person of her ladyship was highly graceful and delicate, and her manners elegantly feminine." I have four portraits of her, all are models of fashion. The finest one is by Sir Joshua Reynolds, and is given on the opposite page; it hangs in the dining hall at "Killerton." One is in a white hood. All the high crises in her life seem to have been connected with America, and these form a series of striking scenes: her coming to America while her husband commanded the British troops during the Revolution ; his capture by the

Lady Harriet Acland.   By Sir Joshua Reynolds.

Continental army while wounded ; her trip overland to join him in the American camp ; her voyage in an open boat, accompanied by the chaplain, down the river, and her journey through the lines of the American forces, till she reached her husband. Major Acland, after the war, lost his life in a duel with an Englishman who called the Americans cowards — an extraordinary tribute to his former enemies.

The shock of his death deprived Lady Acland of her reason, but she recovered enough to marry the chaplain who had accompanied her on her gloomy journey into the camp of General Gates.

The wives of wealthy American officers followed their husbands to camp. Mrs. General Knox was among them — good natured, handsomely dressed, card-playing, fat. It was one of the scandals of the army — the money won and lost at her card-tables. Mrs. John Hancock was more cautious. John Adams wrote to his wife of her : —

Head of Lady Harriet Acland.

" She lives among a hundred men at this house, with modesty, decency, dignity, discretion. Her behavior is easy and genteel. In large and mixed company she is totally silent as a lady ought to be. But whether her eyes are so penetrating, or her attention so quick to the words, gestures, sentiments, looks, &c., of the company as yours would be — saucy as you are this way — I won't say."

"Dorothy Q." Hancock.

Mrs. Hancock was always charmingly dressed. Her portrait by Copley is given facing page 714. A letter exists, written by John Hancock to " Dorothy Q." before they were married, in which he tells of his gift to her of a box containing several pairs of silk and thread stockings, black satin shoes, black callimanco shoes, a very pretty light hat, a neat, airy summer cloak, two capes, and a fan — a very pretty " basket of gallantries," as Saint Simon would call it.

Embroidered Silk Apron.

Though women managed to have scarlet cloaks and feathered topknots, they suffered for petty things in war time. The lack of pins was much cried out upon during the Revolution.

During the scarcity of pins, various home-substitutes took their place; thorns from several thorn-trees were used ; and Franklin examined with inquisitive interest the spines of the prickly pear which General van Cortlandt informed him were used by poor folk instead of pins.

Women seemed absolutely lost without gauze. A high head-dress was a poor thing without it. Money orders and letters, such as lists of articles desired, were given to the masters of privateers, or to tradesmen setting forth for a capital city. The list would have a score of plain but important articles of dress, often shoes, but it would always end with " 3 yards of gaws " — gorz, or goz, or any conceivable or inconceivable spelling of the longed-for article. I have a letter written by a Rhode Island girl to her cousin, the master of a great sloop in the year 1773. It was evident that he, in some way, perhaps by aiding in seizure on the high seas, was in expectation of acquiring some articles of women's dress. She names to him the articles she desires from his stock, a scanty list, however : lutestring "ribands," three yards of scarlet broadcloth ; two pair callimanco shoes, two pair prunella shoes, and four yards of gauze. She closes her letter with this sentence: " The shoes can be spaired, if something must be foreborne ; or even the broadcloth ; but I must have the gauze. I shall be without a Head if you do not send it." The last alarming statement is really very simple ; head in those times meant head-dress.

Those years were the season of gauze. Gauze caps, bonnets, aprons, ribbons, and kerchiefs, were natural ; but cloaks and gowns of gauze, and flounced gauze petticoats seem not only somewhat frail for wear, but they were made things of ill construction by being trimmed with borders and edgings of chintz and calico. A sacque of blue and white copperplate calico, over a blue gauze petticoat, an apron of furbelowed gauze, straw ribbons, and green morocco slippers — this was a dress described by Mrs. John Adams in 1786.

At this period many cheap imitation jewels and

Mrs. Mercy Warren.

much cheap jewelry was worn with the gauze head-dresses. These jewels were often pretty things, and were worn by folk of great dignity. But people of corresponding position would not wear them to-day. Paste jewels were worn by all; and very handsome they were when set in shoe and knee buckles. These paste buckles we often find set with the imitation crystals and the highly polished forms of iron pyrites. This mineral was sold under the name "marcasite" (spelled also marquaset, marcaset, marcosett, marcassite, marchesite, and many other ways), was used for many ornaments, — ear-rings, pins, necklaces, hair ornaments. Another stone was mocho, known also as mocko, morko, mocus, mocchus; this was the dendritic agate or moss agate.

In a chapter entitled Daughters of Liberty, in my book, *Colonial Dames and Good-wives*, I have recounted at length the banding together of American girls and women in the years just previous to the Revolution in a determination to give up all imports from Great Britain except the necessaries of life.

Mercy Warren wrote to John Winthrop, in fine satire upon this resolution of American women to give up the imports of Great Britain, a list of the articles a woman would deem it imperative to retain for her use.

Patriotic Daughters of Liberty proved amply their ability to abstain from British luxuries; so Mrs. Warren's sneer never stung deeply, and is now dead forever. Her list remains of value, however, because it shows the articles of dress then worn by fashionable women. Each one is described and defined in my glossary of terms relating to dress, in my book entitled *Costume of Colonial Times.* Mrs. Warren knew well the dress of good society. Her own portrait is in high London taste. She is in the "dressed negligée" of her rhymes. This negligée is of Copley's favorite green blue tint, forming a fine study with a nasturtium-hung background. The Mechlin lace of her full engageants and her skimpy cap is still owned by her descendants. This negligée with its robings will be recognized as similar to the Levite worn by Mrs. Rudd. It is also almost precisely like the sacque worn by Mrs. Montague of Blue Stocking fame in her portrait by Sir Joshua Reynolds.

One of the inconsistencies of the times was the fact that portrait and miniature painting never ceased. In din of war, in time of siege, in lack of funds, almost of food, there were canvas and colors and men with brushes to use them. Copley's father-in-law was a loyalist, and with Copley and his children went to England in 1774, and never returned. But he painted steadily up to the time of his departure. Gilbert Stuart was in England. Trumbull was a soldier, and thus engaged; but he painted a little. John Woolaston was at work; Cosmo Alexander was in Rhode Island in 1772; Durand and Manly were in Virginia; and Smith in New York; Henry Bembridge in the Carolinas. In Philadelphia Matthew Pratt was painting, and James Peale (who painted chiefly miniatures), and Charles Willson Peale, though he was an officer in the army. Some of the latter's best work was done during the battle-swept years. Rembrandt Peale states that his father was painting a miniature of Washington when news was received of the surrender of Burgoyne.

In 1772 Charles Willson Peale wrote to his friend, Mr. Bordley, from Philadelphia, that he " had in hand one composition of Mr. Cadwalader, Lady and Child in half length which is greatly admired." It is here reproduced.

This painting is not as cold as most of Peale's work; and is a perfect presentation of the dress of the day, in every little detail; not "adjusted," as was often the dress of Copley's sitters. And it also may stand as the dress of the best people; for the Cadwaladers were leaders in Philadelphia social life.

General Cadwalader's daughter Frances married the Secretary to the British Legation, and became Lady Erskine. Her beautiful portrait by Stuart is also reproduced in these pages.

I will quote freely from the diary of Philip Fithian. He was a tutor in 1774 in the home of Robert Carter of " Nomini," a Virginian gentleman of wealth and hospitality, in whose home Fithian met the best of Virginian society. His pages are filled with the doings and sayings of Lees, Carters, Custises, Washingtons, Randolphs, Lanes, Byrds, Hales, and others. Here are some of his descriptions of the dress of Virginians : —

" Thursday, March 3. — Mr. Lane was dressed in black superfine broadcloth, gold-laced hat, laced ruffles, black silk stockings. With his Brooch on his bosom, he wore a Major's badge inscribed, ' Virtue and Silence,' cut in a golden medal. Certainly he was fine ! "

" Friday, June 24. — To-day Mr. Christian's dance takes place here. Miss Jenny Washington came also, and Miss Priscilla Hale while we were at breakfast. Miss Washington is about seventeen : She has not a handsome face, but is neat in her Dress, of an agreeable Size, & well proportioned, and has an easy winning Behaviour. She is not forward to begin a conversation, yet when spoken to she is extremely affable, without assuming any Girlish affectation, or pretending to be over-charg'd with Wit. She has but lately had an opportunity for Instruction in Dancing, yet she moves with propriety when she dances a *Minuet*, and without any *Flirts* or vulgar *Capers* when she dances a Reel or Country-dance."

" Her Dress is rich and well-chosen, but not tawdry, nor yet too plain : She appears to-day in a Chintz Cotton Gown with an elegant blue Stamp, a Sky-blue silk Quilt, and spotted, figured Apron. Her hair is a light brown ; it was crap'd up, with two rolls at each side, and on the top a small cap of beautiful Gauze and rich Lace, with an artificial flower interwoven."

" Mr. Christian very politely requested me to open the dance by stepping a *Minuet* with this amiable girl. I excused myself by assuring him that I never was taught to Dance. Miss Hale is about fourteen ; a slim puny silent Virgin. She has black Eyes, and black Hair, and a good set of Eye-Brows, which are esteemed in Virginia essential to Beauty. She looks innocent of every Human Failing, does not speak five Words in a Week, and I dare say from her Character that her Modesty is Invincible. She is dressed in a white Holland Gown, cotton, Diaper Quilt very fine, a Lawn Apron, has her Hair crap'd up, and on it a small Tuft of Ribbon for a Cap."

Fithian found the governess arrayed in " English dress " : —

" Her huge *Stays*, low *Head Dress*, enormous long *Waist*, was a Dress entirely contrary to the liking of Virginia Ladies. Her *Stays* are suited to come up to the upper part of her shoulders, almost to her Chin, and are swaithed around her as low as they possibly can be, allowing her hardly Liberty to walk at all.   To be sure this is a *vastly Modest* Dress."

Similar stays were worn by Miss Betsey Lee, a young lady who was getting on in years — she was twenty-five; it had been intimated to Fithian that she would make him a good wife, one with a penny in her pocket, too. He looked her over critically as he would a horse for purchase; *but he did not propose : —*

" She is a well-set Maid of a proper Height neither high nor low.   Her aspect when she is sitting is *Masculine* and *Dauntless*.   She sits very erect; she places her feet with great propriety; her Hands she lays carelessly in her Lap and never moves them but when she has occasion to adjust some article of her Dress or to perform some exercise with her Fan.   She has a full Face, sanguine Complection, her Nose rather protuberant than otherwise; her arms resemble those of Juno.   When she has a Bonnet on and walks she is truly elegant : Her Carriage neat and graceful; her Presence soft and beautiful.   Her Hair is a dark Brown, which was crap'd up very high & in it she had a Ribbon interwoven with an Artificial Flower.   At each of her Ears dangled a Brilliant Jewel.   She was pinched up *rather too near* in a pair of new fashioned Stays which, I think, are a Nuisance both to us and themselves.   For the late importation of Stays, said now to be most *fashionable* in *London*, are produced upwards so high we can scarce have any view at all of Lady's snowy necks and, on the contrary, they are extended downwards so low that whenever Ladies wear them, either young or old, have occasion to Walk, the motion necessary for Walking must, I think, cause a disagreeable Friction against the lower edge of the Stays which is so hard and unyielding. I imputed the *Flush* which was visible in her Face, to her being swaithed up, Body, Soul, and Limbs together in her Stays. She wore a light Chintz gown, very fine, with a blue stamp elegantly made, & which set well upon her; a blue silk Quilt: In one word her Dress was rich & fashionable; her Person abstracted from the Embellishments of Dress & Good Breeding, not much handsomer than the Generality of Women."

The mingling of cotton stuffs with silk materials, either gauze, silk or satin, was one of the characteristic fashions of the times. The daughter of General Huntington wrote at this date : —

" I have bought some callico for chints trimmings for old gowns, if you have any that you wish to wear short they are very fashionable at present, & gowns that are trimed with them should be made only to touch the ground, there is enough of the dark stripe for one gown, & enough of the light for one there should be enough white left on the dark stripe to turn down to prevent its *ravelling*. I gave 10 shillings for the callico & have been laughed at for my " foolish bargain " but I am not convinced that it is foolish. The William street merchants ask three shillings a yard for trimmings like the wide stripe & two for the narrow — I guess you will like the narrow."

Through the kind and intelligent helpfulness of families in Baltimore, I have portraits of a group of kinsfolk of the Johnson, Hopkinson, Coale, Duché, and Morgan families, which form a valuable exposition of the dress of people of culture, taste, and ample means of their days. The members of

Ancient Stays.

this cousinry, as Carlyle would call them, form a group of loving intimate folk whose letters are as good to read as their faces are good to see.

These letters and portraits of these vivacious Hopkinson women bring them very near to us; but I wish still more of their words had been preserved; they are like a lively spice in the very dull diet of everyday correspondence which we find in general.

A portrait of the father, Thomas Hopkinson, is given herein; he was a man of importance in the community, a judge. He was born in England, but came to America early in life and married Mary Johnson.

They had a family of children of great intelligence; all were musicians, some were artists — their descendants are both; the best known was Francis Hopkinson, called "the Signer," from his "signature of honour" on the Declaration of Independence. From their mother they inherited great delicacy of features, which in the men members of the family sometimes became too delicate — as in the case of Francis. President John Adams gives a lively picture of the "Signer":—

"He is liberally educated, a painter and poet. He is one of your pretty little curious ingenious men. His head is not bigger than a large apple. I have not met with anything in natural history more amusing and entertaining than his personal appearance, yet he is genteel and well bred and very social."

Facing this page I present the attractive face of his sister, Mary Hopkinson, who became the wife of Dr. John Morgan, the chief surgeon of the Continental army. She is robed in pink satin, with sable and pearls; and the brown and pink are a color-study. Pink gown, pink flowers, pink ribbon, pink cheeks; brown sable and brown lute, for she carries a lute in her hand, as became a member of a musical race. Her intelligent countenance is more indicative of intellect, perception, and thought than of the vivacity, frankness, and light heartedness which she possessed to a degree. Her proud husband, Dr. Morgan, wrote thus to her mother in 1775 of their journey from Philadelphia to Cambridge to join Washington's army:—

"Had Mrs. Morgan been a princess she might have been received with more pomp and magnificence, but not

Mary Hopkinson Morgan.

Dr. John Morgan. By Angelica Kauffmann.

with a heartier welcome. She is an excellent companion at
all times, but, if possible, excels herself in the road. She is
full of spirits. Our horses are gentle as lambs, and yet perform most admirably, and we are truly happy that notwithstanding the heavy rain she escaped getting wet. It would
delight you to get a glimpse of us now — the Colonel at the
violin and she at the harpsichord and singing most sweetly."

Doctor Morgan's portrait is given facing page 724.
It is one of the few portraits of Americans painted
by Angelica Kauffmann. He was a handsome man,
and the artist said he was the best-dressed man she
had ever known. This tribute has an interest and
value in a history of costume, for we may then
assume that his dress was in full fashion. A handsome dress it is, exceedingly well cut and well fitting.

Occasionally we have the pleasure of having proof
that a portrait is in the true dress of the wearer.
Here is an extract from a letter written by Thomas
Duché in London to his aunt, Mrs. John Morgan,
in Philadelphia. He had studied with Sir Benjamin
West and had painted an exquisite portrait of Esther
Duché, his sister.

" I have entrusted to the care of Dr. De Normandie the
portrait of my sister, which I beg you and my Uncle would
accept. I have painted it in her present dress thinking it
would be most agreeable. It is generally thought very like.
I would not send it without Mr. West's approbation and
he is very particular in those of my pictures that are going
to Philadelphia. . . .

                    " Your affectionate
                        " Nephew,
                                " T. Duche.
" 9th June, 1783."

Notwithstanding the vicissitudes of war we learn of some rich wardrobes. An inventory of the wardrobe of Lord Stirling shows him to have had forty-three pairs of breeches, some being of claret color, scarlet or crimson cloth; some were gold-laced and others were of figured velvet; thirty-one coats, some of white or cinnamon silk, and also coats of cloth of every color; fifty-eight waistcoats, of rainbow hues and rich materials and ornamentation; thirty shirts; a hundred and nineteen pair of hose, mostly silk; fifty-four cravats, twenty pair of boots and shoes; and but two pair of gloves. His head-gear is not named. There must have been other lists with hat and gloves; for gloves were universally worn. We know how punctilious Washington was about them.

The attire of the signers of the Declaration of Independence showed no Republican simplicity. The dress of John Hancock was ever of richest material and striking colors; his scarlet velvet suit is still preserved in the Boston State House, possibly the same he wore when he was declared Governor on October 26, 1780, though by William Pyncheon that was called "a suit of crimson velvet-plain." His dress upon an important occasion when he desired to make an impression, and yet not to appear over-carefully dressed, was thus described: —

"He wore a red velvet cap within which was one of fine linen, the last turned up two or three inches over the lower edge of the velvet. He also wore a blue damask gown lined with velvet, a white stock, a white satin embroidered waistcoat, black satin small-clothes, white silk stockings and red morocco slippers."

Esther Duché.

There is no doubt that the influence of Washington largely helped to promote a love of dignified and fine outward appearance. In a degree Washington's attitude to the new nation as to dress was that of Winthrop to the new country, New England.

Orderly and handsome dress was imperative for men in office and authority, that they and the nation should stand well in the eyes of other peoples, that they should impress the simpler of their own folk.

We find him in 1747, when a lad of fifteen, making this careful note for a tailor : —

" Memorandum. To have my coat made by the following Directions, to be made a Frock with a Lapel Breast. The Lapel to contain on each side six Button Holes & to be about 5 or 6 inches wide all the way equal, & to turn as the Breast on the Coat does, to have it made very long Waisted and in Length to come down to or below the bent of the knee, the Waist from the Armpit to the Fold to be exactly as long or Longer than from thence to the Bottom, not to have more than one fold in the Skirt and the top to be made just to turn in and three Button Holes, the Lapel at the top to turn as the Cape of the Coat and Button to come parallel with the Button Holes and the Last Button Hole on the Breast to be right opposite the Button on the Hip."

We have seen the detailed orders for rich attire which he sent to England for the dress of his wife's children, when they were but six and seven years old. Even after the Revolution certain articles of dress were ordered in London.

Just as he set out to ride to Massachusetts on public duties in 1756, he sent a handsome order to London, for livery for his servants. He wished " 2 complete livery suits with a spare cloak, and all other necessary linings for two suits more." " I would have you," he writes, " choose the livery by our arms, only as the field is white, I think the

Martha Washington.

clothes had better be not quite so, but nearly like the enclosed. The trimmings and facings of scarlet, and a scarlet waistcoat. If livery lace is not disused, I should be glad to have the cloaks laced. I like that fashion best and the silver-laced hats." He ordered also handsome " horse-furniture," with crests on the housings ; and for his own wear three handsome scarlet sword-knots, and three others of blue and silver, and a fashionable gold-laced hat. His insistence that each article be " fashionable," that he has the very latest modes, appears in every letter in his many years of London orders.

A long letter of Washington's has been preserved, which he wrote to a nephew, George Steptoe Washington. All its pages are worthy of Chesterfield in expression, and far excel that English master of deportment in moral and æsthetic values. His words on dress deserve quotation — and remembrance — by all. I have been told that much heed was paid to them by his young kinsfolk, and profound observance of his wishes : —

" Decency and cleanliness will always be the first objects in the dress of a judicious and sensible man. — A conformity to the prevailing fashion in a certain degree is necessary — but it does not follow from thence that a man should always get a new coat, or other clothes, upon every trifling change in the mode, when, perhaps, he has two or three very good ones by him. — A person who is anxious to be a leader of the fashion, or one of the first to follow it, will certainly appear, in the eyes of judicious men, to have nothing better than a frequent change of dress to recommend him to notice. — I would always wish you to appear sufficiently decent to entitle you to admission into any company where you may be : — but I cannot too strongly enjoin it upon you — and your own knowledge must convince you of the truth of it — that you should be as little expensive in this respect as you properly can ; — you should always keep some clothes to wear to Church, or on particular occasions, which should not be worn every day."

It is strange, perhaps, to find Washington dwelling so much on these superficial things during the solemn days of his vast responsibility and great apprehension, in the early days of the Revolution, and even in the first racking years of the Republic, but great things and petty jostle each other, nay, keep close company, in this strange and small world of ours. On the Fourth of July, 1776, the day whereon Thomas Jefferson signed that great creation in the formation of which his brain had such a part, — the Declaration of Independence; on that ever-to-be-remembered day of days of his whole life, his sole entry in his day-book and in his own " Signer's " hand is this item : " For Seven pair of Womens Gloves, 20 shillings."

Thus does a woman's glove lie lightly, yet close to the tremendous document which changed the fate of nations, yes — of the whole world. I can find no better symbol to illustrate the importance of the subject of this my book.

CHAPTER XXX

FIRST YEARS OF NATIONAL LIFE

" *I cannot forgive a girl who is not pleased with dress, and does not dress to please.*" —— DOROTHY QUINCY HANCOCK, 1780.

" *Lady Teazle : Lud, Sir Peter, would you have me be out of the fashion?*
Sir Peter : The fashion, indeed ! What had you to do with fashion before you married me?"
"School for Scandal," SHERIDAN.

General Cadwalader, Wife, and Child.

CHAPTER XXX

N 1784 John Adams was sent by the United States as its first minister to England. Mrs. Adams, keen-sighted, quick-witted, with ready tongue and pen, sent many a record of English and French fashions across seas to her sisters, cousins, and friends, and happily her letters were preserved. It was her testimony, as it was that of other Americans who visited London at that time (and of English folk who visited America), that, with the exception of court functions, dress was less regarded and rich dress less universal in England than America. She writes on July 24, 1784 : —

"I am not a little surprised to find dress, unless on public occasions, so little regarded here. The gentlemen are very plainly dressed, the ladies much less so than with us. 'Tis true you must put a hoop on and have your hair dressed, but a common straw hat, no cap, with only a ribbon on the crown is thought sufficient dress to go into company. I have seen many ladies but not one elegant one since I came. There is not that neatness in their appearance which you see in our ladies."

This last statement of Mrs. Adams finds abundant corroboration in the testimony both of French

and English travellers in this country; the one
universal subject of their admiration was the neatness, the cleanliness, of American women. I am
not surprised that they found them neat. I am
surprised that it appeared to them so unusual that
they all noted it. I could give a score of examples.
I will simply quote a Hessian officer's opinion: —

" They are great admirers of cleanliness, and keep themselves well shod. They friz their hair every day and gather
it up on the back of the head into a chignon, at the same
time puffing it up in front. They generally walk about
with their heads uncovered, and sometimes but not often,
wear some light fabric on their hair. Now and then some
country nymph has her hair flowing down behind her,
braided with a piece of ribbon. Should they go out, even
though they be living in a hut, they throw a silk wrap
about themselves and put on gloves."

This is not, unfortunately, all he says of American women; he tempers his praise with a decided
report of extravagance. He runs on: —

" The daughters keep up their stylish dressing because
the mothers desire it. Should the mother die, her last
words are to the effect that the daughter must retain control of the father's money-bags. Nearly all articles necessary for the adornment of the female sex are at present
either very scarce or dear, and for this reason they are now
wearing their Sunday finery."

This accusation of extravagance was too true;
a love of dress ran riot in the new nation. It was
regarded with serious apprehension by all thoughtful citizens, who saw in it a serious menace to the

Nellie Custis.

establishment of such a social life and such public conditions as had been desired by the nation's founders.

Franklin, economical by nature, plain by choice, and frugal by habit, never ceased his warning words. His own dress could not be plainer, but he endeavored to restrain that of his family. He bade his daughter eschew feathers and to choose calicoes instead of silk. For Washington, who loved fine dress, and had ever worn it, it was harder to preach simplicity; but he bravely wore native-made and home-reared cloth; and his wife wore domestic products, and we find her knitting and netting, weaving cloth at home, using up old materials.

Mrs. Joseph Hopper Nicholson.

Foreign economists were severe in their criticisms. The Count de Rochambeau asserted that the wives of American merchants and bankers were clad to the top of the French fashions. Brissot de Warville deplores it as a great misfortune that in republics, women should sacrifice so much time to " trifles." He says : —

" At Mr. Griffin's house, at dinner, I saw seven or eight women, all dressed in great hats, plumes, etc. It was with pain that I remarked much of pretension in some of these women; one acted the giddy, vivacious; another the woman of sentiment. This last had many pruderies and grimaces. Two among them had their bosoms very naked. I was scandalized at this indecency among republicans."

Mrs. Adams tells that the extreme of London fashion was "sapphire blue satin waists spangled with silver, and lace down the back and seams with silver, and white satin petticoats trimmed with rows of black and blue velvet ribbons." She described her own dress as a sapphire blue "*demisaison*," trimmed with black lace; a petticoat flounced with crape edged with blue ribbon leaves, and with black velvet ribbon spotted with steel beads; a cap with wreath of blue ribbon, white flowers, a blue feather, and a black feather.

Elizabeth Russell Johnson.

The tightly frizzed hair and a puffed-out fichu, called a buffont, were the only parts of the dress that stood out. This buffont was confined by the bodice

Marcia Burns, of Washington, D.C. Married John Van Ness, M.C.
from N.Y.

and puffed out above like the breast of a pouter pigeon. In 1784, in the Salem newspapers, " Thread and Net Buffonts " and " Gauze Buffons " were

Mrs. Abigail Adams Smith.

advertised. The portrait of Mrs. Adams's daughter, Mrs. Smith, shows a very moderate buffont.

I have seen several breadths and bits of brocade which were worn by Mrs. Adams; all were tasteful and handsome. One had been cut up into covers for pocket-books. One is given on page 495 as a background for several handsome fans which she owned and carried.

The brocades of these years were very bold in colors and contrasts. I have one with a pink ground with scattered scarlet roses with scant brown foliage and beautiful brown stems; this is intertwined with white roses with curious blue-green stems and foliage. It is a bold combination, and a successful one. A gown of Mrs. John Jay's in the New Haven Historical Society building has white stripes and a scarlet-berried vine on a stripe of purplish pink, a true orchid tint. These striking contrasts were made endurable by the perfection of each tone of color and by the richness of material. A calico in such gay hues would suit only a savage. At one time green morocco shoes were worn with costumes of all colors, which was more endurable than the purple shoes which followed.

Embroidered Plum-colored Crape. Worn by Mrs. John Adams.

Mrs. Adams was exceedingly neat and trim in

Mrs. Robert Gilmour.

dress; as exact in that as in other relations of life. She dressed simply in her home, for John Adams was never rich. A gown of hers, worn probably about 1825, is of soft, fine, plum-colored Chinese crape, embroidered in silk, made with great simplicity.

The following account of the Inauguration Ball, given in April, 1789, has been frequently quoted. It was written by a man — one Colonel Stone.

" Few jewels were then worn in the United States; but in other respects, the dresses were rich and beautiful, according to the fashions of the day. One favorite dress was a plain celestial blue satin gown, with a white satin petticoat. On the neck was worn a very large Italian gauze handkerchief, with border stripes of satin. The head-dress was a *pouf* of gauze, in the form of a globe, the *creneaux* or head-piece of which was composed of white satin, having a double wing, in large plaits, and trimmed with a wreath of artificial roses, falling from the left at the top to the right at the bottom, in front, and the reverse behind. The hair was dressed all over in detached curls, four of which, in two ranks, fell on each side of the neck, and were relieved behind by a floating *chignon*. Another beautiful dress was a perriot, made of gray Indian taffeta, with dark stripes of the same color — having two collars, the one yellow, and the other white, both trimmed with a blue silk fringe, and a reverse trimmed in the same manner. Under the perriot was worn a yellow corset or boddice, with large cross stripes of blue. Some of the ladies with this dress wore hats *à l'Espagnole*, of white satin, with a band of the same material placed on the crown, like the wreath of flowers on the head-dress above mentioned. This hat, which, with a plume, was a very popular article of dress, was relieved on the left side, having two handsome cockades — one of which was at the top, and the other at the bottom.   On the neck was worn a very large plain gauze handkerchief, the ends of which were hid under the bodice."

The dress worn by Mrs. Oliver Ellsworth in her portrait in this book is a perriot.   It had tight sleeves, and flared open over a petticoat.   Sometimes it had lapels and collars, and was much more elaborately trimmed, and had a sacque back.

Colonel Stone noted little jewelry ; but bracelets were deemed very elegant, especially when set with miniatures, or locks of hair.

In 1780 Mrs. George Washington wrote to the artist Peale: "I send my miniature pictures to you and request the favour of you to get them set for me.   I would have them as bracelets to wear round the wrist.   I would have the three set exactly alike and all the same size."   One of these may be the very bracelet seen upon her friend Mrs. Morris's wrist.   A number of Peale's oil portraits — that of Mrs. Walter Stewart, for instance (on page 589) — show the sitter wearing similar bracelets.

I must not fail to speak of the dress of college undergraduates ; and I will give Harvard as an example.   They were under as stiff control as are boys in our great public schools like Saint Paul, Groton, and Andover to-day.   In less than twenty years after Harvard College was founded these rules were prescribed.

" No Schollar shal goe out of his chamber without a Gown, Cloak, or Coat; and everyone everywhere shal were modest and sober Habits, without strange, ruffian-like, or new-fangled fashions, without all lavish Dress, or excess of Apparel whatsoever, nor shal wear any Gold or Silver or jewels without the just permission of the Precident, nor shal it be permitted to wear Long Haire, Locks, Foretops, Curlings, Crispings, Partings, or Powderings of ye Haire."

The Oxford gown was always in favor with the governing body as dress for "publick occasions." At varying intervals strict rules were made; but considerable latitude was given the graduating class in 1748, where one of the Sirs appeared in a rich suit of satin and velvet. In 1784 the coat could be blue gray; the waistcoat could be black, nankeen, or olive green. Freshmen must then wear plain buttonholes; juniors might wear inexpensive frogs but not on their cuffs; the senior was glorious in buttonholes, buttons and frogs *ad libitum*. For many years all decorations of gold and silver lace, cord or edging on hats or waistcoats were fined; in 1816 the fine was not more than $1.60 nor less than thirty cents for each offence.

A century ago a nightgown was permitted except on "the Sabbath, on exhibition, or on other occasions where undress would be improper" — this last rule as late as 1822.

The student's necktie must be black or white — what a trial! — his hat or cap black also; and black shoes and boots must be worn. A senior might wear mourning if necessary. It is interesting to read that in 1768, in Liberty Days, the whole class graduated in homespun and home-made suits — that they might "take their degrees dressed in the manufactures of the country."

CHAPTER XXXI

THE TURN OF THE CENTURY

" In your apparel be modest, and endeavor to accommodate nature rather than procure admiration.   Keep to the fashion of your equals, such as are civil and orderly with respect to time and place.

" Play not the peacock, looking everywhere about you to see if you be well decked, if your shoes fit well, if your stockings sit neatly, and clothes handsomely."

> — " Rules of Courtesy and Decency of Behaviour,"
> GEORGE WASHINGTON.

CHAPTER XXXI

THE TURN OF THE CENTURY

T is well to recall a few of the important conditions and events of the year 1800, as they have a bearing on social life; and their influence is seen in details of costume. In fact, if ever events controlled costume, they did at this turn of the century. It was not a time of elegance or of high-minded and great aims; and life was reflected in dress, which was insignificant.

Rose Bertin and her tirewomen and sempstresses had left France, and were in London. This wonderful woman for years swayed the modes in Paris to a degree wholly unknown in any other person, time, or place in the history of costume. She brought French fashions to England; curiously also through her stay French fashions showed English influences.

It is interesting to read in French histories of dress while Franklin was so popular in the court that "everything American became the vogue." I cannot discover, however, that any "American fashions" were really copied; though straw hats seem to have been regarded as American.

There was a certain tempering of French institution through American ideas. American books were translated into French, not only the writings of Thomas Paine, but political treatises and patriotic poems. Plays with American characters were popular in France. Paine had become a citizen of France; and Franklin's long sojourn there made his name a household word among Frenchmen; at his death public mourning was worn. The Order of the Cincinnati had many Frenchmen enrolled, Frenchmen of great names.

Colonel Brown.

To show the reflex influences at this time we can cite the cockade. Cockades had been, like everything else, originally a French fashion. We have seen them adopted as an important part of the uniform by the Continental army. In turn, Desmoulins, early in the French Revolution, urged France to follow America in adopting a significant and widely worn cockade, the tricolor. When at the turn of the century French influences became so powerful in America, this tricolor French cockade became part of the dress of American citizen and citizeness. In opposition the black cockade of the soldiers of the American Revolution was seized eagerly in 1798 as the symbol of the Federalists.

In America, at this turn of the century, matters seemed in a pretty bad way ; the rage for gambling

Mrs. James Monroe.

and the prevalence of lotteries had had a blasting effect; speculation and jobbery had become regular trades. Many came to doubt the wisdom of separation from England. The yellow fever had afflicted the seaports for years, and lessened their commerce, already subjected to one benumbing embargo, and soon to be by another. American ships were preyed upon and pillaged on the high seas by ships of all nations; ship-masters and ship-owners were desperate.   The shocking and universal prevalence of duelling alarmed all thoughtful folk; it appeared to timid folk that all the really great statesmen, soldiers, lawyers, gentlemen, would kill off each other. And a great sadness had come to all in the death of Washington at the close of the year; he died in December, 1799. Every American was asked to wear a badge of crape; nearly all did so.   Dwellings were hung in black; newspapers were black

St. George Tucker.

bordered. The bells tolled dismally and long in every town. I have seen mourning-badges, cockades, collarettes, sashes, belts, slippers, and gloves which were worn after Washington's death.   Mourning-handkerchiefs stamped with his portrait and bearing words of his virtues were sold in large numbers. " Funeral pieces " in memory of him appeared in china, glass, leather, marble, brass, bronze, pewter, paper, cloth, wood, with emblems and words of patriotic grief.

Oliver Ellsworth and Wife.

We have in America an unusual record of certain details of costume at the close of the eighteenth and beginning of the nineteenth century. It is not a depiction of the entire costume — it is the indoor wear only, and the head and shoulders only; but it is of both men and women. It comes to us through the eight hundred and more likenesses of Americans by Saint Memin, which have been preserved for us in a collection. Let me relate the story of these portraits.

A French artist, Charles Baltha-zar Julien Fevret de Saint Memin, and his father Étienne, French refugees, men of birth and education, came to America in 1797. They had passed through great vicissitudes in France, having turned a hand at many trades besides those of soldier, artist, and gentleman; and they had had to fly. After sore straits and short commons in many American

Walter Ormsby.

towns and at last in New York, the younger Saint Memin, having distinct mechanical skill, constructed a machine, the like of which had been the mode in France since 1786 — a machine for taking a portrait, a " physionotrace "; by it an exact profile of the sitter could be made, life size. By another machine, called a pantograph, this perfect profile could be reduced to any size. This reduced profile Saint Memin then engraved on copper, filling in the outline with shading and added lines of likeness, using another machine of his invention, a roller, for the

shading. So constant was the industry of Saint
Memin, so deft his hand, that he was able to sell,
and at profit, the original drawing (which was life
size) in black crayon on red paper neatly framed,
the copper plate of reduced size, and twelve prints
from this plate, all for $33.

Saint Memin spent two years in New York;
thence in 1798 to Burlington; to Philadelphia in
1803; to Baltimore in 1804; then in 1808 to Richmond and Norfolk. In 1809 he fared to Charleston; again to New York in 1810. These dates of
his wanderings afford probable dates of the execution of the various profiles. In all these cities sitters were plentiful, and welcome was warm. When
he left America in 1814, he carried to France with
him a record of all the portraits he had taken, and a
copy of the plates, each with a name and number;
many with a date of execution.

Saint Memin died in 1850, and a Mr. Robertson
bought all his plates and brought them to New York
and placed them on exhibition and sale. In the
passing years many individuals and families had lost
their plates and prints by various accidents. Some
had a print, but had forgotten or lost the name of
the sitter; so the display of these several hundred
pictures of the aristocracy of the early years of the
century was, as one wrote at the time, "like the
resurrection of the dead." It is easy to imagine
the glad recognition, the infinite sentiment, which
came through the return of these pictures to
America. In 1850 persons living still remembered
the face of their grandparents of 1800, and rejoiced

C. S. Konig.
L. Triplett.

T. Edlitz.
Guy L. Trigg.

in a new possession of their portraits. But it is not this view of the pictures which makes them memorable to us; it is that they afford a perfect record of the dress of head and shoulders of folk of that day; for all are what was then termed "in busto," and of the same size, a perfect circle a trifle over two inches in diameter. All save two are in profile.

None of the men wear hats. In the first five years they wear their hair powdered in various-shaped cues and loops and braids and twists as to the back hair, in curls as to the front; and some wear wigs.

It is often difficult to discern in these portraits whether the natural hair is dressed to imitate a wig, or the wig designed to appear like natural hair. A lock of thick, false hair could be tied with the natural hair to increase the thickness of the cue, which was often turned up in a loop. Sometimes it was braided and turned up like the Cadogan braid worn recently by women.

When the natural hair was carefully " buckled " in a neat, trim roll, and shaped on the forehead advantageously to the contour of the face; when it was kept in trim order and neatly powdered, it was a beautiful and becoming mode of dressing men's hair; far more elegant and more becoming than our modern tight clippings. In this form, if unpowdered, I deem it the very handsomest shape of masculine hair-dressing ever known. Its beauty and fitness are shown on the head of Washington; and to fullest extent in the portrait of Major André, given on page 700. Of course all men are not as handsome as André, but many would be much handsomer were their hair dressed as his is.

The later prints of Saint Memin show natural hair, much longer than it is worn to-day, and as dishevelled as a foot-ball player's, yet studiously so:

the curls at the side brought carefully forward as shown upon Washington Allston and others in these pages.   These heads *à la Brutus*, or *à la Titus*, "like a frightened owl," seemed rude enough after the great stately periwigs or Washington's cue and powder and ribbon.   Another style of hair-cutting seen on young American pates was *en oreilles de chien*, such as was worn by General Bonaparte at the time of the Italian campaign; the hair "banged" at the eyebrows straight across, and left long at the sides to cover the ears.   Exact like-ness is claimed for these Saint Memin portraits ; but I wish to call attention to

F. Beale.

one marked characteristic which I regard with sus-picion.   In the whole six hundred male portraits, but *one* displays a distinctly bald head.   "Mad-dison" is thus stigmatized.   One other old gentle-man has a thinly thatched pate ; the others all have abundant locks.   Can this have been a true record ? If so, what a cruel change has a century brought. The pictures of six hundred prominent men of these cities to-day, of the ages of Saint Memin's sitters, would display at least nine-tenths with bald heads. Those Saint Memin portraits would be one testi-

mony to the truth of the notion that baldness comes
from close cropping the hair; for these eighteenth-
century men had all worn long hair; hair infrequent
of clipping or cutting.

French influences are plainly seen in the shape of
the details of men's attire in these Saint Memin

Washington Allston in Youth.

portraits. Examine French portraits of the period;
look, for instance, at the familiar portrait of Robes-
pierre; look at the dress of the Incroyables. They
were the Republicans of France — so they asserted.
Their aim was extremity of dress. They wore the
highest collars, the biggest puffed cravats, the heaviest sticks, and deemed these fashions so English.
You can see readily from whence came the high-
collared coats and choking neck-cloths which

surrounded the gasping throats of these sturdy
American Republicans. The thin throats and
necks of Frenchmen were better fitted for this
attire than the stout towers and double chins of
Americans. A strangely supercilious look is seen
on many of these Saint Memin likenesses; the head
is held like a camel's, with lip and chin high in the
air. Judge not the fathers for this demeanor;
they really did not mean to be proud; they carried
nose and chin high because they couldn't help it;
the swaddling bands of cambric and lawn, the "pudding," forced them into that carriage.

Southey says in his *Commonplace Book* that
"pudding-cravatts" were invented originally by
some one to hide a poulticed throat. So desirable
was a large-chested effect that coats were padded
to that appearance, and several waistcoats were worn
at the same time.

By 1809 we find a stiff standing collar (called a
dicky in New England) on the necks of all men,
worn with or without the full pudding cravat. The
shirt-frill still continued to be worn. I have portraits wherein a full finely-pleated shirt-frill, a jabot-
shaped chitterling, a pudding cravat, and a dicky
can be seen on one unfortunate wearer. When the
waistcoat stood up fiercely outside this wear, and
an ear-high coat-collar was a wall over all, no wonder men complained that they could not turn their
heads or move their necks a half a degree. It seems
to me a period of exceptional discomfort for men.

One coat which was very fashionable had long,
narrow tails which were twice as long as the waist

portion, which had two rows each of nineteen brilliant buttons. The coat was named "Jean de Bry," for a French statesman. Morning and evening coats were shaped exactly alike till 1830, when a frock-coat was evolved. Overcoats had fur collars, full skirts, and very tight bodies. In 1832 many men wore a picturesque Polish cloak with double cape. The year 1800 saw the invention and introduction

Mrs. Bell.

of rights and lefts in shoes by the fashionable bootmaker William Young of Philadelphia. He advertises these varieties of foot-gear in the *Aurora* of 1801: " Plover and snipe toes, cock and hen toes, goose and gander toes, gosling toes, hog and bear snouts, ox and cow mouths, shovel and stick nose, and others too tedious to mention : Suwarrows, Cossacks, hussars, Carrios, double-tongues, Bonapartes, greaves, fire-buckets, Swiss hunting, full-dress, walking, York."

This year shoe-blacking and polish were first introduced. Ere that " blackball " had been used, made of lamp-black, suet, and tallow, or "dubbing." This greasy mixture ruined ladies' petticoats in dancing.

I have alluded to Eliza Southgate's letters. We

Mrs. Charles Cotesworth Pinckney.

have in them many descriptions of the dress worn by Saint Memin's sitters, for it was in that circle of New York life that the short married years of this fair young girl were spent. She was a lovely, gentle girl, born in Portland, of New England gentlefolk ; going to well-known schools in Massachusetts, visiting the best people; leading a happy, natural life, which she told in a happy, natural way in her letters. On a driving tour to Saratoga, in the year 1798, she met Walter Bowne, a member of an influential and wealthy family of New York and Flushing ; and soon she was married to him. She died

Eliza Southgate Bowne.

when but twenty-four years old. Her letters, preserved sacredly by her daughter, were published in the year 1870 through the affection of a loving and worthy custodian, the late Mrs. Walter Bowne Lawrence of Flushing, Long Island. After their publication Mrs. Lawrence gave me a copy of a miniature of Eliza Southgate which is not in the published book. It is shown on this page. In it the pretty girl wears the wig to which she refers in her letters.

A pretty mode, seen in Madam Scott's portrait
and others by Copley and Stuart, has a high band
of gauze or a ruche around the bare neck. This
with a very low gown has a most charming effect,
becoming to old and young, especially to elderly
women, who thus covered the ugly first lines of old
age, shown ever
under the chin.
Mrs. Madison's
portrait, painted
in old age, proves
her shrewd atten-
tion to this fact.
A fashion note
of the year 1805
reads thus : —

Mrs. James Bowdoin. By Gilbert Stuart.

"Ruffs are much
worn. They are
narrower, but in-
stead of two or three
falls of lace or
worked muslin, our
elegantes now wear
six or seven. The
effect is really ridiculous; but they are fashionable, and a
French woman considers nothing unbecoming or absurd
that is tonish. The double fall of lace at the wrist has
disappeared."

This fine portrait of Mrs. James Bowdoin shows
one of these double ruffs. As the short-waisted
gown was then very plain, this elaborate ruff was
an agreeable addition to its simplicity.

Lorenzo Dow.

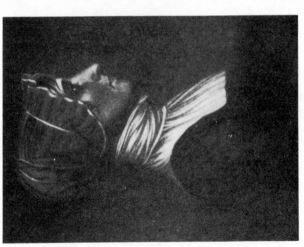

Peggy Dow.

In a single entry in a newspaper of the year 1801, namely: " Perkale and Linen Gloves," is a clew to a detail of fashion which was most strongly accented about the year 1815. I mean the covering of the hand. The cuffs of men's coats hung over the tips of their fingers; the sleeves of women's gowns did likewise. Often long detached sleeves were finished at the hand in a sort of mitt. As early as 1770 linen gloves had been worn, long gloves like sleeves reaching to the shoulder and cut at the hand to leave only the finger-tips exposed; these sometimes were of kid; a pair of plum-colored embroidered kid mitts is given which were worn by Mrs. Robbins, the mother of Caria Robbins. Young girls had glove-bees;

Bolivar Hat.

they met and cut out and made gloves together. A favorite material for these mitts for children's wear was of nankeen. These were tied to the short sleeves of the calico dress, or the spencer. Often these were matched with nankeen pantalets. Stiffly starched for fresh Sunday wear, these clean nankeen or linen mitts must have been trying indeed to a child during the long hours of a New England Sabbath service on a hot summer day.

These sleeves were never so long, however, as the deep cuffs of the sixteenth century given by Viollet-

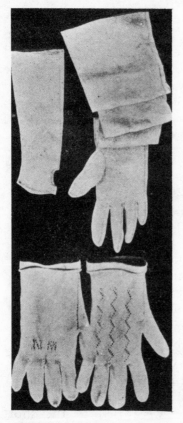

Home-made Linen and Wool Gloves.

le - Duc — cuffs which hung down fourteen inches longer than the hand, thus proving that the wearer never worked.

Eliza Southgate Bowne bore testimony as to these mitts of her day. She wrote in 1803 : —

"Long sleeves are very much worn, made like mitts ; crosswise, only one seam and that in the back of the arm, and a half-drawn sleeve over and a close, very short one up high, drawn up with a cord."

Peter Parley says the women of 1801 wore gowns " close and short-waisted, the breast and shoulder being covered by a full muslin kerchief. Girls ornamented themselves with a large white Vandyke."

We have many portraits of the gowns of these wearers, both simple and rich ; those of the eccentric preacher Lorenzo Dow and his wife Peggy are as good examples of everyday country dress as could be given.

CHAPTER XXXII

THE EVOLUTION OF PANTALOONS AND PANTALETS

> " *Time was when clothing sumptuous or for use*
> *Save their own painted skins, our sons had none.*
> *As yet black breeches were not ; satin smooth*
> *Or velvet soft, or plush with shaggy pile.*"
>
> — "The Task," WILLIAM COWPER.

CHAPTER XXXII

THE EVOLUTION OF PANTALOONS AND PANTALETS

HEN the first settlers came to Virginia and New England, Englishmen's nether garments were in the last stages of a great transformation. The doublet and hose of Tudor times were being laid aside for knee-breeches and stockings. For nearly two hundred years these small-clothes continued to be men's universal wear until, with the closing years of the eighteenth century, trousers became the important question of costume; in the nineteenth century they were adopted. In broad classification we may give the seventeenth and eighteenth centuries to the wear of breeches, and the nineteenth to trousers.

The assumption of both breeches and trousers met with violent opposition; the first bombasted breeches of the reigns of Henry VIII and Elizabeth were so extreme that I cannot wonder they were hated, and that good, sensible, old English gentlemen regarded the dignified gown with long hose as far more suitable and decorous wear.

It must not be forgotten, however, that the ancient Britons, the Anglo-Saxons, and Danes had worn trousers, or something they deemed trousers. I would a London tailor of to-day could behold a pair of them.

The celebrated Bayeux tapestry shows us these ancient trousers; some reaching to the knee, and others to the ankles — the latter held with cross-bandaging. Unshapely as they were, they made an attire of courtly elegance compared with the dress of the rich Irish gentlemen of that day — and indeed for centuries later. Portraits of Irish soldiers and noblemen in full armor with rich buff-coats reaching not half-way to the knees, and with legs and feet absolutely bare, afford a caricature far more ridiculous than any limner could have imagined — the head and shoulders rich in steel and velvet, the feet squalid in dirt.

Thomas Teach, the Pirate.
Blackbeard.

At all times some form of trousers had been known and worn by English workingmen. Laborers in the fields, workers on plantations in America, wore what were known in colonial days as skilts and tongs. They were of coarse tow, and in the Southern states of "negro cloth," or "native-cloth," or "Virginia tow."

In *Margaret*, written by Sylvester Judd, we read of a period previous to the Revolution: —

" The boys were dressed in tongs, a name for pantaloons or overalls that had come into use."

" They wore checked shirts and a sort of brown trousers known as skilts. These were short, reaching just below the knee, and very large, being a full half yard broad at the bottom ; and without braces or gallows were kept up by the hips, sailor fashion."

It is plain that these skilts or tongs were the universal wear of farmers in hot weather. Tight breeches were ill adapted for farm work. John Adams, writing in 1774, in depression of spirits over the lingering war says, " A frock and trousers, spade and hoe, will do for my remaining days. I am melancholy and anxious."

Sailors wore trousers, wide like "petticoat - breeches " ; these reached to the knee. I give a copy of the print

The Sailor and his Sweetheart.

of the pirate Thomas Teach, or Blackbeard, dated 1736, with a bare-footed trousered sailor in the

background.   Blackbeard is really as ideal a pirate
as ever scuttled ship; with his score of pistols fes-
tooned in fringes around him, his burning match
serving as a band for his Monmouth cap, and great
blunderbuss in hand.   His beard, too, is a perfect
forest of horrors in itself.   Another trousered sailor
kisses his sweetheart, who wears a " Duke of York's
nightcap."

Though so recent an event, scarce more than a
century ago, the assumption of trousers for general
wear has a vague history.   With the constant rib-
aldry and newspaper jesting which we daily hear and
read, that women are striving to capture that article
of dress, now held to be so distinctly masculine,
it is somewhat amusing to be told by careful stu-
dents that trousers were first assumed for general
wear, not by men, but by women.   This was in
France during the Reign of Terror.   Distinction
of the sexes in dress was to be put aside by these
reformers, as were distinctions in dress to indicate
birth and rank and wealth.   Trousers were welcomed as an article agreeable to the notions of these
female revolutionary creatures, and proper for their
wear.

This may be untrue, but it certainly is a fact that
women began to wear drawers, and called them
trousers, at the same time that men assumed trousers.   Old men of courtly tastes clung closely to
knee-breeches, and deemed trousers careless, inele-
gant, and vulgar.   Old ladies had a similar horror
of drawers, and never wore them.   Little girls first
put on pantalets for general wear, and naturally they

Adolphus Leffingwell, aged Fourteen Years. About 1815.

continued to wear them when grown.   Little boys, as shown by the boys in the portraits of the Stoddert and Jay children (both given in this chapter), were wearing trousers before their fathers and grandfathers had adopted them wholly.   As early as 1785 the leaving off knee-buckles and lengthening of knee-breeches was the advance note of a change. The breeches were buttoned below the knee or tied with strings, and soon were called pantaloons.   These were generally worn in France, and were copied in America.   They were ugly beyond belief.   I do not like to think that any woman, even a woman of the French Revolution, ever wore them.   They were loose, straight in leg, clumsy at the waist, reaching but little below the calf, and sometimes slit up several inches at the bottom on the outer side of the leg — a very ugly mode.   You may see them in French fashion-plates of the year 1797.

While stockings were largely visible in masculine dress they were, as we have seen, objects of cost, of care and pride.   With the short pantaloons, striped yarn stockings of the French mode were affected. The new trousers went through many mutations of cut and shape — sometimes closely fitted and called tights, sometimes baggy.   Then they were funnel shaped at the ankle, then tight at the ankle only. They were pleated at the waist and side into an absurd fulness, and even had tucks around the bottom.   An old chronicler tells of his first dress pantaloons: " The pantaloons, over which I wore boots, were of non-elastic corduroy.   It would be unjust to the tailor to say that they fitted like my skin, for they sat a great deal closer. When I took them off my legs were like fluted pillars grooved with the cords of the pantaloons."

From 1802 through 1809 trousers were loose and wide and short, reaching scarcely to the ankle. This mode was broken in the year 1810 by a garment

Playing Golf. 1810.

like a continuation of hose and garter which was buttoned on the outside of the leg from the waist to the ankle. An old Quaker preacher, named Jonathan Kirkbride, born in 1739, lived to advanced age; he put on trousers with great reluctance, and complained that they "felt so slawny" flapping around his ankles; this excellent descriptive word, doubtless, voiced the sentiments of many an old gentleman when he gave up small-clothes.

The extraordinary influx of Oriental fabrics into this country, caused by the sudden growth and prosperity of the East Indian trade, was shown distinctly in men's apparel in the wear of nankeen. In one year over $1,000,000 worth of yellow nankeen came to the United States. Nearly all of it was made into trousers, which were worn in summer and winter alike by old and young. They were the constant wear of General Lafayette on his trip through this country in 1824, as may be seen in his portrait in the closing chapter of this volume, and were worn by all our early presidents, often on formal occasions.

Pantaloons and gaiters were made "all in one" in 1810, especially when of nankeen, and were permitted in full dress; while in 1807 nankeen breeches with silk knee-strings were the only evening breeches.

In full-dress assemblies, in polite society, knee-breeches were worn for some years after trousers were everywhere seen on the streets. To enforce this regulation the somewhat startling notice was placed upon the entrance to an assembly hall, "Gentlemen will not be permitted to dance without breeches." In 1814 the Duke of Wellington presented himself at the door of the ballroom at Almack's, and his entrance was barred by an official, who said, "Your Grace cannot be admitted in trousers." The duke, being thus attired, quietly left the building.

I have said in earlier pages in this book that a knowledge of the general history of America was necessary to comprehend the meaning, or explain the importance, of various articles of dress; never was a time when knowledge of history was so necessary in order to comprehend fully the significance of dress as at this period in American history — in the opening years of the nineteenth century.

Dress was then more than a question of taste or fancy or convenience; in fact, it was not in America a question of taste or convenience at all, it was a question of belief, of deep conviction, of political opinion. A man's standing in politics was judged by his nether garments. It was said, complainingly, in American political circles that after the fall of the Bastille every Republican had to dress like a Frenchman — willy-nilly — and every Federalist like an Englishman. If you were a Republican and opposed the administration, you had to tangle your hair in rough locks drawn forward wildly over your forehead, "as if you had been fighting a hurricane backward," and to wear tight pantaloons to the calf of the leg. Wearing knee-breeches and buckled shoes proved that you were an old fogy of a Federalist.

It was not surprising to the Federalists to see Thomas Jefferson discard knee-breeches and shoe-buckles; what could be expected of a Democrat? an atheist? It was the trick of a demagogue to secure the favor of the mob! But he would not wear pantaloons long with *his* shapely legs! But year after year found him in flapping pantaloons and leather shoe-strings, which seem to have been as offensive almost to the Federalists as were the pantaloons.

In 1817 James Monroe became President of the United States. He was a dignified gentleman of

Boy's Tunic and Trousers. 1810.

"the Virginia Dynasty"; his wife was the first mistress of the White House who succeeded in enforcing etiquette in dress and carriage at the President's receptions. A near relative of her own was refused admission because he came not in the decreed small-clothes and silken hose — this, too, when pantaloons and shoe-strings were seen everywhere save at these receptions. She was a stately woman, garbed usually in velvet, with neck and arms bare, and hair dressed high with feathers, or with a turban, as shown in this book. Mr. Monroe was one of the last of the "cocked hats." He sturdily wore the old-time small-clothes till his death — the last man in public life in Washington who dressed thus.

The innovation of French dress, its folly, its extravagance, was a source of much head-shaking and prophesying of evil by lovers of the good old times; the lamentations of the fearful, the raillery of the scornful, the exhortations of the pious, all made special assault on pantaloons. With French dress, they asserted, were sure to come French ideas and French beliefs, or, worse still, French unbeliefs, — so mourned the children of the Puritans.

French "conspiracies," French infidelity, French anarchy, and French "pyrotechny" were darkly hinted at. The massacre of a whole ship-load of American citizens terrified every one, but existed only in imagination. Perhaps the only thing that was real in the list of French influences and invasions were the pantaloons, — yes, and the pantalets, for the two garments walked literally into American life side by side.

A few years ago, a well-known author, engaged upon an historical novel, wrote me this letter of a single line, " What did women wear in the year 1765, from the skin up ? "   I answered him at some length, to receive a second letter, " You do not speak of drawers."   I in return wrote, " I did not speak of drawers, because they did not wear drawers." Much misapprehension exists about the wear of these now universal undergarments for men and women.   Those who desire to read in fulness a discussion upon the subject can turn to *Notes and Queries* for the year 1888, when T. Adolphus Trollope, George Augustus Sala, and other well-known gentlemen and a few ladies give ample pages and full elucidation and illumination to the subject.

In *Lady Chesterfield's Letters to her Daughters* is this sentence, written in the middle of the nineteenth century : —

" I have worn skirts that dragged on the ground, and skirts that ended one inch above my ankles, showing the vandyked or frilled edges of those comfortable garments which we have borrowed from the other sex, and which all of us wear and none of us talk about."

So true is the last clause of this statement that after the first edition of the " Lady Chesterfield " book, the transcription given above was omitted. We have noted that calençons had been worn by French women for riding on horseback ; and Mrs. John Adams wrote from Paris in 1785 of ballet-dancers in gauze, with gauze petticoats "as perfectly showing their garters and drawers as though no pet-

ticoats had been worn " — these are her words.   The
early dislike of drawers was held by some to be from
association with the dress of " opera-dancers," a class
of persons proverbially, though doubtless in many
cases unjustly, of ill-repute.   Though I have never
seen any entry of drawers in any seventeenth-century list of women's garments in America (and I
have examined scores, yes, hundreds, of these inventories), I am surprised to find several explicit references to their wear by Mrs. Pepys in the pages of
Pepys's *Diary*, in the year 1663, in the month
of May.   This is the only allusion I have seen to
these articles for women's wear until the opera-danc-
ing days over a century later, and I note it as difficult of explanation.

The year 1800 can be set as the time when what
were called " women's trousers " first were worn to
any extent.   Their adoption was brought about by
the conditions of women's dress at the time, especially the transparence of the Indian stuffs employed.
A caricature of Gillray's (June 25, 1799) displays
even the garters through the thin, narrow, gauze petticoat.   Wright's *Caricature History of the Georges*
will give you, in caricature, yet in the main in truth,
the conditions of dress which then existed.

From fashion-magazines of the early years of the
nineteenth century I have gathered a few allusions,
which all show pantalets for women's wear were a distinct novelty. *La Belle Assemblée*, June, 1806, says:—

" Pantaloons of corded cambric, trimmed round the
bottom with lace or fine muslin made their appearance
on ladies in the Gardens last Sunday."

A month later the July number of this magazine adds : —

"The pantaloons will have but a short run; being truly ungraceful."

In November the fashion-monger writes : —

"A few of our haut ton have adopted the short frock and the trowsers of the same texture edged with lace. This dress is much too singular to be general. A singular She made her entree at breakfast in a frock of French cambric scarcely reaching below the calf of her leg, with trowsers of the same, at the bottom of which was a broad French lace."

In the year 1811, in Parisian and English fashion-plates, full ball dresses with pantalets are pictured. I copy an "evening dress" of that year. Long, pink satin trousers to the ankle are edged with three ruches of white and pink. Over these, reaching only to the knee, a scant pink satin "chemise-dress," short, edged with the same ruches. The head has an evening array of lace cap which looks like a night-cap. This whole dress seems like a night-dress and looks like an unutterable and grotesque caricature; as absurd for a ball dress as to wear pajamas. The very best of these pantaletted dresses were more ridiculous than a ready-made English bathing-suit at a cheap watering-place.

In July, 1818, a fashionable evening dress was thus described : —

"A blue silk petticoat sufficiently short to display a pair of white satin trousers, finished at the bottom with blue

Evening Dress. 1811.

silk fringe and made very loose. At the bottom of the petticoat was a large rouleau of white satin stiffened in such a manner as to keep it from clinging to the figure. The corsage of white satin was cut low as possible round the bust and ornamented with a narrow fancy trimming. The sleeves, if sleeves they might be called, which scarcely covered the top of the shoulders, were of tulle over white satin. A narrow cestus of lace folded in front by a diamond clasp. If the trousers were omitted and the bosom and arms less exposed the dress would have been truly elegant."

Madame de Beauharnais is described in the year 1807 as having discarded petticoats and put on flesh-colored satin drawers under her clear India muslin and mull gowns.

As the years bring us into the century we find the pantalet plainly in evidence in art. The *Children of the Nobility*, engraved in 1839, gives us many examples. Landseer's charming *Miss Blanche Egerton* also displays them. In the pages of John Leech they appear both on children and young women. I remember a delightful French picture of a ball, by David, wherein the dangling pantalets permit only the veriest tips of the slippers to be seen.

In 1821 the *Lady's Magazine* says that " female children " all wore, in winter, pantaloons of merino with short petticoats. In summer they wore pantaloons of white dimity or colored calico.

These pantaloons for girls' wear were soon called pantalets. They were, at first, only loose flapping frills tied on with drawing-strings below the knee, and hanging over the foot. Untidy things they were. The strings were always breaking or slipping down to the ankle and letting the whole frill draggle under foot; or they unfastened wholly, and had to be placed in a reticule until the child could retire and tie them in place again. The upper part of the garment was finally added to keep these troublesome knee-frills in place.

I have an amusing letter from the young mother of a little girl of eight, written in 1820. Both had begun to wear pantalets, — were forced to do so by fashion. In order to keep the child clad in clean attire, the mother had put upon her, in one week, fifteen pairs of freshly ironed pantalets. Of these, Myrtilla had wholly lost three pairs and an odd one, and a dog had torn off and chewed up another frill. The mother had worn eight pairs, and had only been thus moderate in number because one pair was of blue and brown checked gingham; she writes : —

"They are the ugliest things I ever saw; I will never put them on again. I dragged my dress in the dirt for fear some one would spy them. The gingham I had in the house. My finest dimity pair, with real Swiss lace, is quite useless to me, for I lost off one leg, and did not deem it proper to pick it up, so walked off, leaving it on the street behind me, and the lace was six shillings a yard. I saw that mean Mrs. Spring wearing it last week for a tucker. I told her it was mine, and showed her the mate, but she said she hemmed and made it herself — the bold thing. I hope there will be a short wear of these horrid pantalets; they are too trying. Of course, I must wear them now, for I cannot hold up my dress and show my stockings; no one does. My help says she won't stay if she has to wash

The Osgood Children. About 1820.

more than seven pair a week for Myrtilla, and I feel real
low-spirited about it.   Her legs are so thin she can't keep
her pantalets up.   I am almost ready, after all my trouble
in making them, to take them off, and make her dresses
longer and let her stockings show; but she will look so
dowdy without them, and she is not a pretty age."

In mourning, no lace or embroidery was placed
on children's pantalets, they had three deep tucks
for trimming, or bands of crape.   Fancy a little girl
in crape-bordered pantalets!   In general, the material was the same as the frock, especially if the frock
were cotton.   Sometimes dark-colored pantalets were
used for everyday wear, and white for Sunday.   We
have a letter of a tender grandfather, Judge Saint
George Tucker, — a step-grandfather at that, — written in 1807, telling of his interest in the new dress for
little girls, and his eagerness that his young grandchildren should adopt the latest fashion.   His fine
face is upon an earlier page.   He wrote to his
daughter a masterly description of the dress of the
child of President Monroe : —

" Your mama has refer'd you to me for an account of
little Maria Munroe who is, I believe, a few months older
than our darling Fancilea.   She was dress'd in a short
frock that reach'd about half way between her knees and
ankles, under which she display'd a pair of loose pantaloons,
wide enough for the foot to pass through with ease, frilld
around with the same stuff as her frock and pantaloons.   I
was so pleas'd with it and so convinced you would immediately adopt it for Fancilea and Lisba, that I took more
than ordinary notice of it.   The little monkey did not fail
to know the advantages of her dress.   She had a small

Spaniel dog with whom she was continually engaged in a trial of skill, and the general opinion seemed to be that she turned and twisted about more than the Spaniel."

The teachings of Rousseau brought about a distinctive boys' garb in France, and Marie Antoinette was one of the first to dress her son, the little dauphin, in round jackets and trousers, instead of the formal knee-breeches and brocaded coat and waistcoat boys had hitherto worn.

I do not know precisely when little French boys put on trousers. The Wertmuller portrait of Marie Antoinette with her two children, now in the Royal Gallery at Stockholm, shows her walking in the garden at Trianon with the dauphin — apparently about five years old, in trousers and jacket with open ruffled neck. The portrait by Madame le Brun (now at Versailles) shows the dauphin in similar trousers; this was painted in 1787.

Old portraits and the illustrations of books show how quickly these notions spread, both in France and America.

John Jay was minister at the court of Louis XVI, and his wife on her return to America must have brought the height of the modes to eager New Yorkers. It is said that the change in boys' dress was one of these fashions. Her own boy certainly wore trousers, as may be seen in this portrait of him.

All accounts of Mrs. Jay tell us of a face and figure as queenly as Marie Antoinette's, and of still greater beauty. We all know the engraving of her

Mrs. John Jay and Children. About 1800.

head in straw hat tied down with a kerchief. I have always believed this engraving a wholly inadequate expression of her beauty and charm — but when the original of this head is seen in this portrait group of herself with her two children, it will be found even less pleasing than the engraving. As a study of costume the picture is most interesting; as a work of art it is valueless. The artist was Robert Edge Pine. Peale says he drew his heads from life, but made no study of figure. So when he arranged his final portraits he might put the head of a fat man on a slim body, and *vice versa*. His pictures were a total failure — some were even ridiculous. We know, of course, that this portrait does not give the face nor the figure nor the carriage of the beautiful Mrs. Jay. I may add that I have never seen any painting of Pine's that had the slightest art value. There is a tradition that the coloring of his portraits was fine — but color is of slight value in a portrait compared to drawing.

These first trousers for boys were often a garment of frills; they were tucked, embroidered, and even ruffled; a favored fashion was to draw them in with a puckering-string at the ankle.

An excellent delineation of the dress of a boy at this time is shown in the charming picture of the Stoddert children, painted by Charles Willson Peale. The boy's suit is of nankeen, and the trousers are gathered at the ankle with drawing-strings into a frill. This painting gives a bit of Georgetown life, and was doubtless painted in Bostock House. There is typical Potomac scenery in the background.

The three children are Elizabeth, who married Dr.
Thomas Ewell; the boy, Benjamin Forrest Stoddert,
and the baby Harriet. Their father was Benjamin
Stoddert, appointed Secretary of the Naval Bureau
in May, 1798, — the first Secretary of the Navy.
This picture must have been painted about 1796.
The baby Harriet grew into a lovely girl, the
friend of Marcia Burns Van Ness, whose face in
youth and in age is given in this book. In a delightful costume of orange-colored Canton crape,
Harriet Stoddert so entranced the head of the
Turkish Legation that he promptly asked her at
first sight to become one of his wives. She was
married in 1812 to George Washington Campbell of Tennessee. He had wounded a Mr. Gar-
denhire in a duel. The injured man was carried
into the house of Mrs. Stoddert's grandfather,
Bostock House, and was there carefully nursed.
Mr. Campbell rode out every day to inquire for
his foe, and fell in love as promptly as the Turkish
minister. A few years later Mr. Campbell became
minister to Russia, where his three little children
died of some infantile epidemic at the same time that
the emperor Alexander lost his only surviving child.
Mutual sorrow of the distressed mothers for each
other led to an intimacy, and the little girl who
came to comfort the mourning American parents
was named Liszinka for her imperial godmother.
A portrait of Mrs. Campbell, painted in Russia,
shows a beautiful but sad face, little like the rosy-
cheeked baby in this illustration.

The Stoddert Children.

CHAPTER XXXIII

EMPIRE FASHIONS

*" I'm not denyin' the women are foolish ; God Almighty made
'em to match the men."*

— " Adam Bede," GEORGE ELIOT.

CHAPTER XXXIII

THE Empire was proclaimed in 1804; but the short waist which has become associated with that name had been already worn.

An affected revulsion of feeling against the costly stuffs of the eighteenth century made simpler materials popular for wear even in full dress. Mantua-makers adhered also to plain lines, and less material was used in the manufacture of gowns. The skirt was short, reaching in meagre, clinging folds only to the feet, with but slight flouncing at the lower edge. It was stretched as tightly as possible across the front of the figure, sometimes held across with whalebones placed horizontally. Through the absence of pressure on any part of the figure the dress was far more conducive to health in its shape than in its warmth or weight.

The best-known name in the history of these fashions is Madame Récamier. An English lady describes the dress she wore in the Kensington Gardens, London, in 1802. " She appeared *à l'antique*, her muslin dress clinging to her form like the folds of drapery on a statue, her hair in a plait in the back and falling in small ringlets over her face, and greasy with *huile antique*, a large veil thrown over her head." The last sentence offers some amelioration for the *huile antique*. We can endure the leaders of fashion bare-footed, with rings on their toes, and with

tunics cut up at the side of the skirt even to the belt; we can forgive the absence of chemises; we can overlook many deficiencies of decency, rather than the presence of *huile antique* — it is a little too classical. Since I have known of the *huile*, I seem to see it greasing her face from her dripping ringlets in every portrait of her I encounter.

Dolly Madison in Youth.

I have examined with much interest the winter numbers of *La Belle Assemblée* and the *Lady's Magazine* of the early years of the nineteenth century, and the chief emotion is that any of our grandmothers survived those years, so lightly were they dressed. In January, 1807, the walking-dresses were of white jaconet muslin or cambric, with brown velvet or " orange-blossom " shoes. The hat was of straw or tiger fur. Another favorite was a " Chinese robe " of India twill or French dimity trimmed with a border of tambour, with loose back or scalloped at the bottom. White kid and rose-colored silk low shoes were worn, with silver rosettes, and variegated sarcenet silk " cottage cloaks " pretended to give warmth. In the spring pink muslin mantles appeared. But in general the neck and portions of the arms were left bare, even for outdoor wear, hence a scarf became a grateful adjunct to the scanty toilet.

One old lady tells me she often went to church in winter in a French cambric gown, with a shawl but a yard square as the only outdoor covering. The wife of Governor Joseph Trumbull remembered riding from Middletown, Connecticut, to Berlin in an open sleigh one bitter winter's night, in an organdy gown, low-necked and sleeveless, her only extra covering a cloth cape without lining. That fell curse of New England — consumption — was nourished and increased by this scanty dress. A rhyme of the day begins : —

> " Plump and rosy was my face
> And graceful was my form ;
> Till fashion deemed it a disgrace
> To keep my body warm."

When cloth was announced for gowns in 1828, a writer in the *Lady's Magazine* urges the readers never to wear them indoors, as they " were not a fireside costume."

All the underwear worn with the scanty empire gowns was of slight texture, close cut, and consisted of very few pieces. Especially with the antique models was it necessary to abandon ample or thick underclothing.   Thus wrote a rhymester of the day: —

> " Many, filled 'tis said with pride,
> Have laid their underclothes aside ;
> Such healthful dress they do dispise,
> And naught but gauze and muslin prize."

In a letter dated February 17, 1812, Miss Morris wrote of Madame Bonaparte, who had been Miss Patterson of Baltimore : —

" I never beheld a human form so faultless.   To the utmost symmetry of feature is added so much vivacity, such captivating sweetness; and her sylphic form thinly veiled displays all the graces of a Venus de Medici.   She appears particularly in a fine crepe robe of a beautiful azure color interwoven with silver; in this attire she is truly celestial, and it is impossible to look on anyone else when she is present."

A contemporary description of her dress at her marriage runs thus : —

" All the clothes worn by the bride might have been put in my pocket.   Her dress was of muslin richly embroidered, of extremely fine texture.   Beneath her dress she wore but a single garment."

It was told that this beautiful but certainly reckless young woman, going to the extreme of French modes, wore no chemise.   But this daring fashion lasted even in Paris but a single week.   A certain little demure scrap of mull used as a tucker was

Dolly Madison.

known as a " modesty " or a " modesty bit " ; and a
satirical poem of the day ran thus : —

> " And where their bosoms you do view
> The truth I do declare, O !
> A modesty they all must have
> If ne'er a smock they wear, O ! "

The miniature of Madame Bonaparte painted by
Jean Baptiste Augustine, is one of the least-clad

portraits I have ever seen, either French or American. There is so little a waist-portion to the dress, so slight in extent, so slight in weight, — merely a tiny scrap of organdy an inch or so wide, and very loosely applied, — not fixed on the person. Another tapelike scrap hangs out from the arm halfway down to the elbow, carrying out (if it had a waist) what might be termed the line of the belt. This scrap of mull of Madame Patterson Bonaparte might well be called an immodesty bit. She is seated — and apparently had to be; for the moment Madame Bonaparte stood up, that empire gown would certainly fall to the ground; it was half fallen as she was seated.

The "chemise dress," well named, was a favorite form for day wear, and was equally proper for evening dress. It was shaped precisely like a sack-chemise, and was seldom fuller than the ordinary French-gored chemise of our present underwear. It was also of similar material, thin linen lawn, or sheer percale, and was no more trimmed at the neck and sleeves, though the skirt might be scantily flounced.

A magazine declared that the "chemise-dress must be made tight to form of bosom, drawn very low at each corner of neck and worn with crooked pearl slide to separate the bosom." A very vulgar-looking accessory consisted of a golden net confining the breast.

One of these chemise-dresses, and not an extreme one, is shown in these pages. Both figures would appear to us more properly garbed for bed than for the opera.

Opera Dress of Mother and Daughter. 1808.

In the years 1805–10 a one-sided effect was much sought after in dress as in hair-dressing. In one case the top of one boot only was turned over to show a fur edging. With the thin robes one garter was ordered, a beribboned and buckled garter, proving plainly that garters did not blush unseen, but peeped out shyly — or boldly for all we know — through a cloud of gauze or mull. A one-sided, irregular garment may be graceful ; it must not be a studied irregularity ; it must appear to be accidental. The directions to wearers of these modes, to hold a certain corner of the garment in one hand, to catch the corner of a scarf to the girdle by a bit of the fringe " lightly yet firmly," all savor too much of strained effect. Mantles and manteaus were all one-sided. These sentences are taken from English fashion-notes of the year 1807 : —

" In the Danish mantle the left arm is confined in a long loose sleeve, the back is fulled on the right shoulder leaving simply an armhole. The mantle on the left side reaches to the bottom of the dress."

" A Cardinal is draped to form a hood on one side and hangs in loose drapery on the other. One corner is rounded off small and must be held in one hand."

" French cloak of white floss net fulled into a narrow band of lilack sarsenet fashioned high on left shoulder with strips of sarsenet and tassels."

" Mantle of orange and purple velvet with but one arm-hole, the right side rounded down from neck in a long point. Trimmed all round with spotted leopard fur."

Even the skirts of gowns were of uneven length on either side, being very deep on right side always, while the left was made shorter either by being looped up or slashed up very sharply. Sometimes the sleeve of the robe was opened up to the arm-

Mrs. Richard C. Derby as Saint Cecilia.

scye. I find no reference to a petticoat being worn under this open tunic, which, I must say frankly, is precisely like the most severely reprehended dress of one of our modern spectacular plays; a dress that was finally discarded in deference to public opinion. Yet this robe was worn calmly by our discreet and proper great-grandmothers.

Perhaps the wearer could not have stepped in the gown had it not been thus slashed. I have seen these robes brought out of old trunks in staid New England homes — gowns of fine organdie or mull, scant, with a narrow tail-like train; so low necked that they were indeed incroyable; slit up at one side nearly to the waist. One was a wedding-gown of a parson's wife; it was like Madame Bonaparte's. A certain "sheath" slip was worn under this outer cobweb — desperately immodest attire, it would seem to us to-day. Two of these old, scant, narrow-tailed gowns were chosen last summer for wear at a fancy-dress party. They were exquisitely fine and beautiful. Though our modern underclothing was of course added to the "sheath slip," and a deep tucker was sewn into the neck, yet when the evening came, and the robes were put on, neither young girl who was to wear one could make her mind up to appear thus clad. The gowns were really far from proper wear, according to our present estimates. Still, the short-waisted empire gowns could be very charming. Two exquisite portraits given in this book show the simple empire dress at its best; one is of the lovely woman who was known in her Boston home as "the beautiful Mrs.

Derby." She was twenty-two years old in 1806, when this portrait was painted. She is seated at a

A Ferronnière and Turban Pins.

harp, and is painted as Saint Cecilia in order to show to advantage her perfect eyes and arms. Her

Mrs. John Ridgely. 1805. By Sully.

dress still exists. It is of finest white mull, or India muslin, and is edged with a band of gold embroidery; it is buttoned on the sleeve with gold buttons.

The second portrait shows an equally graceful figure standing by a harp. This is the beautiful Eliza Ridgely, who married John Ridgely, who was not related to her; the ancestor of each came to Maryland in the seventeenth century, unknown to the other. This portrait is deemed Sully's masterpiece. It hangs in the great hall at Hampton, the Ridgely mansion-house in Baltimore County, Maryland.

One graceful ornament was just being revived into popularity in 1820; I mean the ferronnière, or band around the head, from which depended a jewel in the middle of the forehead. Pearls and rubies were favorite stones. A well-known portrait of the wife of President Tyler has this ferronnière. It gives to every countenance a curiously submissive look, as if the jewel were hung on a slave. It was originally an Oriental fashion, but had been most popular in France in the seventeenth century. The ferronnière was generally a fine gold Venetian chain, but might be made of velvet ribbon, of silken cord, of strings of beads, or tiny vines of artificial flowers.

CHAPTER XXXIV

THE ROMANCE OF OLD CLOTHES

" *Dress does make a difference, Davy.*"

— " Bob Acres," in *The Rivals*, RICHARD BRINSLEY SHERIDAN, 1775.

CHAPTER XXXIV

THE ROMANCE OF OLD CLOTHES

OLD portraits, old letters, and old garments! these bring us very close to those who have been gone for centuries. Here is the modest, girlish wardrobe of Caria Robbins; the outfit made for her when she went from her country home to visit in the growing city of New York. It was in 1812, a five or six days' journey by coach. It might be a day shorter if one went to Providence by coach and then by boat on the Sound. I have a diary kept during a trip made from New York to Newport on a passenger sloop, by a great-grandfather and his family, in 1780. It took eight days.

Caria — I like to say her pretty name — was the youngest girl in the family of Stephen and Abigail Robbins of West Lexington, that pleasant and historic old Massachusetts town. She was born in 1794, and was therefore eighteen years of age when she made this visit. The wardrobe which she had for her journey has been wonderfully preserved. She never married, and of course we fancy there was a romance and a reason for her single life. There certainly was in her youth a favored lover. I like to think that the romance was connected with this trip to New York, and that it affords a reason why this special set of garments was saved, and so little worn — while innumerable dresses of other years went the way of gowns in general. She died when over eighty years old, but she will never be remembered as a feeble, withered old woman; she lives in cheerful, pretty girlhood forever, through the power of her salmon-pink and sea-green finery.

Gown, Hat, and Slippers worn by Caria Robbins.

Here is a charming little scant tamboured India muslin, labelled in her own hand-writing, "The Dress I made to walk down Broadway in." This, like all the thin mull and muslin gowns of the day, is too poorly represented by photography to be worth reproducing.

Here, on this page, is one of her simple gowns that she carried to New York, with hat and slippers that matched. The dress is salmon-pink lutestring, a favorite color and favorite stuff of the day. The hat is sea-green silk edged with blond-lace and trimmed with salmon-pink and white ribbons. The white silk stockings and mitts, and a charming salmon-pink gauze shawl, with a stamped black and white border, have been kept always with the dress. The little flat slippers are salmon-pink kid. They were bought in Boston, "Near the Old South Meeting House." A tiny label says, "Rips mended Gratis."

Plum-colored Kid Mitts worn by Mrs. Robbins.

Another page bears the sea-green silk spencer that was worn with the silk gown and hat. Another spencer for morning wear is of brown and white cotton chintz. The spencer may be called the characteristic garment of this quarter of a century. Every fashion-bulletin from the year 1800 to 1830 has a reference to spencers. Here is one fashion-note for the year 1803 : —

"Spencers are worn both for walking and carriage dress. Levantines, spotted silks, and striped lutestrings are the favorite materials. The trimming is always satin. The Augusta spencer is one of the prettiest dress spencers. The waist is finished with tabs cut in the form of leaves. In velvet spencers, black, purple, and bottle green are favorite colors. The velvet is cut byas. Perkale dresses are

worn with these (December).   Pelisses called Carricks are
worn trimmed with swan's down and steel."

Spencers worn by Caria Robbins.

The Persian
spencer was much
recommended and
was termed com-
mendable because
it "demands a
correct neatness of
the robe with which
it is worn, as well
as a delicate and
chaste attention to
the decoration of
the foot and leg."
As the spencer was
always cut short
at the waist, I can-
not understand
why it had any
special trend upon
the dress of the
foot and leg. Nor
should I think
neatness specially
indispensable to
this Persian form
of garment.

I copy in this chapter two fashion-plates from
Ackermann's Repository for February, 1816.   These
seem to me very elegant dresses, "quite the jant,"

Marquis de Lafayette. 1824.

as the editor of that publication says of them. One, a spencer of dark mulberry velvet, has what is termed a "half-sleeve" of puffed satin with white silk balls which are duplicated in the trimming on the edge of the petticoat, on the bonnet, and in the shoe-knots. The great white satin and swan's-down muff is called a Roxburgh muff. Half-sleeves or epaulettes were worn with many of these spencers. White velvet spencers trimmed with swan's-down were elegant indeed. Purple and orange was a favorite combination of color in spencers; with this, coral ornaments, writes one fashionmonger.

Swan's-down Stole. Brought from Russia in 1800.

The spencer has an interesting origin. It was originally a man's coat, a short, scant top-coat, not so long as the wearer's body-coat, and often sleeveless; a very skimpy, pinched garment, invented by Lord Spencer at about the same time that Lord

Sandwich invented a form of food which would be nourishing and could be eaten quickly and conveniently while he was at the gambling-table. An English rhyme ran:—

> "Two noble lords, whom if I quote
>   Some folks might call me sinner,
> The one invented half a coat,
>   The other half a dinner.
>
> "The plan was good, as some will say,
>   And fitted to console one,
> Because in this poor starving day
>   Few can afford a whole one."

Lord Spencer made a bet with Sir Edward Chetwynd that he could set a fashion which would be adopted as a ruling mode within six months. This should be a form of dress wholly meaningless and unnecessary. Spencer called for a pair of shears, cut off the entire tails of the long coat he was wearing, put on the unhemmed, unfinished garment, and went out for a stroll. He was a handsome, dashing man; and in three days several young men were seen in the streets wearing similar "spencers." In two weeks all London was wearing the garment; and in two months all England, men, women, and children; and in scarcely less time all America.

English people have ever had a fancy for short jackets, and the longing was not wholly filled after the loss of the beloved jerkin and doublet, until we had the spencer. Since the day of the spencer, men have not been able to carry out that notion, unless the dinner coat may be given as a half-fulfilment.

Women have had zouaves, and Spanish jackets, and Eton coats, and boleros, and various short spencer-like garments.

This bet must have taken place in 1792, for there is a caricature of Earl Spencer by Gillray, published in May, 1792, in which the earl wears a blue spencer; below which show the tails of a red coat with brass buttons.

The climax of interest in American life in the year 1824 was the visit of Lafayette in his old age to the scene of his career of sentiment and love of liberty in early life. I have told in another chapter of the romantic affection and hero-worship which all Americans held for him. The garments which he wore on this memorable visit may fitly close this record of the masculine dress of two centuries. Blue coat with brass buttons and rather wide nankeen trousers are well depicted in his portrait by

Walking Costumes with Muffs and Spencers.

Professor Morse of telegraph fame; the dress he
wore at the laying of the corner-stone of Bunker
Hill Monument, when Daniel Webster delivered
his memorable oration. The dress worn by Mrs.
Webster at this great occasion has been preserved
in her portrait (reproduced facing this page). In it

Embroidered Linen and Lace
Capes.

she wears a pearl-gray
silk hat and gown. Her
costume is not only rich,
but thoroughly elegant,
and in the full height
not only of the best
American, but the best
French fashions which
succeeded the empire
modes. The hat is the
shape known as the Res-
tauration. No elegante
of the Champs Élysées
wore a more distinctive
hat than this of Mrs.
Webster's. A younger
woman might have added
an ostrich plume to the
bow of ribbon, but it

would be in no better style. This costume may (as
fitly as that of Lafayette for men), close the series
of women's gowns of two centuries.

As I turn from one picture to another in these
volumes they speak with clearer voice than do the
printed pages, telling many and varied stories.
They remind me of friends who have shared with

Mrs. Daniel Webster.   1824.

me the ownership of cherished family portraits; they speak of thoughtful helpers who have gathered far and wide for me; they tell of happy journeys to see the portraits, the clogs, the spencers; to read old diaries, old letters, old news; they lead me along pleasant ways by New England roads and lanes to old New England homes.

There is written "between the lines" of these pages *The Romance of Old Clothes*. Memory and sentiment give to many of the pictures both an æsthetic and a spiritual value. What harmless jealousies, what gentle vanities, what modest hopes linger in the folds of these pictured garments! They have other threads than that warp and woof which makes them silk or homespun. I recall the old dim garret and the rarely opened hair trunks and cedar chests where I found many of them. These yellowed mull baby dresses and linen shirts, what heart-aches do they figure, for they are unworn! But they cannot touch the tenderest depth of sympathy, as do these faded red morocco shoes; for these are worn to shabbiness with the many little pattering foot-steps that ran eagerly and trustingly after the young mother, but suddenly followed her no more. And here is the bride's bonnet-veil; home worked, it hung long and narrow, giving glimpses of her blushing face as she walked proudly up the aisle of the old church on the coming-out Sunday. The veil was the frailest thing in her bridal outfit, but it has outlasted her substantial dress.

Here is the boy's first suit of "boughten" cloth, which he had when he went to college. This suit and the standing iron candlestand with long-handled fire-shovel and tongs, that were forged for him by the village blacksmith, were the chief glories of his outfit. The cut and make of the garments show that Miss Polly Patten, the town tailoress, fashioned them, and upon the same principles that the smith used in making the candlestand, broad at the base, with legs well spread, the arms firmly fastened and standing out squarely — made in every part to last forever; both have done so. Here is the satin court-suit which the boy wore in London when he was grown middle-aged, and full of cares and dignities. The silk is faded, the tinsel is rusted, but his elderly sister at home on the farm is proud to keep it. Here is the cloak of the younger brother; he went to college, full of eager ambitions, when the red leaves turned in autumn. He was drowned through heedless skating on the first thin November ice. His mother folded this cloak, and pinned an old sheet around it, and marked it "John's Last Cloak." You can feel a pang in your heart for her, though she joined her boy fifty years ago, and perhaps understands at last why a life so needful, so noble, and, above all, so full of the simple joy of existing, was ended so early.

Old letters and old garments bring us in close touch with the past; there is in them a lingering presence, a very essence of life. Here the hand pressed that held the pen; here it lingered in dainty stitches. The very substance of these garments, spun and woven ere cheating makeshifts were known, seems true and good. These rich brocades, these

The Romance of Old Clothes.

bits of cherished laces, tell of the gathered egg-money or petty legacy sent across seas to France for bridal finery ; these India muslins speak of the home garden's tribute of sage or the wildwood's unwilling yield of ginseng, which journeyed on a venture to far Cathay under the judgment of the supercargo, that obsolete officer who was in old-time trade what might be termed a commercial neighbor.   And some are homespun.   There still clings to the firm all-wool stuff, unfaded hand-stamped calico, the lustrous homespun linen, something of the vitality of the enduring women who raised the wool, the cotton, the flax, even the silk ; who prepared each for the wheel by many exhausting labors ; who spun the yarn and thread, and wove the warp and woof; who bleached and dyed ; who cut and sewed these ancient garments.   All these honest stuffs, with their quaint fashionings, render them a true expression of old-time life ; and their impalpable and finer beauty through sentiment puts me truly in touch with the life of my forbears.

INDEX

INDEX